THE RIGHT TIME

D1596142

THE RIGHT TIME

*John Henry "Pop" Lloyd
and Black Baseball*

Wes Singletary

McFarland & Company, Inc., Publishers
Jefferson, North Carolina, and London

ALSO BY WES SINGLETARY AND FROM MCFARLAND
Al Lopez: The Life of Baseball's El Señor (1999)

Frontispiece: Pop Lloyd: "...if you mean ALL baseball, organized and unorganized, the answer is John Henry Lloyd" (courtesy John Henry "Pop" Lloyd Committee).

LIBRARY OF CONGRESS CATALOGUING-IN-PUBLICATION DATA

Singletary, Wes, 1960–
    The right time : John Henry "Pop" Lloyd and
Black baseball / Wes Singletary.
        p.   cm.
    Includes bibliographical references and index.

    ISBN 978-0-7864-3572-2
    softcover : 50# alkaline paper ∞

    1. Lloyd, John Henry, 1884–1954.   2. African American
baseball players — Biography.   3. Negro leagues — History.
4. Baseball — United States — History.   I. Title.
GV865.L55S57   2011
796.357092 — dc22 [B]   2011009704

BRITISH LIBRARY CATALOGUING DATA ARE AVAILABLE

© 2011 Wes Singletary. All rights reserved

*No part of this book may be reproduced or transmitted in any form
or by any means, electronic or mechanical, including photocopying
or recording, or by any information storage and retrieval system,
without permission in writing from the publisher.*

Front cover image: *John Henry "Pop" Lloyd* by Kadir Nelson
(reproduced by permission of the artist)

Manufactured in the United States of America

McFarland & Company, Inc., Publishers
  Box 611, Jefferson, North Carolina 28640
    www.mcfarlandpub.com

For Nelson and Patricia

Table of Contents

There is no such thing as part freedom.
— Nelson Mandela

Preface

John Henry "Pop" Lloyd was an icon of black baseball, a Hall of Fame player whose improbable success in a highly visible yet segregated venture secured pathways for others of his race to follow. Raised by a grandmother in the Jim Crow South, Lloyd chose baseball as his way out, defying hardships at every turn. A gifted infielder and hitter, he became one of the great players of his era, white or black. He was also a forerunner to the modern baseball player one not tied to a binding reserve clause, but free to ply his trade wherever the money was — what there was of it. It is ironic that Lloyd and other black ballplayers, while relegated to less than major league status, were freer in some respects than their white counterparts. But such freedom came with a price. Black baseball was a grind — a hardscrabble, difficult trek, played under racism's constant yoke. It led many astray, most notably from themselves. Lloyd, however, seemed born to it, and his exceptional talent, kind nature, and friendly gestures won for him a cadre of supporters, carving a niche among the game's great players. Yet, today, those without a serious interest in the history of black baseball know very little about him.

The first time that I became aware of John Henry "Pop" Lloyd was in the fall of 1994, when as a graduate student at Florida State University I took a class on African American history from Professor Maxine Jones. Dr. Jones had just co-authored a book titled *African Americans in Florida*, and there, on page 59, in a section devoted to sports, was a brief note on Lloyd, who, to hear tell it, must have been one hell of a ballplayer. Unlike Ray Charles, "Bullet" Bob Hayes, Zora Neale Hurston, and other popular contemporaries, each of whom had been the subject of a multi-page profile, Lloyd's life and career were covered in the space of four sentences.

That I had never heard of Lloyd told me something as well. After all, I grew up playing — and reading a great deal about — baseball in Florida. I had even tendered a master's thesis on the life of Hall of Fame manager Al Lopez. Yet here was this man, who entered Baseball's Hall of Fame on the

1

same day as the erstwhile "Señor," and I had never heard of him. It was embarrassing!

I immediately set out to learn what I could about Lloyd, and black baseball in general, devouring Robert Peterson's homage to the game, *Only the Ball Was White*, James Riley's *Biographical Encyclopedia of the Negro Leagues*, and everything John Holway had in print. I reviewed Whitey Gruhler's *Atlantic City Press* clippings on file what the National Baseball Library and phoned Lawrence Hogan and Michael Everett of SABR's Pop Lloyd Committee seeking even more information.

When a paper that I produced for Dr. Jones's course revealed some of the possibilities enhanced research might produce, I promised myself that at some point in the future I would give Lloyd's life and legacy the attention that was due. That was 17 years ago. While the task of writing this book was never far from my mind, life, as the saying goes, got in the way. From time to time I came across information that could be squirreled away, or spoke to someone with an insight to share — but other than that, it sat there. What ultimately got the ball rolling was a brief visit in 2006 with Lawrence Hogan, author of *Shades of Glory*, who agreed to visit with me while on a trip to Tampa. Dr. Hogan was in town as part of the special Negro Leagues Committee assigned the task of selecting a group of players from baseball's Jim Crow era for admission to the National Baseball Hall of Fame. (Sixteen men and one woman were ultimately chosen.)

After I picked him up at a Laundromat — he had laundry to do — and explaining that I hoped to write a book on Lloyd, Dr. Hogan advised that I again get in touch with Michael Everett, his colleague with SABR's Pop Lloyd Committee; visit the Peterson Collection in the National Baseball Library (NBL) at Cooperstown; scour the black press; and get my hands on a copy of Riley's encyclopedia, which I had. He later provided me with his own clippings file on Lloyd, which included two non-published biographical essays. Dr. Hogan's suggestions formed the basis of my research outline. His advice regarding Michael Everett was especially helpful.

Michael Everett, a teacher in Linwood, NJ, is an avid baseball fan and educator. As part of an oral history project, he had videotaped extensive first-person interviews on life in Atlantic City with individuals who had lived there a generation after Lloyd, but who had memories of him and the community. After spending an afternoon reviewing the material and talking baseball, Michael directed me to Lloyd's burial site at Pleasantville, and to "Pop Lloyd Stadium," which I promptly visited. I then drove north, spent an evening with my aunt Marjorie outside Manhattan, and headed to Cooperstown to review the Peterson files, of which Nan Lloyd's taped interview was of particular interest. Without Hogan and Everett's assistance this book would not have been written.

Once I returned to Tallahassee, I began the grunt work of researching each of Lloyd's baseball seasons — one game at a time — the result of which rests here. Doing this in the black press, which for the most part were weeklies whose coverage of games varied wildly — calls upon skills of a forensic nature to determine the flow of a respective contest. As long as a box score contains a line showing which innings the runs were scored in, and the innings pitched by a respective hurler, finding the results is not difficult. But, depending on the quality of the copies reviewed, whether or not a narrative accompanies the box, and other issues, the research at times can become patchwork, calling upon the researcher to have at least a fair knowledge of the game, and how it flows, so as to bring it together. I hope that I have been able to do this.

Aside from Dr. Hogan and Michael Everett, there are many others to thank. Linda Pulliam, Deborah Mekeel, Cynthia Killingsworth and Kathy Toon at the State Library of Florida have all been tremendous in obtaining needed research through the inter-library loan program. Adam Watson of the Florida State Archives, Larry Lester with NoirTech Research, Ray Doswell of the Negro Leagues Baseball Museum, and the staff of the National Baseball Library and Archives have all been generous with their time and support in helping to gather images for this volume.

Dr. Jim Jones at the Florida State University and Todd Thomas at Georgia Military College both took time from their summer breaks to read the manuscript and offer needed suggestions. It was a big assist on their part, one that is much appreciated. Other individuals who have been helpful include Maxine Jones at the Florida State University; Will Benedicks and Monte Finklestein of Tallahassee Community College; Robert Cassanello at the University of Central Florida; Mike Salario, Joe Knetsch, Ken Crawford, and Gerald Ensley. Thanks to each of them.

My large, clannish family continues to provide a great deal of encouragement, especially in a pinch. They are always there, and as always, I am proud to be one of them: Charles W. Singletary Sr. and Judith A. Corbett, Ray and Judy Fojaco, Manuel and Patricia Zarate, Joe, Amy, Brock, Jake and Alex Singletary, Lorraine, Frankie and Devin Fernandez, Lee, Marlene, Tiffany and Taylor Singletary, Marjorie Teel, Cliff and Cynthia May, Danny and Marilyn Zarate, Paul, Candy, Mike, and Carol Singletary, John D. Singletary, "Razor" Herrero, "Danny Boy" Herrero, "Louie" Herrero, Michelle Highnote, Stan McIntosh, "Stevie" McIntosh, Sam McIntosh, Sabrina Noyes, Gloria McIntosh, Hazel Singletary, "Bubba" Singletary, Billy Singletary, Cheri, Calvin, Cy and Casey Jarel, Mark Teel, Rod Teel, and Lauren Teel-Handler,

Floyd Ferguson, Robin McIntosh-Stokes, and Erin McIntosh. Also the late Bertha L. Singletary, Raymond Singletary, Howard Singletary, Glen McIntosh, Cal and Rose Carter, Raymond Gonzalez, and Patrick Michael Foley, a sweet boy who loved baseball.

Thanks again to the following friends *across the miles*: Bob Lotane, "Big Scott" Harward, John and Carol Calacino, Joel Overton, Tyler Turkle, Boo Taylor, Sandy Shaughnessy, Art and Tammy Skafidas, James and Jodee McIver, Brian Lynch, Peter Harris, George and Vicki Drady, Stuart Goldberg, Jackie Pons, Marianne Valenti, Joe and Susan Martelli, Lyle and Chris Rauh, Jimmy and Vicky Bryson, Tommy and Ann Hopkins, Pete and Karen Butler, Rich and Annette Williams, Orlando and Carrie Evora, Doug Fields, Joe Bulgarella, Richard and Lori Crowe, Andy and Lisa Miller, David and Kelly DiSalvo, Lou Leinhauser, Susan Stratton, Nick Gray, Mark Solomon, Ronnie Rodriguez, Gary Rodriguez, Frank Fernandez, K. R. Lombardia, Bobby and Linda Johnson, Joe Vallese, Chris Milstead, Mitch Davidson, D. Norton, Chris Warfel, Dean Palmer, Stephen Veliz, Bruce Williams, Joe Karels, Rick Moulton, Willis Perry, Traci Cash, Hillary and Junior Hodges, David Culligan, Robin Barber, Vasili Efimov, Mark Herron, Bob Harris, Eric Urra and Johanna Ganem, Fred and Beth Tedio, Jay McConnell, all of my students — you know who you are; and the late Alex Abaroa, Thierry Kobes, and Alone "Ray" Harrison — I miss you guys.

Toni Zarate Singletary, my wife of thirty years, remains the love of my life. I cannot do or say enough to thank her for all that she does for our family. My girl is a blessing! Then there are these kids who have taken over our lives, Patricia and Nelson. Who would have thunk it? We went years without children, but now ... their joyful, noisy presence makes it hard to recall what life was like before they arrived. Every moment with them is incredible. What great kids they are, a testament to their mother. I am so proud of them. I love my family and remain thankful for it.

ONE

Slow Glide

The janitor was a kind, soft-spoken old man with a falsetto voice and "a tired look in his eyes." He was tall, with a lantern jaw, long arms and large hands, moving with a deliberate "slow glide" as he walked the buffed corridors of Atlantic City's segregated Indiana Avenue School. "Pop," the children called him, had played big-time baseball. They bunched about him, begging to hear stories of his past until the bell rang, prompting "Pop" to physically carry them back to their classes. To these children he was special, conveying a prideful dignity and honor belying the conditions of his own everyday employment. When some, unfamiliar with Jim Crow's legacy, wondered aloud why he had not played in the major leagues, he would smile and respond that it was not meant to be, leaving it at that. His focus was on these kids. They had a tough road ahead, and "Pop" would help guide them, becoming "a role model in every sense of the word."[1]

*   *   *

In the September, 1938, issue of *Esquire* magazine, Alvin Harlow, a St. Louis baseball writer, responding to a question about who was baseball's greatest all-time player, replied, "If you mean the greatest in organized baseball, my answer would be Babe Ruth; but if you mean ALL baseball, organized and unorganized, the answer is John Henry Lloyd." Babe Ruth went further, eliminating the color distinction when he stated that Lloyd was his choice as the greatest baseball player of all time. These were remarkable sentiments given that black players were largely overlooked and would not be integrated into the organized "lily-white" game until 1947, with Jackie Robinson's "Great Experiment." They also bore an indication of the respect garnered by Lloyd, an outstanding baseball player whose "kind, patient, soft-spoken, well mannered" ways rendered him highly thought of, both within and outside of the game.[2]

Were it not for segregation, John Henry Lloyd would certainly have been

5

a star in major league baseball. At the least, he would have been afforded the opportunity. John McGraw, iconic manager of New York's baseball Giants, on more than one occasion rued this fact aloud, longing to place Lloyd in the middle of his vaunted lineup. Perhaps as a Cuban, he thought, or an Indian. It never happened. An angular man, Lloyd had the cut of an athlete, with a "protruding jaw" and hands like shovels.[3] In Cuba, where Lloyd played winter ball, they called him *Bemba de Cuchara* or "the spoon," for the way he lapped up grounders — pebbles and dirt sprayed as he tossed the ball across the diamond for the putout.[4] His approach so closely resembled that of Honus Wagner, Pittsburgh's "Flying Dutchman," that Lloyd was favorably likened to him by Connie Mack, the Philadelphia Athletics' Hall of Fame manager. Upon being told that Mack had made the comparison and that Lloyd was being called the "Black Wagner," the Pirates shortstop replied, "I am honored to have John Lloyd called the Black Wagner. It is a privilege to have been compared with him."[5]

Lloyd played at the highest level of Negro baseball for 27 years He loved the game, playing and managing until he was 58 years old. At an age when men ease into retirement, Lloyd was still out there, taking his hacks for the Farley Stars, one of the strongest clubs in southern New Jersey. Al Lopez, the Hall of Fame manager, recalled seeing an aged Lloyd in Cuba, when Lopez

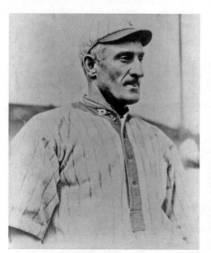

Left: Honus Wagner. Upon being told that Lloyd was being called the "Black Wagner," the Pirates shortstop replied, "I am honored to have John Lloyd called the Black Wagner. It is a privilege to have been compared with him." *Right:* John McGraw, iconic manager of New York's baseball Giants, dreamed of placing Lloyd in the middle of his vaunted lineup.

was there barnstorming in 1930. "He was getting old," said Lopez, "but he could still hit."[6]

A southpaw, Lloyd held the bat in the "crook of his left elbow," swinging easily, gracefully, while generating considerable bat speed and power. The available batting averages, while incomplete, indicate that Lloyd, during his prime, hovered near .400. His lifetime recorded batting average was .368 with a single season high of .564 coming in 1928, when he was already 34.

On the base paths, Lloyd was deceptively fast and became known as a dangerous base runner, despite the fact that at 5'11", 180 pounds, he was big for a shortstop. His defensive range was considerable, and with his long arms and big hands, he stabbed many balls that other shortstops flailed at. Once, when Lloyd stretched his left arm out to take a hit away from a batter, a fan shouted, "That's not baseball, that's *Jai Alai!*" Judy Johnson, the Hall of Fame third baseman who played for Lloyd at Hilldale in 1921, recalled that Lloyd "just looked like he was sliding over to the ball — you could hardly see his feet move." When comparing black baseball's great shortstops, only Luis Bustamante, Willie Wells and Dick Lundy are mentioned in the same breath as Lloyd.[7]

Judy Johnson (above), the Hall of Fame third baseman who played for Lloyd at Hilldale in 1921, recalled that Lloyd "just looked like he was sliding over to the ball — you could hardly see his feet move."

Lloyd was more than a shortstop. He was by all accounts a kind, well-liked man who looked for the best in people, even when it was hidden. "He always had a good word for everyone, a pat on the back," said pitcher Arthur Hardy, who played with Lloyd in 1914. "I never saw him get ruffled."[8]

* * *

John Henry Lloyd was born in Palatka, Florida, on April 25, 1884. This is the place and time provided by Robert Peterson, in his groundbreaking study of black baseball, *Only the Ball Was White*.[9] Peterson gleaned this detail from a 1967 interview he conducted with Nan Lloyd, John Henry's widow. In it she claimed that Lloyd, who had not known his father, the latter having died when Lloyd was an infant, was taken to be raised by his grandmother in Palatka following the subsequent marriage of Lloyd's mother.[10] Nan Lloyd altered her story a few years later, asserting that Lloyd was not born in Palatka, but rather forty or so miles away in Gainesville.[11]

Lloyd was a descendant of slaves. As was custom for black folk in Florida at that time, there is no state "record of event" concerning Lloyd's birth to confirm a location, nor a census record or city directory acknowledging him. Most birth records in Palatka were not recorded there but rather with the state, even though there was an established Health Department in Putnam County. Some birth records can be found in the newspapers, but mostly for whites. Only the best-known African Americans in the county were ever listed.[12] The first mention of Lloyd in any official record comes in the 1900 Federal Census for Duval County where, as a 16-year-old, he lived in Jacksonville with Maria Jenkins, his maternal grandmother.[13]

Twice on federal applications Lloyd (when he was 58 and 71) listed his birthplace as Jacksonville.[14] This inconsistency is understandable, as the available evidence suggests that he had been taken to the city as a small child and resided there until he was a teenager. It might also explain why Whitey Gruhler of the *Atlantic City Press*, a man who had covered Lloyd as a player and knew him well, wrote in a 1938 article that Lloyd was born in Jacksonville. Ed Nichterlein, however, also of the *Atlantic City Press*, confirmed for Cliff Kachline of the National Baseball Hall of Fame that Lloyd "personally told him" that he was born in Palatka. "On one or two occasions" Lloyd had given Jacksonville as his birthplace "because the name was more familiar to [the] general public."[15] This revelation, Peterson's research, the claims by Palatka officials that Lloyd was born there, as well as the ballplayer's return to the town during the offseason, make it highly plausible that John Henry Lloyd came into the world at the cattle crossing 55 miles upriver or south of Jacksonville in the spring of 1884.

Palatka was chartered in 1853. Over the next three decades, the city became a major center for transportation, freight, lumber, citrus, and tourism on the St. John's River, hosting steamboat and railway lines. Along with local citrus production, Palatka developed a diversified and well-rounded slave-based economy. By 1860, slaves made up 52 percent of the city's total population.[16]

Two signature events ultimately stymied Palatka's growth, a great fire on November 7, 1884, and a yellow fever outbreak four years later. These two calamities nearly wiped out the town. The fire reduced Palatka's largely wooden business section to ashes, destroying 65 houses. Damages were estimated at $1,000,000, an enormous sum for the day. While a brief renaissance took place in the aftermath — brick buildings replaced wood structures and first class hotels such as the Putnam House and the Saratoga were erected — it was short-lived. By the 1890s, the railroad had taken much of its business to Jacksonville, and the steamships were reduced to operating only during the tourist season. Terrific freezes in 1894-1895 added to the woes, forcing Palatka's citrus industry south forever.[17]

Perhaps this is why Maria Jenkins, a widow by 1890, took her grandson to Hansontown, one of Jacksonville's Negro sections, seeking a safer life or a return home. Maria had been born a slave in Loudoun, Virginia in 1845. By 1880 she was married and living in Jacksonville with her husband Isaac Jenkins and children Isaac, age 7, and Emma, age 14. Isaac's sister Mary was also living in the home with them. Isaac, who had been born in Florida, was employed as a stevedore or longshoreman, while Maria worked as a washerwoman. Mary Jane, Lloyd's mother, was already out of the home in 1880.[18] Sometime between 1880 and 1890, Isaac died, leaving Maria to follow Mary Jane to Palatka. But with the death of Mary Jane's husband, John Lloyd, and her subsequent remarriage, Maria, now with a grandson in tow, returned to Hansontown, a black slum on the northwest fringe of downtown Jacksonville.[19]

By 1900, Jacksonville's black population, comprising nearly 60 percent of an urban populace that was Florida's largest, lived mostly in poverty on the edge of downtown, with a large concentration in Hansontown, and other smaller settlements in Oakland, LaVilla, and Brooklyn. Their mortality rate was almost twice that of whites. Pools of stagnant water, piles of garbage, and overflowing privies contributed to 75 percent of all typhoid fever cases coming in Hansontown alone. Most adults did menial jobs with little opportunity for advancement. Jim Crow segregation ruled, and an onerous poll tax limited political activity. Black children attended seven segregated elementary schools; there were no public high schools open to them. Such secondary schooling was afforded by the private academies — Edward Waters College, Cookman Institute, Florida Baptist Academy, and Boylan Industrial School.[20]

Maria Jenkins and her grandson lived a life common to blacks in Jacksonville, one where menial tasks, self-help, and limited opportunity was the norm. In 1900, Maria worked as a washerwoman, while the 16-year-old John Henry were out of work, and had been for six months. This was remarkable given that Lloyd had a record of employment dating to early childhood when he had dropped out of elementary school and taken a job, first as a delivery boy, then as a red cap in the railroad terminal. He was later hired to push a freight wagon for the Southern Express Company.[21]

In the spring of 1901, Jacksonville was devastated by a great fire. The *Florida-Times Union & Citizen* described it as "a roaring furnace, without any prospect of being put under control." The flames were so fierce "that millions of sparks and flying burning shingles spread over five or six blocks," torching homes like cigar boxes, "like chaff, as the thundering, mighty, lurid, storm-wave of fire rolled to the east," sweeping the city bare.[22]

It was the largest metropolitan fire in the American South. A total of 2,368 buildings, including 1,700 homes, lay in ruins; seven residents died,

Jacksonville, during the 1901 "Great fire." The flames were so fierce "that millions of sparks and flying burning shingles spread over five or six blocks," torching homes "like chaff, as the thundering, mighty, lurid, storm-wave of fire rolled to the east," sweeping the city bare (courtesy State Archives of Florida).

while 10,000 were left homeless. In all, 146 city blocks were destroyed. The homes or businesses of 9,500 people were also destroyed. Over half of the tax base was gone. Estimated property losses totaled $12 to $15 million, with insurance covering about $5 million. But the recovery began immediately, with pledges of support pouring in; $225,000 came from around the country, and $15,000 from Jacksonville relief agencies.

As Jacksonville "began to live again," downtown streets were cleaned, tents were set up for government offices, trains arrived with needed supplies, and temporary structures were erected for local business operations and Sunday worship. Within weeks, workmen had cut down all burned trees and telegraph poles, dug up stumps, cut and removed tangled and useless wires, cleared and begun filling the bulkheads along the river, torn down dangerous walls and chimneys, and cleaned and sorted brick. The drive to rebuild was all-consuming; within six months more than half of the homes had been rebuilt and one-third of the offices and shops replaced. Within ten years, largely assisted by laborers moving to the city for work, Jacksonville's population doubled, from 28,429 to 57,699.[23]

As Jacksonville prospered in the fire's wake, increased opportunities for leisure activities such as sports arose. Local fans reveled in the spring training efforts of the Philadelphia Athletics, Cincinnati Reds, Boston Nationals, and

Jacksonville, after the 1901 "Great fire." It was the largest metropolitan fire in the American South. A total of 2,368 buildings, including 1,700 homes, lay in ruins; seven residents died, while 10,000 were left homeless. In all, 146 city blocks were destroyed (courtesy State Archives of Florida).

Brooklyn Superbas, who each trained there over the following decade. Judge Morris Dzialynski and former Mayor J. E. T. Bowden organized the Jacksonville baseball team that became a charter member of the South Atlantic League in 1904. Attendance that first season averaged 1,000 fans per game, with the club playing near .500 ball over 117 tilts. Four years later, the Jacksonville Scouts won their first Sally League pennant.[24]

African Americans in Jacksonville loved the game as well, and like minority communities elsewhere, filled local lots with amateur nines competing against one another. Clubs such as the Jacksonville Eagles, the Jacksonville Red Caps and the Duval Giants — who would move to Atlantic City, New Jersey, reborn as the Bacharach Giants — brought the fans out in large numbers, where they shared fish fries, barbeque, baseball, and fellowship. One such club was the Jacksonville Old Receivers and it was on this team that Lloyd got his first real taste of competition.[25]

Napoleon "Chance" Cummings, who later played for Lloyd in Atlantic City with the Bacharach Giants, but had known him since the former was a boy in Jacksonville, remembered Lloyd as a great guy, someone that everybody got along with. "They always called Lloyd 'Just-in-time,'" Cummings said. "You'd be running, he'd take the ball and throw you out and then stand at shortstop and laugh at you. He'd say, 'Just in time.' That's how he got his name." When Cummings was a boy, the kindly Lloyd would get him into ballparks by letting him carry his glove and shoes past the gate so that he could watch the game. "He was a man practically everybody could get along with," Cummings recalled.[26]

In 1905, at the age of 21, Lloyd, who by this time was a 5'11", 180-pound catcher, traveled a few hours north to Macon, Georgia to begin playing with the Acmes, a semiprofessional club featuring southern black baseball pioneers "Georgia Rabbit" and "Big Foot Mary." As the team was too poor to afford a mask or chest protector, Lloyd ignorantly assumed the position without the requisite tools. Cary B. Peterson of the *Indianapolis Freeman*, as quoted by Robert Peterson, spoke years later of the consequences, recalling that Lloyd in a game against Augusta took such a beating behind the plate from foul balls that both of his eyes were swollen shut, forcing him to leave the field. The "next day," Peterson wrote, "he purchased a wire paper basket, enclosed his mug, and finished the series."[27]

While Lloyd was happy for the chance to play with a top team, it did not take him long to realize that if he was going to lead with his face, he should at least put some distance between himself and the opposing bat. By the following year, playing with the Philadelphia Cuban X Giants, Lloyd was a second baseman.

There is still some uncertainty as to when and how Lloyd made his way north to pursue a baseball career. What is probable is that during the winter following his season in Macon, Lloyd either joined other players waiting tables at resort hotels in Palm Beach, playing baseball on the side to entertain guests, or was spotted when playing in the area by one of these professionals. In the early 1900s, railroad baron Henry Flagler built two baseball fields in Palm Beach, one at his Royal Poinciana Hotel and another at the Breakers. These diamonds became winter home to some of the finest black ballplayers of the era. Albert Spalding, who played organ at Whitehall, Flagler's home, to entertain Flagler, his wife, Mary Lily Kenan, and their wealthy guests, recalled in a 1907 letter to his sister that he had seen baseball played like nothing he had ever witnessed before:

> Both teams are colored and composed of employees of the Breakers and Poinciana hotels, who however are hired because of their baseball ability and then incidentally given employment as waiters or porters. Many of them play on the Cuban Giants team during the summer so that the quality of baseball ranked with professional white teams.
>
> The greatest sport was in listening to the coaching and watching the antics of a full grandstand back of first base. Their sympathies were pretty evenly divided between the two teams, so accordingly, whenever either team would make a hit, then was the time to watch the bleachers. The crowd would yell themselves hoarse, stand up in their seats, bang each other over the head, and even the girls would go into a perfect frenzy as if they were in a Methodist camp meeting.[28]

The Breakers, 1901. In the early 1900s, railroad baron Henry Flagler built two baseball fields in Palm Beach, one at his Royal Poinciana Hotel and another at the Breakers. These diamonds became winter homes to some of the finest black ballplayers of the era.

This "waiter-baseball" phenomenon found its way to Palm Beach from Long Island, where Frank Thompson, headwaiter at the Argyle Hotel, had formed a team of black waiters to play for amusement. This was the start of the Cuban Giants, one of the best early black clubs. By 1888, the trend had reached Jacksonville; a *Sporting News* wag reported that the players were equal to any white players on the ball field. "If you don't think so," he wrote, "go and see the Cuban Giants play" (McIver, "Cooks to Catchers," *Fort Lauderdale Sun-Sentinal*, August 22, 1993).

Ed Andrews, a former centerfielder with the Philadelphia Phillies, had moved to West Palm Beach in 1899 after a freeze wiped out his Indian River pineapple business. Flagler, who liked the ballplayer and knew that his father had been a Great Lakes boat captain, hired him to manage his yacht basin. Flagler also knew that Andrews was a man who could run his baseball program. Andrews subsequently began recruiting black players from teams such as the Cuban Giants, the Cuban X Giants, Brooklyn's Royal Giants, and Chicago's Leland Giants to field two competing squads, one for the Royal Poinciana and the other for the Breakers. This rivalry, dubbed the "Coconut League" by some, continued until 1931.

Highly regarded players like Oscar Charleston, Louis Santop, Dick Redding and Cyclone Williams were brought in to boost the level of play. The players were in turn paid $23 to $33 a month as waiters or up to $40 for captains, while headwaiters could receive $75. Meals and housing were provided on the grounds. The rich hotel guests loved it, lapping up sunshine, scotch, and wagers, all in the shadows of men who might have played big league baseball were it not for the game's segregation practices.[29]

Newspaper accounts of the baseball games between the two squads were sparse at best during the early years. The first recorded mention came in the Palm Beach *Daily News* on Thursday, January 27, 1898. The reason of course was that the games were intended as entertainment for the bored hotel guests, and the players were assumed to be merely waiters and such. No one other than hotel insiders had any idea who it was they were watching. The best games were the ones matching an all-star crew from the hotels against white big leaguers from the Palm Beach resort and the Miami resort. As historian William McNeil notes, "These were among the first integrated professional baseball games of their kind in the United States."[30]

Lloyd's success on the diamond during the winter of 1905-1906 drew attention. Some sources indicate that E. B. Lamar, Jr., the owner of the Cuban X Giants, saw Lloyd play while the Giants were in Palm Beach that winter, opting to bring him north and paying his fare to Philadelphia. Lloyd's widow, however, told Robert Peterson that he went north at the urging of his fellow

Breakers cab drivers. The baseball games were intended as entertainment for the bored hotel guests, and the players were assumed to be merely waiters, cab drivers and such. No one other than hotel insiders had any idea who it was they were watching (courtesy State Archives of Florida).

porters in Jacksonville, arriving in Philadelphia with $1.50 in his pocket and no assurance of employment. Regardless, Lloyd was on his way.[31]

It has been written that Lloyd began his 1906 rookie season with the Cuban X Giants as an understudy to Charlie Grant, the so-called "Chief Tokahoma," who five years earlier McGraw had tried to pass off as an Indian on his Baltimore Orioles.[32] But Grant was the second baseman for the Philadelphia Giants, the city's other professional black baseball club, not the Cuban X Giants. Accounts of the Cuban X Giants that season have Lloyd listed as a part-time second baseman, with John Hill at short. Lloyd batted a meager .108, but in his first game drove in the winning run with a double in the tenth inning to beat Charles "Kid" Carter and the Wilmington Giants.[33]

On August 14, Lloyd's Cuban X Giants posted a 5–0 shutout against the Professionals at the Athletic Grounds in Philadelphia. For six innings Lefty Biggins held the X Giants even, allowing no runs. But in the seventh, the X Giants got to him for a double, triple, and three singles, netting four of their five runs. Perez got the win for the X Giants, keeping the Professionals guessing, allowing just two hits while fanning eight.[34]

On Labor Day, before an overflow crowd at Athletics Park, the Philadelphia Giants twice bested the Cuban X Giants for the league championship. It was the morning contest, won by the Giants 3–1, which both clubs badly wanted, for that was the game in which the championship was decided. Andrew "Rube" Foster of the Giants was brilliant in the lid-lifter, twice pitching out of bases-loaded situations. The big Texan also got two hits. Harry Buckner, pitching for the Cuban X Giants, had no such luck, allowing three run-scoring singles. In game two, a sequence of hits off Perez in the second and third innings gave the Giants all of their runs in a 4–1 win. Dan McClellan picked up the win for the Giants, buffaloing the Cuban X Giants until the seventh inning when they were able to scratch across one run.[35]

Following the season, the Cuban X Giants played an exhibition game

with a Philadelphia Athletics squad that included future Hall of Famers Eddie Plank and Rube Waddell plus Jack Coombs and Andy Coakley. While the X Giants lost, the young Lloyd, batting leadoff, had a great day with four hits in five at-bats, all coming against Coakley, a 20-game winner in 1905.[36]

A dramatic shakeup took place in eastern black baseball that off-season, namely the jumping of Rube Foster to Frank Leland's Chicago Giants, bringing four of his Philadelphia teammates with him — Pete Hill, Pete Booker, Nate Harris, and Mike Moore. They were joined by Bobby Winston, Lloyd's teammate on the Cuban X Giants, along with Bill Gatewood and Jap Payne of the Royal Giants. Historian John Holway notes the westerners'

Andrew "Rube" Foster, a great pitcher and "the mastermind" of black baseball, "perhaps the most colorful figure the game has known" (courtesy the Negro Leagues Baseball Museum).

utter amazement at their first look at Foster. He quotes the Chicago *Inter-Ocean* as observing that Foster was a pitcher with the guile, speed and coolness of future Hall of Famers Hoss Radbourn, Amos Rusie, and Cy Young. "What does that make him?" they asked. "Why the greatest baseball pitcher in the country; that's what the greatest baseball players of white persuasion who have gone against him say."[37]

With the upheaval came the disbanding of the Cuban X Giants, an incredible turn for E. B. Lamar's storied club. They had been champions of the East from 1897 through 1903, and champions of all black baseball in 1899. In 1899 Lamar had taken the X Giants west,

Bill Gatewood. A tremendous pitcher in the early years of black baseball, he played for 15 teams in his 24-year career.

winning the first challenge playoff championship series. It was also the longest trip ever taken by a black ballclub to that point.[38]

The break-up led Lloyd to sign with the rival Philadelphia Giants, managed by black baseball pioneer and future Hall of Famer Sol White, who were in need of a shortstop with the defection of Nate Harris. Lloyd proved a great investment for White. An ex-shortstop himself, White taught Lloyd the secrets of playing the position. Lloyd responded, rounding out an excellent infield that included White at first, Charlie Grant on second, and Bill "Brodie" Francis at third. Bruce Petway was the catcher, and lefty Danny McClellan the ace.[39]

While there is no record of the games played between eastern clubs that season, a group comprised of Giants, Royals and Lelands did travel to Cuba for play that winter. The squad included Lloyd, Bobby Winston, Grant "Home Run" Johnson, Pete Hill, and Bruce Petway, with Rube Foster, John Davis, and Danny McClellan pitching. They faced a stellar collection of

Cubans including future major leaguers Rafael Almeida and Armando Marsans, as well as pitchers José Méndez and Joséito Muñoz. The Americans won six and lost five in Cuba. In 43 recorded at-bats that season, including the exhibition with Cuba, Lloyd collected 12 hits, batting .279. Excluding an injury-marred year in 1912, 1907 was the last season for ten years in which Lloyd did not hit .300 or better.[40]

As noted earlier, in Cuba, Lloyd was referred to as *Bemba de Cuchara*, or the spoon. While *Bemba* can mean fat lips or "nigger" lips, Cuban baseball historian Roberto Echevarria does not believe the Cubans applied it to Lloyd negatively, trusting rather that it was applied to compliment his fielding. Cubans, however, also referred to Lloyd as "Sam," which was short for the racist "Sambo." It was a name that stayed with Lloyd throughout the 1910s. Given the times, it is probable that *Bemba de Cuchara* and "Sam" began as racial slurs, with the former later changed to a compliment about his fielding.[41]

Pete Hill, Lloyd's teammate in Cuba, was once described by Cum Posey, the legendary owner of the Homestead Grays, as the "most consistent hitter of his lifetime." He was a stalwart for Rube Foster's Chicago American Giants teams for close to 20 years. A lefty at bat, Hill consistently shot line drives to all parts of the park, seldom striking out. In 1911, he hit safely in 115 of 116 games. "The first great outfielder in black baseball history," Hill was often compared with the Detroit Tigers' Ty Cobb. James Riley, in his *Biographical Encyclopedia of the Negro Leagues*, writes that if an all-star outfield was composed of players from the deadball era, Pete Hill would have joined Cobb in flanking Tris Speaker "to form the outfield constellation."[42]

Pete Hill. "The most consistent hitter of his lifetime," in 1911 he was credited as batting safely in 115 of 116 games.

The 1908 season was a breakout campaign for Lloyd, who led his team into an East-West "World Series" against Rube Foster and the Leland Giants. The Lelands had just finished an incredible swing during which they had traveled through much of the South in a private Pullman car amassing a 64–21 record against semipro opponents, as well as playing in the competitive Chicago City League, which also included the Colts, owned by Cap Anson. Anson, widely blamed for baseball's color line, and by this time 52 years old and playing first base, ironically exhibited no problems in facing the Lelands. As John Holway noted, the game's history may have been significantly altered were his attitude different in 1887 when he played the key role in segregating baseball.[43]

As they traveled west to face the Lelands, the young Giants squad must have felt some trepidation, and it showed, as the Lelands jumped out to a game one victory. The next day, the Giants fought back, taking an 11-inning contest 5–4. Bob Garrison scattered four hits in the affair, while Nux James, who batted .348 in the series, bagged four hits. Game three found the Lelands rallying from behind as Bobby Winston singled home the game-winner with two outs in the ninth inning. Pete Booker had three hits for the Lelands.[44]

With the Lelands up two games to one, Rube Foster went to the hill on August 3, facing off against Danny McClellan. It was a lopsided affair, Foster confounding his old team in an 11–1 rout. But two days later, with Foster pitching on short rest, the Giants struck back, touching Foster for eight runs and handing him his worst defeat since coming to Chicago. Lloyd, developing as a hitter before everyone's eyes, had four hits on the day. The Giants were further braced by their pitcher, "Martin." Martin's only other appearance in the baseball record was with the Chicago Giants in 1913. Yet he clearly was on top of his game in this series, for the next day he went again, this time opposing the excellent spitballer Walter Ball in a 7–4 Giants victory. Lloyd banged out two more hits in the contest, bringing his total for the series to ten, finishing with a .500 average. The series ended abruptly tied at three games apiece when Foster, angered over suspect officiating, led his team off the field, refusing to finish it. For his efforts, Lloyd received the "Rube Foster Award" for most outstanding player in the series.[45]

Upon their return to Philadelphia, the Giants played Connie Mack's venerable Philadelphia Athletics in a one-game exhibition. Mack was no stranger to black baseball and understood the level of talent that it possessed. According to Al Harvin, in a 1973 *Black Sports Magazine* piece, Connie Mack, in speaking with Judy Johnson about bringing blacks to the major leagues, once said, "Judy, there's just too many of you! If we let you in, then we'd knock a lot of white boys out of jobs."[46] This was a common assumption held among black players at the time, but did little to alter the economic reality of their situation. Mack's Athletics, with future Hall of Famer Eddie Collins,

Harry Davis, and Cy Morgan, a 14-game winner for Boston in 1908, won the game 5–2. Lloyd had two hits against Morgan.[47]

Again with the Philadelphia Giants the following year, Lloyd began the season with a bang, rapping two hits and scoring three runs, leading his club to a 12–2 win over the Brooklyn Ridgewoods. At home in Meyerrose Park for the early set, the Giants turned 16 hits into 12 runs, while Danny McClellan held the Ridgewoods to a pair of runs on seven hits. This sent a strong message to the New York media, some of whom might have questioned the Giants' readiness for the season. "The Quaker team is one to be seriously reckoned with," they said.[48] The following week the Giants assault continued, besting New Brunswick 11–5. Fisher, the Philadelphia hurler, scattered nine hits in the contest, but was helped by the losers' sloppy defense.[49]

Lloyd was impressive with his glove as well as his bat, fielding sensationally at times. In a twin-bill against Hoboken and Ridgewood on Sunday, June 13, Lloyd made two putouts with three assists in game one, while getting two hits, one a double. He followed suit with a double in the second game, a 6–1 win for Philadelphia. In game two, the Giants gathered four runs in the first inning. Neuer, the Ridgewood hurler, then settled in, blanking his opponents until the sixth when the Giants pushed two more runs across. Fisher allowed a scant three hits for the Giants. Two weeks later, Fisher cooled somewhat, posting a 5–4 loss to New Brunswick.[50]

On July 4 the "Genuine" Cuban Giants came to town, a club that had been winning most of its games in the West, but proved not as strong in the east. Danny McClellan, "in great form," and bolstered by an offense that brought ten runs, allowed but a single run on six hits to the Cubans. Lloyd, McClellan and Patton, the light-hitting right fielder, had three hits each for the Giants, while Bill Bedford, the ill-fated second baseman and pitcher, had two hits for the Cuban Giants.[51]

On Sunday, July 18, the Giants traveled to Manhattan Field, located uptown near 300th Street, to take on the Manhattans, a squad featuring Andy Coakley, the now former Philadelphia Athletics and Chicago Cubs hurler who was doing time in the bushes, hoping to find a way back to prominence.[52] The Manhattans, who other than Coakley fielded a mediocre squad, scored three runs in the fifth against a shaky Giants defense, including an error by the usually stellar Lloyd. The Giants battled back, however, plating three in the sixth and touching Coakley for several hits, including a double by Lloyd, one of his two hits on the day. The score stayed knotted at three as the game was called on account of darkness.[53]

The season evolved through the summer with a provisional schedule, the Philadelphia Giants, Royal Giants, and Cuban Stars all playing teams with lesser credentials simply to pick up games. On July 25, the Giants won both halves of a split-bill doubleheader at Meyerrose Park, the first against Hoboken, 7–3 and the latter against Ridgewood, 4–3; this in spite of the Giants not using either of their top pitchers, McClellan or Fisher. Lloyd "carried off the batting honors" in game one, getting three hits.[54] It was then announced that they would travel to Detroit to take on Rube Foster's powerful Chicago Leland Giants at Bennett Park, home of the Detroit Tigers. The games were also to be played during the National Elks Convention, the series advertised as East vs. West, a series to settle the colored championship.[55]

The Giants traveled west by bus, and while difficult, they made the best of it. "Bus travel brought players closer," recalled Max Manning, a later pitcher for the Newark Eagles who played for Lloyd when coming up outside of Atlantic City. "It was a shared experience, with singing and joking." Lloyd clearly enjoyed the travel, which did not affect his play or approach. He was consistent. "Don't jump up and down when you win," he said, "or cry when you lose. Determine why you lost and then correct it." Lloyd was a "quality man," especially when games or conditions were tough.[56]

In the August 9 lid-lifter, the Lelands took control, winning 3–1. The Giants "went to pieces" in the sixth, allowing the Lelands to score three runs behind hits by George Wright and first baseman Chappie Johnson. Making matters worse, Ray Wilson, the Giants' first baseman and team captain, was forced out of the series with a badly wrenched foot. Walter Ball, the great spitballer, got the win for the Lelands. With "Bugs" Hayman allowing a scant four hits in the second game, the Giants fought back, easily beating the Lelands, and Ball, 5–2. Lloyd and Petway led the way for the Giants, each with a double. Spot Poles and Nux James both stole a base. So elated was Hayman over his team's success that the following day he asked to be allowed to pitch, and again he beat the Lelands, this time 9–1. A triple play by Lloyd, Brodie Francis and Nux James was the highlight of the game. Lloyd had three hits, one a triple, while James, the team's star second baseman, banged a grand slam.[57]

John McGraw once said that if the color line were not in place, he would take Lloyd, Dick Redding, Joe Williams and Spot Poles to the major leagues for his club. Spot Poles, like Pete Hill, was a slightly bowlegged bullet of an outfielder who was considered one of the greatest athletes of his day. Known as the "black Ty Cobb," Poles usually batted leadoff, which because of his speed gave his team a great chance of scoring first when he got on — and he got on a lot. During World War I, Poles joined the Army infantry, serving with distinction in Europe, ultimately earning five battle star decorations and a Purple Heart for his combat experience in France as a sergeant in the 369th

Infantry. Poles, a great hitter, would muster a career batting average of over .400 against all competition, and .594 against big leaguers.[58]

Having dispatched the Lelands, the Giants returned home to top the Brooklyn Royals, a team that they had found no success against in 1909. Lloyd had three hits in the affair, one a double, and Bill Francis contributed a triple. Following the victory, the Giants finished up their regular season with another win, this one over the Ridgewoods, a 3–0 shutout tossed by Fisher. Lloyd belted a triple in the game, bringing his average to .409 for the season.[59]

That fall Lloyd traveled to Cuba for the first of his ten seasons there.[60] In spite of the nicknames he was tagged with, he loved it in Cuba and eventually the feeling became mutual. There were those in Cuba who wanted the soft-spoken, line drive–hitting Lloyd to stay permanently, becoming a citizen of the island nation.[61] Lloyd was easy to like. His friends called him "slow glide" for the deliberate manner in which he spoke. "He would think a lot," recalled Nan Lloyd. "You would have to pull the words out of him." Even if frustrated, he would just scratch his head and say "Dad burn!" It was his favorite expression, and the closest he ever came to using profanity. But on the field, his bat and glove spoke for him. "You can never win a ballgame with your mouth," Lloyd would say.[62]

Lloyd was a Christian man, so ill manners and unseemliness rubbed against him. He was a well-built guy and could have been imposing or overbearing had he gone that route, but he was not like that. Lloyd was a kind, respectable fellow and he looked the part. "He always matched," Nan recalled. "He was well-dressed, his fingernails were always groomed, he was immaculate in every way." Lloyd was also meticulous in washing his hands, "especially after shaking hands with everybody out in the street." Given the yellow fever and malaria outbreaks of his childhood, such fastidiousness was prudent, and no doubt served him well in the 1918 influenza pandemic, as well as those that followed in the next decade.[63]

Traveling with Lloyd to Cuba was Bruce Petway, the outstanding catcher and Lloyd's best friend in baseball. "They were very close, like brothers," Nan recalled. "They roomed together wherever they would go, and lie awake at night talking about what they were going to do the next day."[64]

Bruce Petway was lean and deceptively fast for a catcher, especially then, the stereotype calling for a catcher who was squat and heavy-legged. On offense, Petway was "better known as a base stealing threat than as a slugger," but it was on defense where he excelled. A student of the game, the "scrappy" Petway used his knowledge and abilities to become the best catcher in the business, truly the first great catcher in black baseball history. He was an exceptional receiver with a strong, accurate arm that forced runners to cling to the bases rather than be picked off, which Petway would do while throwing from his knees.[65]

The *Liga General de Base Ball de la República de Cuba* had four teams in 1909, Havana, Almendares, Fe and Matanzas. Petway played for Fe, which usually employed more American blacks than the other clubs, while Lloyd was assigned to Matanzas. Games were played at Almendares Park and Palmar del Junco in Matanzas, at least until January, when the latter club folded. Lloyd subsequently joined Pete Hill on the Havana club, which won the league championship. Each of the surviving teams played 46 games that year.[66]

After the season, Petway joined Lloyd and Hill with Havana to take on the barnstorming Detroit Tigers, the 1909 American League champions. The Tigers, confident enough to have left their two stars, Ty Cobb and Sam Crawford, back home, must not have expected much in the way of competition on the island.

Even without Cobb and Crawford, the Tigers were fierce, boasting a rotation of George Mullin (29–8), Ed Willet (21–10), and Ed Summers (19–9). But it was Detroit's rookie right-hander Bill Lelivelt (0–1) who opened the series before a crowd "so thick it overflowed the stands and covered part of the outfield." The teams battled for nine innings, locked in a 2–2 tie, before the Tigers pushed three runs across in the top of the tenth. In the bottom of the frame, with one on, Lloyd gave the Havana hopefuls something to cheer about, blasting a triple into the crowd, making it 5–3. The inning and game ended, however, with Lloyd on third.[67]

In the six games played against the Tigers, Havana won four and lost two. Lloyd picked up five hits in 24 at-bats. Yet the Tigers were humiliated. In 12 games against Havana and Almendares they went 4–8, one loss an 11-inning no-hitter tossed by "Bombín" Pedroso, who beat them, 2–1. The Tigers' lone run came on an error in the seventh. Luis Bustamante, for Havana, led the series with a .415 average, followed by Augustín Parpetti at .336, and Chino Morán at .333. The Cubans and their black American *compádres* had come to play![68]

Following the Tigers came an all-star squad of major leaguers including Fred "Boner" Merkle at first, Sherry Magee in left, and Jimmy Archer behind the plate, as well as hurlers Mordecai "Three-Finger" Brown (27–9), Nap Rucker (13–19), Addie Joss (14–13), and Howard Camnitz (25–6).[69] In game one, Lloyd got a hit in three trips to help beat Joss 2–1. Chicho González got the win for the Cubans in a contest decided by Mulo Padrón's homer in the fifth inning. Brooklyn's Nap Rucker bested Joséito Muñoz in game two although he allowed nine hits in the process. Pastor Pareda next blanked the all-stars 5–0, with Lloyd picking up a single. Jose Méndez starred in the game four, scattering two hits and one run while Julián Castillo doubled and tripled to lead the attack. The all-stars broke through in a big way on the final day of the set with Addie Joss, Brown and Camnitz combining for a 7–2 "onslaught." Lloyd had a nondescript single in two at-bats.[70]

If Lloyd learned anything that winter in Cuba, it was that he could play baseball with anyone. Others had already figured this out, and in Chicago, Rube Foster, having kept an eye on the happenings in Cuba, moved to act. The next spring, 1910, Foster signed Lloyd, Pete Hill, and Bruce Petway to the Lelands, as well as Jap Payne and Grant "Home Run" Johnson. A year later, Foster split with Frank Leland, organizing his own club, the famous Chicago American Giants, of which Lloyd at shortstop proved to be a lynchpin.[71]

TWO

The Black Wagner

The *Chicago Defender* bemoaned 1909 as one of the worst on record for the lynching of 325 Negro men and women, "killed and burned at the stake." While the violence was not limited to those "coarser whites" residing in the south, Lloyd's birthplace, Florida, had the highest lynching rate in the nation. The brutality fostered an atmosphere of unease, fear and intimidation among black folk, particularly when approaching Jim Crow's racial barriers, which they did in remarkable numbers. White, organized baseball, with its own invisible line, was such a frontier, but a no man's land of exclusion had existed for twenty years. "Had it not been for rabid race prejudice," Lloyd later recalled, "many of those fellows would have been in the big leagues."[1]

In the years following the Civil War, baseball became a true national pastime, one where blacks and whites played together, neither deprived of the competition they sought. Bud Fowler, the first black professional baseball player, spent many years barnstorming wherever a game could be found. Moses Fleetwood Walker and his brother Welday Wilberforce Walker made it into the major leagues in 1884, with the Toledo club of the American Association. Frank Grant, said to have been the "best of the Negro players in the White leagues," led the International League in batting in 1887.[2]

As Jim Crow segregation spread across the land, however, prompted by an elitist need to keep working class blacks and whites apart, and codified by the 1896 United States Supreme Court in *Plessy v. Ferguson*, opportunities for African American ballplayers in the White game diminished. By 1887, the racist actions of Adrian "Cap" Anson, the future Hall of Fame leader of the Chicago White Stockings, and others led to the door to major league baseball closing on black players, remaining so for the next sixty years. Instead, these players sought work elsewhere, either barnstorming the back roads or abroad, or in colored leagues formed in the nation's major cities. The dream remained and was ubiquitous — that one day talent alone would allow them to ply their profession at the highest level possible.[3]

In 1910 Chicago's Leland Giants readied itself for its first season without Frank Leland, the club's founder and president. Following the 1909 season Leland and Rube Foster had a falling out, resulting in the two men forming separate rival clubs. Foster, who won the legal right to retain the name Leland Giants for 1910, opted to hold it for a year before changing it to the Chicago American Giants in 1911. Leland's new club, the Chicago Giants, which ultimately became a charter member of the Negro National League in 1920, became known in the press throughout the season as Leland's Chicago Giants, causing a certain amount of confusion.[4]

That spring, Rube Foster took his club to Florida to round them into form while swinging up through the south on an exhibition tour. Foster, pitching for the Lelands in a 4–1 victory over the Royal Giants in Palm Beach that February, was said to have "added grace and dignity" to the affair. In the game he struck out four, allowing a scant three singles, behind 11 Lelands hits. The *Chicago Defender* noted that Foster's 1910 Leland Giants looked like the "real goods."[5]

The first mention of Lloyd in the Chicago press came on April 30 in an advertisement placed by Foster announcing the new season and the May 15 "Grand Opening" of its park at 69th and Halsted Streets. Foster, marketing his Lelands to "the most select audiences in the city," noted that games would be played with the best talent he could find:

> Come visit our park and see Rube Foster, the world's greatest pitcher, assisted by Wickware and Dougherty, the season's sensation; Petway and Booker, the stars; Hill and Payne, outfield phenomenon; Duncan, Prior, Hutchinson, Lloyd and Home Run Johnson, celebrities who can only be seen on our diamond.

The Lelands began their season on a high note, besting a local squad known as the Gunthers. The infield, with Lloyd and Grant Johnson up the middle, was spectacular, comprising what very well could have been the top double play combination in America at the time, better even than the Cubs' Johnny Evers and Joe Tinker, of Tinker to Evers to Chance fame.[6]

Grant Johnson, black baseball's greatest shortstop prior to Lloyd, might have served as a role model to the latter shortstop, their similarities were so striking. Johnson was a hard hitter, garnering the moniker "Home Run," at least until age and experience led fans and other players to call him "Dad." Johnson was also a good man, not prone to vices such as drinking and gambling. He kept himself in fine physical condition and played out his baseball days with semi-professional teams before retiring as a player in 1932 at age 58.[7]

By July 29 the Lelands were on cruise control, besting the Stars of Cuba, 7–0. The Lelands broke up the game in the third inning with four runs, scored on four hits. Two more runs came across in the ninth when Pete Hill hit his second triple of the game, a shot to right-center, scoring two runs. A day earlier, the two clubs had played to an 11-inning 4–4 draw at "old White Sox park," but the game had been called on account of darkness. Rube Foster had

Grant Johnson, black baseball's greatest shortstop prior to Lloyd, might have served as a role model to the latter player, their similarities were so striking.

gone to the bump for the Lelands, opposed by José Méndez for the Cubans. Lloyd stroked five hits over the two games, a double in each, and turned a double play. Only Pete Hill fared better on offense, with seven hits.[8]

Over the next few weeks the Lelands remained hot, topping an all-star team at Gunther Park in both ends of a doubleheader, 3–1 and 6–3. They then posted a 9–4 victory over the Gunthers in the "Third Annual Monster Ball Game" played at Comiskey Park, this time 9–4. After dropping one to the Gunthers, 6–5, they rounded out the month by beating the Athletics, filling in for the Louisville Cubs, 4–3. Bruce Petway led the way with a triple for the Lelands.[9]

On September 2, the Lelands played at Normal Park and topped a team called the Oklahoma Giants, 3–1. The visitors scored in the second inning on a home run from their own "Hill." The Lelands battled back, tying the game in the fifth, and icing it in the seventh on a Grant Johnson sacrifice fly that scored Duncan. Dougherty struck out ten "Okies" in the game, against only one walk. The Lelands were at it again a few days later, this time topping the "Okies," 5–0. Rube Foster went the distance for Chicago in the shutout, but the game's remarkable feature was the triple play posted by the Lelands. The play occurred in the fourth inning, when Oklahoma's Bennett was passed and Donald singled. Bolden, the "Okie" catcher, then blasted a shot to centerfielder Pete Hill, who trapped the ball and fired it to third, where it was relayed to second and first, getting the woefully slow Bolden to finish the play.[10]

In the season's final tally between the Lelands and the Gunthers, the Lelands won, 6–4. It was announced shortly thereafter that the Lelands had signed to play the Stars of Cuba in a game at Comiskey Park. The game, to benefit United States War Veterans at Camp Allyn K. Capron, Jr., No. 6, was a Saturday afternoon affair. In the contest, the Lelands, with Lindsay on the hill, beat the "Islanders," 4–1. Lindsay, "Rube Foster's new pitcher," struck out ten, holding the Cubans all the way with the exception of the fifth inning, when hits by Figarola, Guerra, and Perera scored their only run. "Jap" Payne and Grant Johnson had doubles for the Lelands, with Lloyd, Hill, Duncan and Petway all contributing at the plate.[11]

Having finished their season in Chicago, the Lelands traveled east, playing an impressive 18-game schedule and winning all of them. The final tilt came against the Ridgewood club, billed that fall as the "Champions of New York." The game took place on October 1, the date on which the Lelands had been scheduled to sail for Havana, before receiving a large guarantee to remain over. The earnings and time spent were worth it for the Chicago team who, with Frank "Red Ant" Wickware on the mound, shut out Ridgewood, 7–0. Following the contest the Lelands departed for Jacksonville for a two-game set, playing one, an 8–2 victory, before continuing on to Cuba.[12] By the time 1910 wrapped up, this version of the Lelands had proven to be one of Rube Foster's greatest teams, winning 123 games against six losses on the year. Lloyd batted .324, with Pete Hill at .457, Bruce Petway at .433 and "Jap" Payne at .368.

Frank "Red Ant" Wickware was Foster's ace in the hole. He came from Coffeyville, Kansas, home of the Dalton Gang and Walter Johnson.[13] A lanky right-hander "with a blazing fastball," he was best known for his match-ups against Johnson, outdueling him in two out of three games in 1913 and 1914. Called the "black Walter Johnson," Wickware was composed on the bump, firing the ball with an unfailingly "smooth delivery." A star gate attraction for obvious reasons, the "Red Ant" was "formidable!"[14]

The autumn of 1910 brought not only the Lelands' return to Cuba, but the Detroit Tigers as well, fresh from a third place finish and this time with star outfielder "Wahoo" Sam Crawford. Ty Cobb, the Tigers' star outfielder and hit king, also came, but traveled on a later ship. In a series rank with tension, Lloyd shined, batting .500 while performing brilliantly in the field, despite aggressive, hostile attempts to take him out at second base when covering the bag. Lloyd's teammates were up for the challenge as well, with Grant Johnson batting .412 and Bruce Petway .389. In five games, Cobb batted .368 and was thrown out three times attempting to steal second. On November 28, he was held hitless in three at-bats by the Cuban hurler Chiché

González, while Crawford got a single in four trips. "Wahoo" Sam batted .360 in 12 games.[15]

Ty Cobb, considered by many to be the greatest baseball player of his day, and one of the five original inductees into the National Baseball Hall of Fame, was said to have been so disgusted with his performance that he left Cuba, never again taking the field against black players. His hard sliding was also said to have prompted Lloyd to wear shin guards under his pant legs to fend off Cobb's flying spikes. John Holway, however, a historian on black baseball, refutes the story, arguing that the newspapers at that time never mentioned it. For his part, Lloyd "insisted that 'Cobb was a good fellow, on and off the field.'" Buck O'Neil — later manager of the Kansas City Monarchs — disagreed, recalling

SAM CRAWFORD.

In the autumn of 1910 "Wahoo" Sam Crawford, star outfielder of the Detroit Tigers, batted .360 in 12 games against Cuban and black American players in Cuba, just behind his teammate Ty Cobb, who batted .368. At the same time, Lloyd batted .500, Grant Johnson .412 and Bruce Petway .389.

that Cobb had an urgency about him, born of a need to get out of Georgia. "He had to fight his way out and this was why he had this great competitive spirit." Cobb viewed blacks the way all poor whites did, O'Neil asserted, as competition. "We weren't competition to the affluent, to the educated. No. But the other man ... we were competition to him ... but a lot of other people felt the same way — the majority of people felt that way."[16]

Connie Mack's World Champion Philadelphia Athletics followed the Tigers into town, but to little effect as Lloyd and his teammates continued to paste the ball, stymieing the opposition. In game one, Lloyd gathered

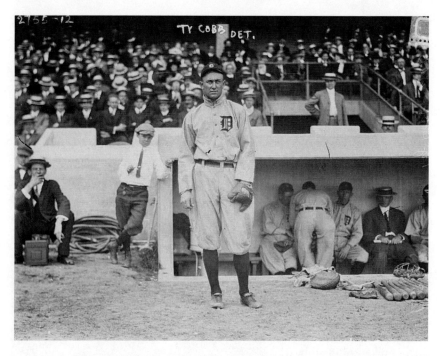

Ty Cobb, considered by many to be the greatest baseball player of his day, was said to have been so disgusted with his performance in Cuba that he left the island, never again taking the field against black players.

a single in two at-bats against the Athletics' Chief Bender, a 23-game winner that season, Havana winning, 2–0. Pastor Pareda got the shutout for Havana, allowing just one hit. The A's sent 16-game-winner Eddie Plank to the mound in game two, but with little consequence and a similar result, losing 5–3. Havana scored the tying and go-ahead runs in the sixth off Plank. Grant Johnson, who hit .458 that fall against white big leaguers, raced home on an error by Stuffy McInnis, who was playing out of position at third base. For his part, Lloyd was silenced by "Gentleman Eddie," going 0-for-4.[17]

With the A's down two games to none versus Havana, and with 31-game-winner Jack Coombs on the hill, they fought through an exciting ten-inning, 5–4 victory. The winning tally came on a walk, a single by Coombs, and the game-winning hit by Topsy Hartsell. The A's took it to Havana once again three days later, with Bender earning the 6–4 win. Lloyd got his bat going in the final game facing Bender again, rattling a double and a single in the 6–2 rout. The win gave Havana a 3–2 advantage over the champions. For the series, Lloyd batted .300, three for ten. His batting average that winter,

Jugadores del Habana. "Players from Havana" 1911. 1— Gonzalo Sanchez, catcher, 2 — Sam Lloyd, short stop, 3 — Ricardo Hernandez, outfielder, 4 — Preston Hill, outfielder, 5 — Grant Johnson, short stop and second base, 6 — Luis Padron, right fielder, 7 — J. H. Magronat, outfielder, 8 — Carlos Moran, third base, 9 — Camilo Valdes, mascot. Havana went 3–2 against Connie Mack's World Champion Philadelphia Athletics that winter, with Lloyd batting .300. His batting average that winter, coming largely against Hall of Fame pitching, was a remarkable .356. Grant Johnson led all hitters at .458.

coming largely against Hall of Fame–caliber pitching, was a remarkable .356. Grant Johnson led all hitters at .458.[18]

*   *   *

In 1911, Sol White lured the 27-year-old Lloyd back east to the New York Lincoln Giants as field manager and captain of the club. The Lincolns, owned by white boxing promoter Jess McMahon and his brother Rod, were the dominant club in the east, "a powerhouse." Spot Poles batted leadoff and played centerfield. The fleet Jimmy Lyons was in left. Lloyd played shortstop and batted clean-up, in front of "slugging" Louis Santop, the catcher. Pitching for the Lincolns, coming over from the Philadelphia Giants after the season began, was a 20-year-old fireballer from Georgia named "Cannonball" Dick Redding who could neither read nor write, but could chuck it with anyone. The 1911 Lincoln Giants boasted an offense featuring four .400 hitters: Poles .440, Lyons .450, Santop .470 and Lloyd .475. Against the best competition available, they won 105 games, losing only 17.[19]

"Cannonball" Redding was one of black baseball's most dominant pitchers throughout the era. His overpowering speed earned him his nickname. Along with the hard stuff, Redding used a no-windup delivery, and a hesitation

pitch with devastating effect. In 1911, relying on his "blinding speed" and exceptional command, Redding reeled off 17 straight wins. The following season, when paired with "Smokey" Joe Williams, Redding boasted a 43–12 record, with several no-hitters, including one against the Cuban Stars.[20]

With cold weather forcing the postponement of many games scheduled in the New York area during the first week of the season, the Lincolns opened up

A young John Henry Lloyd stands for a studio shot at New York's Apeda Studios. Apeda was a diversified corporate studio located in New York City and organized in 1906.

on Sunday, April 16, against Mike Donlin's All-Stars, winning 11–1. The Lincolns gathered 16 hits in the game; Poles and Lloyd led the way with four and three hits respectively. The Lincolns followed it up two weeks later, besting Paterson, 5–4. "Captain Lloyd" banged a homer in the affair, playing flawlessly in the field.[21]

At the same time, the New York press trumpeted the return to action of Brooklyn's Royal Giants, reporting on their "very successful" trip in the south and west where they won 43 of 46 games. The Royals met and defeated Rube Foster's American Giants in Jacksonville, also winning games in Pensacola, New Orleans, Memphis, Mobile, Montgomery, Birmingham, Hot Springs, St. Louis, Detroit and Buffalo. Manager J. W. Connors predicted that his team would win the colored championship and would undoubtedly be the team

Described as the "Bronze Behemoth of Brooklyn," Cannonball Dick Redding was one of the great pitchers of black baseball. In 1912, Redding boasted a 43–12 record, with several no-hitters, including one against the Cuban Stars (courtesy Negro Leagues Baseball Museum).

to beat in the New York area. The Lincolns, hearing the news, clearly believed that Connors had overstated the value of his club, and planned their own say regarding who would be the beast in the east.[22]

The Royals' predictions took a hit a week later when the Cuban Stars came to town and, fronted by José Méndez, shut them out, 5–0. At the same time the Lincolns pounded the All-Stars, 16–0, before dispatching Allentown, 11–2, and Ironsides, 5–0. The Lincolns played errorless ball against Ironsides behind Danny McClellan's four-hitter. Lloyd, "living up to his reputation as a slugger," hammered three hits and was robbed of a homer in his fourth at bat when Lang, the Ironsides centerfielder, made a spectacular catch. Spot Poles was active on the bases for the Lincolns, stealing two.[23]

José Méndez, nicknamed *el Diamante Negro*, or the "black diamond," hailed from Cardenas, Matanzas, Cuba. He was a lithe, wiry pitcher with a tremendous heater. His strength, however, lay in his ability to throw a rising fastball offset by a cutting bender, and a quick release that kept hitters off balance. Later in his career, as a manager with the Kansas City Monarchs,

Mendez would lead his team to pennants in 1923, 1924 and 1925. In the 1924 World Series victory over Hilldale, Mendez, back from the hurlers' bone yard, pitched in four games, including a shutout in his only start, picking up two victories in the process. Lloyd, who faced most of the era's great pitchers, claimed that he never saw anyone better than Méndez.[24]

On May 28, the Lincolns routed Paterson, 12–1, before a well-dressed Sunday afternoon crowd at Olympic Field. It was a one-sided affair in which the visitors were unable to get to Charles Bradford's breaking pitches, particularly when runners were in scoring position. Bradford also had a double for the Lincolns. It was Bradford's second win in a week during which the Lincolns also beat Wilmington, 6–0, and Newburg, 12–3.

The Lincolns blistered the opposition during this stretch, outscoring opponents 30–4 over six days.[25] In fact, "so rude, heartless and cruel" had been the Lincolns batters to opposing pitching, that a club called the All-Manhattans hired "Knockout Brown," a boxer of some local repute, to umpire its game with the Lincolns. Brown, having no experience with baseball, called everything a strike and so seemed to favor the home team that fans began to believe that they were playing with ten men rather than nine. By the fourth inning the Lincolns had had it with Brown, "so perturbed" with his calls that they came to bat with "blood in their eyes." Fagan, pitching for the All-Manhattans, must have felt something "dreadful" was about to occur because he moved his infielders far out. But the "Giants cared naught," and after scoring five runs on numerous hits, drove Fagan from the box. Fagan later returned to the bump after his reliever proved ineffective, but the Giants won, 14–1. As for Brown, when asked

José Méndez, nicknamed *el Diamante Negro*, or the Black Diamond, was a "wiry" pitcher with a tremendous heater. His strength, however, lay in his ability to throw a rising fastball, which was offset by a cutting bender, and a quick release that kept hitters off balance (courtesy Negro Leagues Baseball Museum).

following the game if he had found a new profession, he replied, "Never again, believe me, never again." Lloyd and Poles had three hits each for the victors, both with a double. Charles Bradford got the win.[26]

With Lloyd leading the way at the plate and in the field, the Lincolns continued to blast the opposition, beating Ironsides, 6–0, Pottstown, 3–2, New London, 5–4, and Duquesne, 11–1. The Royal Giants, over the same stretch, stumbled twice, losing to the Cuban Giants, 3–2, and to Ridgewood, 6–1. The Lincolns continued to win, next topping New London, 3–1, and taking two more games, one from the Philadelphia Professionals, 5–4, and another from Yonkers, 12–5. A key moment against the Professionals came late in the game with the mop-up duty of the Lincolns' recently acquired pitcher, Dick Redding, who got the final two outs.[27]

With the July sun beating down on Olympic Field, the Lincolns did the same, scoring two shutouts, a 3–0 win over New London, Dick Redding's first win with the team, and a 1–0 affair with the Central Islip club. Pitching was getting hot all over, as José Méndez struck out 14 in his 3–1 victory against Ridgewood. Méndez needed his good stuff, for on the horizon was the All Cubans, a club made of Havana all-stars who had been beating the opposition across the south on their trip north. They were led by Eustaquio "Bombín" Pedroso, who had tossed the 11-inning victory against the Reds two autumns earlier. This was the first time that two Cuban teams had met in the United States. In the game, played at the Bronx Catholic Protectory Oval, "el Diamante Negro" bested Pedroso and his fellow countrymen, 5–4.[28]

Black baseball happenings in mid–July found some talk of a new league being formed out west. A committee consisting of Frank Leland (Chicago), Charles A. Mills (St. Louis), and F. J. Weaver (Kansas City), agreed to come together in September to discuss further plans for the organization of a colored baseball league. The Royal Giants also found a new home, moving into the Harlem Oval at 142nd Street and Lenox Avenue. The deal was consummated when Royals owner John W. Connors took possession of the ball park for five years. It was believed that the new grounds would be popular with fans because of the location's convenience. The deal marked the first time in the history of New York City that an African-American ball club had complete possession of up-to-date ball grounds, rather than leasing the off dates of a white club's stadium. Two games were immediately scheduled for the Oval.[29]

The Lincolns continued, for another week, playing varied clubs of reputable standing. On the final weekend in July they traveled down to Asbury Park, New Jersey, to play a local white team before a large crowd of summer visitors. The score ended up 10–0 in favor of the Lincolns. The manager of the local club became so disgusted with his team's effort that after the game, he fired everyone. He told them that to put up with such a one-sided affair would spoil his business. Later that day, the Lincolns beat the Loughlin Lyceum team, 10–2. The Lincolns rapped 20 hits in the game, Louis Santop and Bill Francis leading the way with four hits each and Lloyd with three.[30]

By mid-season, much of the baseball talk in the black press surrounded the vaunted St. Louis Giants. This was a club not counted on at the beginning of the season to be in contention with the better teams, yet by adopting the hustling, inside baseball tactics of the crosstown St. Louis Cardinals, had found a way to do so. The Chicago Giants learned this the hard way. When Frank Leland took his club into St. Louis for a three-game set, they were swept before record-breaking crowds. St. Louis also had its way with the Indianapolis ABCs, while splitting a set with the tough All Cubans. With the veterans Frank Wickware, who had come over from Rube Foster's American Giants, and Chappie Johnson, to go along with a team of young unknowns, Manager Charlie Mills had a team which threatened a "reckoning."[31]

On August 6, the reckoning came to Olympic Field, posing a test for the Lincoln Giants. Before the largest Sunday afternoon gate of the season (10,000) and a crowd that caused some problems for the defense, the Lincolns lost their first game of the year to St. Louis, a close 10–7 affair. The heavy hitting youngsters from "the Mound City" had their bats with them, getting 17 hits and driving Buckner from the box early in the game. Danny McClellan, in relief of Buckner, was knocked about freely as well. Ben Taylor "did the slab duty for the visitors," earning the win, with Chappie Johnson in relief, saving Taylor's arm for the second game if needed.[32]

The Lincolns bounced back in game two, scoring 12 runs on 16 hits, winning 12–1. After striking out the side in the first inning, the Giants' "Steel Arm" John Taylor — Ben's older brother — gave way to Chappie Johnson, but to no avail. Johnson was then removed for Ben Taylor, on for the second time of the day. None of them could match Dick Redding, who poured it in, allowing one run, a bomb by Ben Taylor, on a scant three hits. Mercifully for the Giants, the game was called in the seventh inning on account of darkness. Redding also led the way at the plate with three hits, one a double. Pete Booker had three hits and Lloyd had two.[33]

"Steel" Taylor, as he was known to most, and his brothers Ben, Candy Jim and C. I. were black baseball royalty in a way that few other families could hope to be. Natives of Anderson, South Carolina and sons of a preacher who never witnessed a ballgame, the boys followed C. I. Taylor, the oldest of the brothers, into the game. "Steel" Taylor, who began his baseball career in 1898 when he was just 16, acted as both coach and pitcher for Biddle University in Charlotte, N.C. In 1899, in front of home crowds at Latta Park in Charlotte,

"Steel" Taylor pitched on two consecutive days against Shaw University of North Carolina, winning both, 5–3 and 4–2. A sportswriter from the *Charlotte Observer*, a white paper, was impressed enough with the feat and with Taylor's "exceptional speed" to dub him "Steel Arm Johnny." For 17 years "Steel Arm Johnny" Taylor went to the mound, pitching anywhere from 45 to 65 games a season, finishing 15 to 20 of them. He was known to have pitched in as many as three games in one day. In 1907 he pitched 72 successive scoreless innings. "Steel" Taylor was a horse![34]

A week later, the Lincolns played St. Louis before another Olympic Field record-breaking crowd, again splitting a doubleheader, 5–11 and 2–0. In game one, T. Johnson was hit hard by the Giants, prompting a wild Redding to come on in relief. After stamping four passes in game one, Redding dominated the second, allowing one hit for the shutout. The split brought the Lincolns' record for the season to an impressive 62–9.[35]

It was then announced that the Cuban Stars were coming to town to face the Lincolns. The fans of greater New York had been clamoring for such a series all season, especially given the ease with which the Cubans had defeated the Royal Giants and the Philadelphia Giants earlier that season. A meeting was held between white booking agent Nat Strong, representing the Cuban Stars, and the McMahons, to arrange a series of games between the two clubs for the "colored championship of the United States and Cuba." The games, as per the gauntlet thrown by Nat Strong, would be played for $1,000 each, a bet eagerly grasped by Sol White and the McMahons. They were held uptown at Hilltop Park, also known as American League Park, home of the Highlanders, the first coming on August 19. It was also announced that a big league umpire would be on hand for the game one match-up featuring Dick Redding, winner of 17 straight games, and Jose Méndez.[36]

Whether because of rain or otherwise, game one was the only contest in the series reported in the New York papers. Further, the anticipated pitching duel between Méndez and Redding never materialized as the Cubans won, 14–8. Lloyd and Francis played stylishly on the left side of the infield, but the Lincolns' piecemeal offense could not counter the Cubans' 16-hit attack. The "Islanders" got things going in the first inning, scoring a run, with five more coming in the second, three in the third, and two more in the fourth. Danny McClellan replaced Redding in the third inning, and stymied the Cubans until the eighth when they pushed three more runs across. Most of the Lincolns' damage came in innings three, four, and five, when they scored seven runs, but they tallied only one after that. Méndez scattered 13 hits, three by Lloyd, but shutting down the Lincolns in the sixth, seventh and eighth proving the difference. John McGraw, venerable manager of the New York Giants, who had seen Méndez work, claimed that if the Black Diamond were white he would pay $30,000 for his release.[37]

A Labor Day baseball showcase pitted the Lincolns against the Chicago American Giants in game one of a holiday doubleheader, with the winner facing the Cuban Stars later that day. As with the earlier set, the games were played at Hilltop Park, this time before 12,000 fans. This day proved the high point for the Lincolns in 1911 with Danny McClellan topping Frank Wickware, back with the American Giants, in game one, 6–4, and Redding scattering eight hits while getting the best of Méndez and the Cubans, 6–5.[38]

In the first game, Chicago's defense failed, logging three errors as well as a couple of poor throws. Taking advantage, the Lincolns scored three in the fourth inning, one in the fifth and two in the seventh, all on five hits. Rookie first baseman LeRoy Grant led the way for Chicago with three hits. In game two Redding was in good form, proving the difference, "an ambition he has been trying to realize all season." He also had some timely hits, belting the game-winning triple in the ninth inning off of Lico Mederos, who had come on in relief of Méndez in the fifth, scoring Gordon and George Wright. The Lincolns swept another double dip six days later, besting the Philadelphia Giants 3–1, and Ridgewood, 10–1. Lloyd continued to hit well, getting three hits in each game.[39]

Two weeks later the Cubans got their revenge, winning the last game of the season between the two clubs, 10–5. The Lincolns, said to be "dull" and "listless," played sloppy ball, kicking eight errors in the game, something no team could afford to do when opposing Méndez. Were it not for the snappy fielding of Jimmy Lyons and Spot Poles, things would have been worse. Buckner started the game for the Lincolns, but with little support gave way to "Green River" Johnson in the fourth. After the Cubans scored five runs in the fifth inning, Méndez breezed the rest of the way, striking out 11, including Lloyd twice.[40]

It had been a tough week in general for the Lincolns, who had lost to the Royal Giants, 12–3, in game one of a pair that was to determine the local colored championship. Manager J. W. Connors of the Royals claimed his team could have earned another run, but his players were superstitious about scoring 13 runs. McClellan got the start for the Lincolns but was booted from the box, replaced by Redding who was treated equally rude. Meanwhile, "Pop" Andrews had his slow ball working for the Royals, and the Lincolns could do little with it, only one player getting more than one hit. The closest they came was in the eighth inning, when with two men on Lloyd blasted a sharp liner that was certain to be a triple into the right-center gap, only to have it snared by Bill Kindle, who was "quick as a cat," and playing deep at second. Two days later, against the same Royals, the Lincolns could only muster a 5–5 draw in a game called in the ninth inning because of darkness.[41]

Despite their doldrums, the Lincolns managed to put it together the following weekend, beating the Royals twice, 4–1 and 9–4, proving once and for all who New York's best team was in 1911. Dick Redding, who had been knocked all over the lot in the prior match-up, was the star of the doubleheader, pitching both games in an "iron man" effort. He allowed the Royals five hits in the first game and nine in the second, striking out 17 over both.[42]

Frank Earl began the game for the Royals, but was relieved by Sam Crawford in the second inning after giving up four runs. Crawford, in a yeoman's performance, held the Lincolns the rest of the way, allowing no further runs. His attempt to shadow Redding and go in game two, however, proved disastrous as he tired early and was hit hard and often, the Lincolns scoring two in the first, one in the second, third and fourth, then five more in the seventh and eighth. Lloyd led the way, getting three hits in the first game with one more in the second. Spot Poles also had five hits on the day.[43]

At a time when big league managers were bringing more light-skinned Cubans to their rosters, men like Rafael Almeida and Armando Marsans, claims were being made by followers of the black game that the best non–major league players were American blacks. If the previous winter in Cuba against the Tigers had not shown it, Lloyd's play with the Lincolns that summer, as well as the performance of others, continued to support that contention. The *St. Louis Post-Dispatch* must have agreed, writing in respect to white baseball that "we play it, to be sure, but the colored people play it so much better that the time is apparently coming when it shall be known as the great African game." Unfortunately, the *Post-Dispatch* then attributed it to the fact that "the descendant of Ham ... less removed from the anthropoid ape ... gets down on ground balls better, springs higher for liners, has a much stronger and surer grip, and can get in and out of a base on all fours in a way that makes the higher product of evolution look like a bush leaguer." The racism, not the game or the skills it required, kept blacks from being accepted in it.[44]

On Tuesday, October 3, an unusual scene took place in Key West, Florida, one in which the mingling of white and black ballplayers generated a great deal of interest. A hand-picked team from the white schools of Monroe County crossed bats with the colored players of the Douglass School on Jackson Square. The colored team won, paced by the stalwart pitching of a young man named Hepburn, 2–0. In allowing a scant 27 batters to face him, Hepburn struck out 18 and allowed but one player to reach first base in the game, which lasted a mere 48 minutes. The only runs scored were in the last half of the first inning, when Soto and Prichard of the Douglass team were walked and scored on Stevens' double to right, the only hit of the game. Like Hepburn, Aselido was classy on the bump for the white team, striking out 12 and allowing a single hit. It was a tough game to lose. The game's only error was made by Albury of the Douglass squad, who missed a fly in center, allowing the only player on the white team to get to first. It was a great day, one proving again that a ball field was a place for races to come together, not to be driven apart.[45]

When Dick Redding had left the Philadelphia Giants to join the Lincolns in July, it was said by some who had watched him closely that it took him six or seven innings before he began to warm up, to pitch effectively. This assumption was resoundingly refuted as the season unwound, Redding proving to be one of the top "long distance pitchers" in the game. Further proof came on October 8 when the Lincolns, again demonstrating the quality of baseball being played by African Americans, took on the white Jersey City Skeeters of the Eastern (now International) League in a four-game set.[46]

The Lincolns won game one with Redding on the hill, but dropped the second contest, 5–0, behind Danny McClellan. Redding pitched the final two games, a doubleheader, winning the first, 6–3, and the last, a 5–0 shutout. It was a dominating performance by Redding, but he didn't start out that way, allowing two runs in the first inning before shutting it down until the ninth, when he allowed one more. In the meantime, Redding continued to help out at the plate with two hits, to go along with a bomb from Bill Francis, four hits from Santop and two from Lloyd. In the second game, it was no contest with Redding finding "his gate," allowing but three hits and shutting them out by the time the affair was called for darkness. The Lincolns rapped ten hits, including three by Wright, and also had three stolen bases, one each by Poles, Lyons, and Lloyd.[47]

The Lincolns followed up the series with the Skeeters by taking on the big boys, a team of major league all-stars including Walter Johnson and Honus Wagner. Johnson, known as the "Big Train," was the premier pitcher in the American League, boasting a 25–13 record that season with an earned run average of 1.89. Johnson brought Gabby Street with him to do the catching. Wagner, who had just won his eighth National League batting championship, hitting .334, was once called the "nearest approach to a baseball machine ever constructed." And Lloyd was the nearest thing to him. "Connie Mack used to say, 'If you put Lloyd and Wagner in a bag together, whichever one you picked out first, you wouldn't go wrong.'"[48] The "Black Wagner," as Lloyd had become known, was facing his namesake on the diamond for the first time.[49]

The game's buildup proved bigger than the outcome, the All-Stars winning 5–3 against an abbreviated Lincolns squad. Johnson was just about unstoppable, striking out 14 and allowing six hits, with Lloyd wearing a collar, going 0–4. With Dick Redding already back in Atlanta, it was up to Danny McClellan to face the white stars, but the little lefty did not have much in him, allowing 12 hits, including a triple by Wagner. Aside from Redding, others having already left town and missing the game were Poles and Santop.[50]

The loss against the All-Stars was the Lincolns' last game of the season. As with Redding and Santop, the other players, including Lloyd, began leaving town. Lloyd announced that he planned on getting some "good rest" before gathering his club in

Walter Johnson was just about unstoppable. Known as the "Big Train," Johnson was the premier pitcher in the American League, boasting a 25–13 record in 1911.

January to play winter ball in Palm Beach. With his wife "Lizzie," Lloyd left the Big Apple for the shaded serenity of Palatka, Florida, where, he wrote, "the sun is shining on both sides of the street." Lloyd also noted that he had received a letter from the manager of the Havana team, requesting his services in Cuba that winter. He again surmised that he would likely remain in Florida to play in the hotel league.[51]

Anna Amelia Key was Lloyd's first wife. Known as Lizzie, she was a native of Pittsburgh, but it is not known how they met or when they married. Nan Lloyd, Lloyd's third wife and widow, recalled that Lizzie did not have a job and so traveled everywhere with her husband.[52] They were together that winter in Palatka, living in a modest rented home at 115 N. 9th Street, in the black quarter. Lloyd was frugal regarding where he stayed, particularly when on the road; he was on salary. Palatka and its low cost of living was affordable, providing the restful southern setting he longed for: sable palms, moss-laden oaks, sandy streets and a strong river that ran north — like Lloyd. Their home

"Baseball Today," Palatka, Florida, 1916. Palatka and its low cost of living provided the restful southern setting Lloyd longed for: sable palms, moss-laden oaks, sandy streets and a strong river that ran north—like Lloyd (courtesy the State of Florida Archives).

was two blocks from the East Palatka Railroad Depot, providing another exit, and a block west of the "New" AME Bethel Missionary church, where the two may have worshipped. It was a quaint neighborhood with black schools, banks, barbershops, grocers and other ventures catering to the needs of its town folk or those just visiting. Lloyd and Lizzie returned to Palatka for many winters, where he sometimes worked as a bird dog looking for promising baseball players.[53]

* * *

Sol White left the Lincolns during the middle of the 1911 season, prompting Lloyd to assume the full-time managerial duties. For some reason, however, there must have been some friction between Lloyd and certain other teammates, because a week after he wrote from Palatka full of sunshine and attesting his plans to be with the club in Palm Beach that winter, he abruptly resigned as manager and captain. Was Lloyd suited for the job? He was a thoughtful man, but not much of a speaker, often having to have his words pulled out of him.[54] At age 27, he may not have had the maturity or the desire to assert himself in such a role.

In a letter to Rod McMahon, Lloyd stated that he was resigning his two positions with the club because some of his teammates did not give him the proper support as head. In a letter to the *New York Age*, Lloyd explained that because the players had not shown the right spirit toward him since he had been appointed manager, and rather than force another player to do his best, he would give up the positions. "There are some players," he wrote, "who believe in doing their best for any they are under," while others do not. Clearly, the latter frustrated the diligent, professional Lloyd, who then prematurely exclaimed, "I never expect to be at the head of another team as long as I am in baseball, regardless of what kind of salary is offered me ... I have had my fill in such a position." Lloyd assured readers that he expected to be with the Lincolns the following season, "or with some other good club," but as a player only.[55]

In spite of statements to the contrary, Lloyd opted out of Palm Beach during the winter of 1911-12, traveling instead to Cuba, where by mid–February

ruary he was performing brilliantly with the Havana Reds, who were averaging nearly eight runs per game. "Lloyd's fielding cannot be improved," the *Age* reported. "He can cover lots of ground and then some." The Reds were playing in a three-club league which also included Almendares with Méndez and "Bombín" Pedroso, and Fé, who featured Dick Redding, Spot Poles and Frank "Red Ant" Wickware. As in the prior year, Lloyd was joined on the Havana roster by veterans Pete Hill, Bruce Petway and Grant Johnson, who "like whiskey" got better with age. Havana also brought in "Smokey" Joe Williams to front its staff. The league was rugged.[56]

Joe Williams, alternately known as "Cyclone" or "Smokey Joe," was the greatest pitcher not named Satchel Paige in the history of black baseball. A 1952 survey conducted by the *Pittsburgh*

Joe Williams, alternately known as "Cyclone" or "Smokey Joe," has been called the greatest pitcher not named Satchel Paige in the history of black baseball.

Courier had him outpolling Paige as black ball's greatest pitcher. Williams, who was part Indian, was tall at 6'4" and possessed a monster fastball. But he also was shrewd, using his exceptional command and composure to pitch until 1932. Ty Cobb thought that Williams would have been a "sure 30-game winner" in the major leagues, and with good cause, given the games Williams won when facing major league competition. In his final season, Williams played on one of the great black teams of all time, the Homestead Grays, featuring the powerful Josh Gibson, Oscar Charleston, and Jud Wilson.[57]

Reflecting on the competition in Cuba that winter, the *New York Age* opined that "any team can beat the Havana Reds, provided they can score more runs. But where's the team? ... Havana will drop from her place just as soon as Johnson, Lloyd ... Petway and Hill enter into a batting slump, and just as soon as Williams breaks his pitching arm."[58] It had not happened three weeks later as the Reds continued to dominate, besting Almendares and Méndez, 5–3. Nine hits were collected from Méndez, two each by Petway and Mulo Padrón, while Lloyd, Johnson, Hill, Chino Morán and Hernandez had one apiece. The Fé club, with Poles, Jimmy Lyons, shortstop Luis "Anguila" Bustamante, and Wickware on the bump, had also recently topped Almendares, 2–1.[59]

All of black baseball was not restricted to Cuba that winter. Having severed all ties with the Lincolns, Sol White announced that he would be putting a team in Brooklyn to be named, of course, the Giants. They would play across the bridge at the old Wallace Grounds in Ridgewood, which held 15,000 fans. At the same time, Rod McMahon was working hard to secure the lease at Olympic Park and believed it would be done soon. And in Florida, the Poincianas won the hotel league championship, besting the Breakers with eight wins to five over a total of 13 games played.[60]

When Lloyd announced in November that he would not return to the Lincolns as a manager, nor would he ever manage again, it was greeted with some skepticism. The cynics were borne out in April when it was announced that Lloyd would in fact be back with the Lincolns as captain and manager. Writing from Cuba, Lloyd expressed his gratitude to Jess McMahon and his belief that the Lincolns would have a strong team in the coming year. This was an understatement given the Lincolns pitching staff that season, one of the finest ever assembled, featuring "Smokey" Joe Williams, "Cannonball" Dick Redding and Danny McClellan. As for Redding, Lloyd wrote that he was in fine shape and would be leaving Cuba for Atlanta within the next week. "When the big pitcher appears in Harlem," Lloyd said, "he will have on a new Panama hat that will set the natives along 135th Street to talking." Lloyd expected to be back in New York within a few days.[61]

In early May, with Redding in the box and allowing a meager three hits, the Lincolns scored an easy 13–0 shutout over the Murray Hills. Lloyd led the team on offense with three hits, including a home run, while Poles, Santop, and Wright got two hits each. Bill Francis, back at third base for the Lincolns, failed to get a hit. There was some speculation that Francis was about to jump the Lincolns, along with Danny McClellan, to play for Dick Cogan and the Smart Set Nine of Paterson, New Jersey. Cogan, an ex-ballplayer and politico who had come into some money, was putting together the new team and throwing around salaries in an attempt to woo quality talent. Lloyd denied that any of his players would be going with Cogan, insisting that his roster would include Francis and McClellan as well as Booker, Santop, Poles, Grant, Redding, Williams and McClellan. A short time later, the Lincolns beat a team from Passaic, 12–1, on the arms of Williams and Redding.[62]

Very quickly thereafter, however, Danny McClellan left the Lincolns for Paterson, and was pitching for them against the New York Giants of the National League on May 26 at Olympic Park in Paterson, N.J., when a riot nearly ensued due in part to Wilbert Robinson pulling his team from the field with the score tied 3–3 in the ninth. Dick Cogan had arranged to have several members of the Giants visit Paterson to play, but controversy arose almost from the start when Drucke, one of the Giants pitchers, who hailed from the South, objected to playing under his name, preferring to appear under the name O'Brien. Another concern arose in the seventh inning when the Giants reacted angrily to the umpire's calling foul a would-be double by McCormick, the Giants right fielder. McCormick and Warner, the umpire, were about to fight before the Paterson Chief of Police intervened, threatening to arrest McCormick if he struck Warner. In the ninth, with the scored tied three-all and daylight fading, the Giants began another row, this time over a new ball. "Uncle Robbie," John McGraw's long-time assistant and managing the Giants for the day, pulled his club off the field. Many in attendance believed that it was done to preserve the tie rather than risk a loss. Angry fans began pelting the retreating Giants with rocks and sticks until order was restored.[63]

At this time, the volatile Ty Cobb was again in the press, his suspension for assaulting a cripple while the Tigers were playing in New York being upheld by American League President Ban Johnson. Johnson's ruling came in spite of threats by Cobb's Tigers teammates to strike, and the support for Cobb of the Georgia delegation in Congress, who were "deeply wrought up" over the suspension. The incident had occurred when Cobb, angered over heckling by a fan, had charged into the grandstand and pummeled the man to the ground even though he lacked a hand with which to defend himself.[64]

After trouncing a squad from Pennsylvania, 16–0, a game in which

"Smokey" Joe Williams was invincible, the Lincolns met the Washington team of the United States League at Olympic Field, winning 4–1. Redding pitched for the Lincolns, while Big Jeff Pfeffer, an old big league pitcher, went for Washington. Both pitched good ball, but every time Washington posed a threat, Redding would wriggle out of it. Ashby Dunbar, the Lincolns part-time center fielder, "put the game on ice" in the third with a two-run double. Bill Francis added three hits for the Lincolns, with Lloyd and Poles getting two each. The Cuban Stars were next up and received much the same treatment from the Lincolns, losing 11–1. The Lincolns beat them in every facet of the game. "Smokey" Joe was again the star of the day, allowing six hits and blasting a three-run bomb in the bottom of the second inning. Wright had three hits for the Lincolns, with Lloyd adding another as well as a stolen base. Spot Poles, the "Black Ty Cobb," in an oddity of sorts, went hitless.[65]

A day later the Lincolns faced New London, which boasted of its own string of victories. When the latter returned to Connecticut, however, its reputation was somewhat lessened, losing to the Lincolns, 10–3. Lloyd, Wright and Dunbar all had three hits, with Spot Poles getting a hit and two stolen bases. "Smokey" Joe Williams struck out ten.[66]

During the game, Lloyd and Poles became embroiled in an argument that apparently led to Poles leaving the Lincolns and joining the Brooklyn Royal Giants. It was said that within a few hours of the incident, Poles had contacted Brooklyn and made plans to join them in Detroit. (Making matters worse, it was believed that Redding might join him.) What the two men argued about is not known, but one can surmise that given the events of the preceding year, Lloyd may have thought that Poles had not given everything he had on the field, and when confronted, Poles must have disagreed. Lloyd had made it clear that if he was going to manage again it would be on his terms, and with no mention of the McMahons intervening, it is clear that management felt the same way. The shame of it was that the Lincolns had lost one of the best all-around players in the game.[67]

If the McMahons required incentive to hold onto Redding, it came the following week. Dick Redding was 21 years old in 1912. He had been signed by the Philadelphia Giants the previous year when the club traveling north had stopped over in Atlanta, Redding's home town. As noted above, when the Giants began to struggle late in the 1911 season, both Redding and Santop were secured by the McMahons to play for the Lincolns. Regardless of the outstanding winter that Redding had enjoyed in Cuba, there were few who could have predicted the ease and speed at which his star would ascend. On June 16, Redding, firing at will, hung up a new record for strikeouts at Olympic Field with 24, allowing three hits in posting a 6–0 shutout. Of the three hits, Redding had two strikes and a ball on each batter before lapsing. The major league record for strikeouts at the time was 19, set by Charlie Sweeney of the Providence team in the 1880s. Lloyd and Santop had two hits each for the Lincolns.[68]

The Lincolns continued to play well into mid-season, beating a team known as the Pittsburg Giants, 8–1, and the New York Colored Giants, 6–3. On July 4, the Lincolns clashed with Spot Poles and the Royal Giants, losing 11–9. It had been billed as game one of the eastern colored championship, but given the situation with Poles, more was clearly at stake. The Lincolns were anxious to get a rematch with the Royals to even up matters, but the Royals were in no hurry, boasting that they would win again regardless.

The contest, played at Hilltop Park, took place on July 27, and while a "red hot game" was expected, a long, drawn-out one ensued. With Dick Redding striking out six, the Lincolns did enough offensively, coming away with the 10–8 win. In the third inning, the Lincolns drove Jesse Shipp from the mound. Andrews followed but fared little better, giving up eight hits in 51/3 innings. The Royals battled all day, collecting 11 hits off Redding, including two bombs by Brown, the back-up right fielder. Lloyd had one hit in the game, a home run, and was hit by a pitch his next time up. Poles went hitless with a stolen base for the losers.

The Lincolns' win tied the series at one-all. J. W. Connors of the Royals, however, made it clear that there was only a slim chance of the series resuming in light of the fact that he was getting a very small share at the gate. It was not worth it to play the game, he offered, and so they moved on. Spot Poles must have disagreed because following a startling reconciliation with Lloyd and the McMahon brothers, he was back with the Lincolns the following day, batting lead-off against the Smart Set.

In "one of the most exciting games ever witnessed at Olympic Park," Lloyd, welcoming Poles back into the fold, rapped a double and a walk-off knock flying over the scoreboard to win it in the ninth inning, 9–8. The Smart Set had tied the game in the top of the ninth, and when "Green River" Buckner, on in relief of McClellan, got his second strike over on Lloyd, the crowd anticipated extra innings. But it did not happen. When Buckner tried to get his quick underhand delivery across on Lloyd, the Captain struck, "landing it with such force that it made for the East River in great haste." Having pitched against the Royals a day earlier, Redding was not at his best, uncharacteristically allowing eight runs on 12 hits, including a home run to Bradley, the catcher. In six games against the Smart Set that season, the Lincolns won five.[69]

With the season staggering into August swelter, many in the nation turned their attention toward the Presidential nominations and the race to the White House. The Republicans chose incumbent President William Howard Taft over former President Theodore Roosevelt, forcing the latter to jump to the newly formed Progressive Party, forever known as the Bull Moose Party. It would be an important election for African Americans. By 1912, the 50th anniversary of the Emancipation Proclamation, there were 2.5 million African American men of voting age. The question for them was which candidate would "do right by us?" The early line said Roosevelt.

To his credit, Roosevelt had worked somewhat as President to ease race relations in the country, particularly by turning to Booker T. Washington as an advisor on race matters. Roosevelt had once even invited Washington to dinner in the White House, becoming the first President to have extended such a courtesy to an African American, in spite of the controversy and political costs. But as President, he had done nothing to protect the voting rights of African Americans or to suppress lynching, 600 of which occurred on his watch while in the White House.

Despite his record, it still surprised some when in 1912 Roosevelt opted to support southern states in their segregation of the Progressive Party convention, where "not a single colored delegate" was admitted from the south. In a lengthy letter addressed to *Uncle Remus's*, a magazine published by Julian Harris, son of the author of the "Uncle Remus" tales, Joel Chandler Harris, Roosevelt took the easy road, leaving the issue of race at the convention to the "best white men" in the south. Despite black delegates appealing to Roosevelt to change his position, he never did. Illustrators such as W. Russell in Booker T. Washington's *New York Age* ran unfavorable images of Roosevelt booting African Americans out of the convention. While many in the north gave scant attention to the controversy, Roosevelt's siding with southerners on this issue hurt his chances in 1912, the election ultimately going to Woodrow Wilson, New Jersey's Democratic governor, running against the split loyalties of Taft and Roosevelt supporters. Roosevelt's conversion was a sign of the times. With former "Agrarian Rebel" Tom Watson and others, he continued a precedent in which normalizing race relations would not prove worth the effort and would remain a matter of political expediency.[70]

Fast behind Lloyd's ninth-inning heroics to beat the Smart Set came another walk-off win for the resilient Lincolns, this time against the St. Louis Giants. With the game tied, two outs in the ninth, men on first and second, and the crowd settling in for what they believed would be a round of free baseball, "Smokey" Joe Williams' single to right drove in Bill Francis from second base to win it. The hit, one that everyone in the park thought was a sure out to right field—outfielder Jimmy Lyons failed to see it until the ball hit the ground — fell in, giving Francis time to score the winning run. The game itself had been a pitchers duel between Williams and a young hurler for St. Louis named Frank Harvey. "Both twirlers had the opposing batsmen guessing" (*New York Age*, August 8, 15, 1912). Three more contests were scheduled between the two clubs over the coming week.

The Lincolns split the next two with St. Louis, losing the first, 2–0, and winning game two, 4–3, in ten innings. In the bottom of the tenth, Redding, who had allowed the visitors to tie the score in the sixth by dropping a high fly, made up for it with a two-out single driving in the winning run. The Lincolns had been ruined in game one by right-handed submariner Dizzy Dismukes. Dismukes, the Birmingham, Alabama, native, credited with teaching Carl Mays the submarine style of pitching, scattered four hits and had the Lincolns "eating out of his hand" in the shutout.[71]

New York's Polo Grounds was the scene of the August 24 match-up between the Lincolns and the Cuban Stars featuring two of the best pitchers in the game, "Smokey" Joe Williams and José Méndez, both with "an abundance of speed, a large assortment of curves and good control." The game figured to be a pitchers duel and it was, the Cubans winning, 2–1. For eight innings neither side scored, the contest "nip and tuck." In the eighth, however, Chino Morán singled, went to second on Garcia's infield out, and scored on Jabuco Hidalgo's base hit to left. Hidalgo came home on Kiko Magrinat's double. An inning later, the Lincolns tried to get things going by using pinch hitters, scratching out a run in the process. Frank Grant batted for Zach Pettus and singled. "Steel Arm" Taylor then batted for Mike Moore and also singled, with Grant moving to third. While Taylor was thrown out trying to steal second, Grant came home. That was all they would get in the loss. Also, in a rare moment when another shortstop was actually noticed with Lloyd on the field, the press commended the stylish work of the Cubans' Pelayo Chacón at short.[72]

The following day at Olympic Park the Lincolns split a dip with the Royals, 2–3 and 3–0. Dick Redding and Frank Wickware tossed both games for their respective clubs, which for 18 innings was a burden on a hot day in August. Most of the offense came early, with the Royals getting all of their runs by the second inning in the first affair, and the Lincolns doing the same in the second. The two teams had played four games to that point in the season, with each winning two. They were back at it in less than two weeks, again splitting a doubleheader, 1–0 and 6–0. Frank Wickware had the "Indian sign" on the Lincolns in game one, besting Redding for the second time in a month, this time a shutout. Williams bought the Lincolns back in a fast-paced game two, scattering seven hits with nine strikeouts. Spot Poles led the offensive attack with four hits.[73]

After running out the schedule with wins over Trenton and Jamaica Woodhills, the Lincolns readied themselves for the National League Champion New York Giants, or at least a "hand-picked" squad led by team captain Larry Doyle. The game was played at Olympic Field on Sunday, October 27, and with "Smokey" Joe Williams on the bump the Lincolns won it, 6–0. Johnson and Lloyd had two hits each for the Lincolns. In winning, the Lincolns did more than defeat the white professionals; they showed them what black baseball was all about. Williams allowed the Giants but four hits in the shutout, striking out nine men with an assortment of gas and "puzzling" benders. He was so dominant that Doyle, Moose McCormick, Josh Devore and Red Murray all were reminded of another "Smokey Joe," Boston's masterly Joe Wood, who had just beaten New York three times in the World Series. Walter Johnson once said that there was not a man alive faster than "Smokey Joe" Wood. These Giants may have disagreed.[74]

Hal Chase and a team known as the All-Stars, few of whom represented Chase's New York Yankees, met a similar fate during a Tuesday afternoon twilight affair at Olympic Field, the last baseball played in New York in 1912. The Lincolns, with Williams again on the mound, smoked Chase's crew in a shutout, 6–0. Chase and his team could do nothing with Cyclone, securing but four hits. The Lincolns, on the other hand, rapped seven timely hits

In defeating John McGraw and the New York Giants, the 1912 Lincoln Giants showed white America what black baseball was all about. Lloyd is at the center, standing.

against the All-Star's hurlers, including Chalmers of the Philadelphia Nationals. They bunched four of their runs in the eighth and ninth innings to win it going away.[75]

Over the course of the year Lloyd batted remarkably well, hitting .376, while playing shortstop and managing his team to the best record in the east. It was a time to be commended, but there were few moments for it because within weeks Lloyd had his team back in Cuba, where they played 14 games as the Lincoln Giants before being scattered across the "Liga" filling rosters. The schedule was hectic, a grind, but baseball and the motion that came with it was the life Lloyd had chosen for himself and his wife. He considered it a blessing. Lloyd and Lizzie would live and play wherever the money took them, and when his playing days were over, he would have no regrets. Asked how long he planned on playing baseball the left-handed-hitting Lloyd replied, "Until a lefthander strikes me out." It would not happen anytime soon.[76]

THREE

A Baseball Drivin' Man

Historian Lawrence Hogan once identified similarities between John Henry Lloyd and the mighty John Henry of folk legend and song. That John Henry was a rugged, "steel driving man" who on behalf of his fellow workers fought the advance of technology in a rail setting contest against a powerful steam drill. In the race, John Henry, with *Lightnin'* in his eye, urged his *Cap'n'* to *bet yo' las' red cent on me, Fo' I'll beat it to de bottom or I'll die.* Max Manning, a later pupil of Lloyd's on the Newark Eagles, recalled that Lloyd was much like the folk hero, "a gentle giant, strong in character, an honest man, a wonderful person.... He was a gentleman, that's what he truly was. It seemed as if adversity would just fall off his shoulders.... He would always go to the brighter side of whatever would come up." It was a trait that Lloyd carried with him throughout his life.[1]

In Cuba during the winter of 1912-13, the Lincolns battled Almendares and Havana in a string of 14 games lasting several weeks. Over the first week of the season the teams were fairly well balanced, but with Redding and Santop yet to arrive, the Lincolns were shorthanded. Lloyd was not worried, believing that a rotation of Redding, Wickware and Williams would be too much for the other clubs once a full squad was in place. It looked good on paper, but it did not materialize. Santop never arrived, going home instead to Ft. Worth, Texas, while Wickware, Booker and Wright left Cuba for Palm Beach, prompting Lloyd to recruit several Cubans to take their place.[2]

The roster shifts posed some concerns for those following the Lincolns back in New York that Lloyd might be replacing his players with Cubans. It bothered Lloyd enough that he was compelled to respond in print. On February 13, in a letter to the Sporting Editor of *The Age*, Lloyd wrote that his hiring of Cubans had nothing to do with the coming season, and was in fact necessitated by the earlier departures of some of his players, all of whom, he reiterated, would be with the Lincolns in the spring. Because of the departures, the short version of the Lincolns only played 14 games before Poles, Jude

Gans, Redding and Lloyd signed on to play out the remainder of the season with Fé, which was owned and controlled by Cuban promoters. Lloyd next assured that he would be in New York again with the Lincolns for the 1913 season, and would lead the team to victory over all other colored teams. Responding to queries regarding those players who might not return, Lloyd, in no-nonsense fashion, wrote, "I pay my players on the first and fifteenth of each month and therefore am compelled to have their services. When they get so they can't deliver the goods I am just like any other manager who has a winning team — pin the pink slip on them when they don't show.... I will have a good or better team than ever and no Cuban will be added."[3]

The Fé team that Lloyd, Poles, Redding and Gans signed on to play with won the Cuban National League championship that season, which closed on March 23. It was clearly a result of the African Americans on the roster, especially given that Fé had been the league's unwanted stepchild for some time. Lloyd, with 31 games under his belt, played as much as anyone, batting .378. Only the major leaguers Marsans and Almeida hit for a higher average, but both in fewer at-bats. Poles followed Lloyd at .355, with Gans at .353. That March, writing from his home in Palatka, Lloyd informed the press that he would be in New York by early April, where he would address any personnel concerns, especially those caused by a number of his players holding out for higher wages.[4]

*   *   *

That winter, mob violence continued to haunt the American landscape, with lynchings reported in the Midwest and South. Near Montgomery, Alabama, an African American named Charles Carson, a man well-liked in the community, was hogtied and beaten to death by five white men, his mutilated body left to rot in a cabbage crate. Alice Carson, his wife, who had been pistol whipped for attempting to intervene, explained that her husband had been taken from his bed and dragged outside where his body was bound into a stooped position. He was then beaten with heavy buggy whips, interspersed with kicks to the ribs so vicious that they led the ribs to tear though the body. Recognizing that her husband was being murdered and there was nothing she could do, Alice ran for her own life. Adding insult to murder, the killers refused to allow Carson's family to take charge of the corpse for burial, choosing their own means to do it. Change was a slow thing in coming.[5]

*   *   *

There was very little coverage of black baseball in the New York press during the early part of the 1913 campaign. In fact, the first mention of the

Lincolns did not come until June 12 when *The Age* reported that the Lincolns had beaten the T.A.R.S. team from Elizabeth, New Jersey, 8–4. Pitcher Doc Scanlan, who had recently played for Brooklyn in the National League, hung a bender to Louis Santop, who belted it for the longest homer in park history. Santop had three hits on the day and Lloyd two. The game was played in Elizabeth because the McMahons had not been able to procure a lease for Sunday baseball at Olympic Park. The inability of the McMahons to secure the lease and the retirement from baseball of John W. Connors, owner of the Royal Giants, were blamed for a lack of interest in black baseball in the early part of the season. All of that changed on June 15, however, when the local authorities, having changed their attitude, agreed to the lease and Sunday baseball was restored in Harlem. That day, the Lincolns won a twin bill, taking it to Passaic and the Elizabeth Stars, 5–3 and 9–1 respectively. "Smokey" Joe Williams struck out 21 batters in the second game, after pitching five innings of relief in game one. Jude Gans had four hits against the Stars, with Doc Wiley getting three and Lloyd and Poles two each.[6]

A week later, the Lincolns, with Williams again on the mound, shut out the Royals in a hard-fought affair, 3–0. A large Sunday crowd turned out to watch the game, with "partisanship running high," a sign that interest in black baseball was again on the upswing. The Lincolns got to Frank Harvey for 12 hits, three apiece from Lloyd and Wiley, while the Royals did nothing with Williams, who struck out nine. "Smokey Joe" struck out 12 in another win, 5–1, this time against Bayonne, then followed that up by sitting down 11 in a 5–4 win over T.A.R.S.[7]

"Smokey Joe" Williams was an "iron man" in 1913, pitching 11 of 15 games that season against Rube Foster's Chicago American Giants, all played within 20 days, winning seven and losing two. He also saved one and posted a no-decision. Six of the games were played in five days, with Williams going five complete in the process. Williams split a pair on July 31 and won two games on August 2, the final a 1–0 shutout. His herculean efforts won him the George Stovey Award as the league's top pitcher. Not to be outdone, Lloyd finished second in the league in batting at .325, and led his team to a 101–6 record. For this he was named to the East All-Star team.[8]

The games against the American Giants were of particular note that season, above all to Rube Foster, who the next year would lure Lloyd, Jude Gans, and Bill Francis to Chicago. Foster was shrewd that way. He knew what he wanted for his team and he worked the inside game to get it. Buck O'Neil recalled:

> Foster had an excellent mind and was more or less two innings ahead of everybody else. He devised a system that had never been seen in baseball before.

Rube picked all the men to play. He put on all of the plays and he had the type of men that could do just what he wanted them to do.... This was the Chicago American Giants.... Rube would score runs without a base hit. If you walked the lead off man, he'd bunt the ball, bunt and run, hit and run, steal home base. It changed the way a pitcher had to pitch.[9]

Games played between the Chicago club and the Lincolns were also dipped in controversy, as evidenced by a series played late in July. The two teams had agreed to play a five-game set for the colored championship, but only three games were played as Foster and the McMahons spent the rest of the time arguing. In it, the Lincolns won two games and Chicago one. The initial argument came when Foster attempted to start Frank Wickware on the hill in game one. The McMahons, angry over the fact that they had just paid Wickware, who was officially on the roster of the Mohawk Giants, $100 to pitch in this series, only to find him now "togged up" in an American Giants suit, refused to take the field against him, arguing that he should be with the Lincolns. McMahon and Foster argued the issue for over an hour before the game was called off.[10]

"Smokey" Joe Williams was brilliant in the series, winning the two games he pitched, 8–3 and 5–4. Chicago won game two, 6–5, before about 4,500 people. The final game was called off when Foster objected to the McMahons bringing in Frank Earle from the Royal Giants to play in place of Jude Gans, who was sick. This scenario, more than most, shows the flexibility in personnel taking place in black baseball, where the focus was to field a competitive team, and the axiom that you "dance with the one that brung you" was not necessarily the case.[11]

Much of the attention in black baseball that summer was directed at the success being enjoyed by Cuban ballplayers in the big leagues. The Cincinnati Reds already had Rafael Almeida and Armando Marsans, both of whom were excellent players, but a lot of notice was being afforded to a durable young pitcher named Adolfo Luque. Luque, who became legendary in Cuba as "Papá Montero," named for a celebrated Afro-Cuban rumba dancer and pimp, was known in the United States as the "Havana Perfecto," a reference to a fine cigar. In 12 years with the Reds Luque posted double-digit wins ten times. In 1923 he had a standout season, going 27–8, with a 1.93 ERA. In his 20 years in the majors, Luque won 194 games before going on to enjoy a successful run as a winter leagues manager and major league pitching coach. He was said to have taught Sal Maglie of the Giants, known as "The Barber," to pitch inside. Maglie then passed it down to Don Drysdale, a future Hall of Famer who developed his own reputation for pitching inside.[12]

Luque did not have the stereotypical dark skin appearance of other

Cuban players, looking "more like an Italian than a full-blooded Cuban." Clearly, this allowed him to pass through segregated doors that others among his countrymen found closed. He had been pitching in the New York area with the Long Branch Cubans, where he was the best hurler in the league, winning 12 out of 13 games, three of them shutouts. Luque had beaten the Pittsburgh Pirates at Long Branch the season before, and had bested the New York Giants in Cuba that same winter. The Yankees, Senators and Boston Braves had all been in the mix for his services.[13]

The Lincolns hit the road in August, winning a majority of their games and impressing the fans as being a "classy bunch" of players. In a series with the American Giants the Lincolns took a majority of the wins, though contending that they had received a "raw deal" from an umpire in one of the contests. Upon their return to Harlem, and for their good show, the Lincolns were presented with a large floral offering in the shape of a horseshoe by former owner J. W. Connors. The Lincolns kindly responded by splitting a doubleheader with the Royals, winning 9–2 and losing 12–4. Williams struck out six in game one for the win, with Poles getting four hits. Lloyd was not in the lineup.[14]

Perhaps Connors purchased the floral for the Lincolns because they could not afford it themselves. *The Age* reported that the Lincolns were in the "throes of financial troubles" which could bring about a disruption of the club before season's end. It was reported that many of the players had not been paid their full salaries for weeks. Further, within the past month, a number of judgments had been rendered against the McMahon brothers, and the outlook was bleak. The McMahons had spread themselves thin across several ventures, including fight promotions. While attendance was good, gate money was used to pay other debts. J. W. Connors was said to have advanced money to several players on the Lincolns, while Nat Strong of the Royals rendered financial assistance to the club as well. It would not be the last time that Strong would come to the financial assistance of the franchise.[15]

With Lloyd sidelined with a bum ankle, the Lincolns topped the Philadelphia Professionals, 6–0. Williams was again dominant on the mound, scattering three hits in the shutout. At the same time, the Lincolns were finding it to hard schedule home games at Olympic Field because of their financial problems. Nat Strong, in particular, flatly refused to have the Royals play a game at Olympic Field until all moneys owed to him were paid. It must not have occurred to him that a home gate for the Lincolns would allow the McMahons to make a payment. Or perhaps Strong did not trust the McMahons to be good for it were a home gate afforded. The only reason he had loaned them money in the first place was because it was good business to keep his chief competitor afloat, at least until season's end.

The Lincolns next dropped a game to Phillipsburg, 3–0, but with Lloyd back in the lineup the following week, getting a hit in a 3–2 win, the Lincolns began to surge. A week later, with several major league scouts in attendance to get a look at Matty Sheridan, Phillipsburg's "crack pitcher," "Smokey" Joe Williams wowed them, allowing just four hits and striking out 17. Sheridan did not help his cause, giving up 11 hits, and allowing the winning run to score in the ninth inning on a wild pitch, the Lincolns winning, 3–2. On offense it was a team effort for the Lincolns, with everyone but the pitcher taking part; Poles and Johnson had two hits each, while Lloyd added a hit and two stolen bases.[16]

As the season wound down, the Lincolns took on a white team of all-stars led by "Turkey" Mike Donlin, formerly of the New York Giants, winning, 9–1 behind Williams' 16 strikeouts. The closest anyone got to touching Williams was when Donlin's pitcher, Barberich, plunked him. The Lincolns, for their part, drove 18 hits off Barberich, three each coming from Santop and Grant, with Lloyd, Poles, Johnson, Wiley and Francis getting two apiece. Lloyd and Poles each had a stolen base as well.[17]

The Lincolns' biggest show of the year came against the Philadelphia Phillies or Nationals as they were called, the second-best team in the National League. The Phillies were led that day by their pitching phenom, Grover Cleveland Alexander, who had won 22 games that year, and included part-time players Vern Duncan, Beals Becker and Bobby Byrne. If the white big leaguers expected an easy go of it they were mistaken. The Lincolns won in a rout, 9–2, with Williams out-dueling Alexander, "who looked like any other pitcher" and was hit hard. Williams posted nine strikeouts in the game and hit a home run. Lloyd, running increasingly well, got two hits and stole more four bases.[18]

On the same day, Frank Wickware and the Mohawk Giants, playing in Schenectady, New York, defeated Walter Johnson and a team of minor leaguers, 1–0. Wickware and Johnson were both strong—Johnson allowed just two hits—but the "Red Ant" was a little better, posting his third shutout in four days. The game began late as the Mohawks, demanding $900 in back pay, struck just as Johnson and his team arrived. The only thing preventing a cancellation and subsequent riot of fans was a $500 partial payment quickly made by the Mohawks owner. The game was called by darkness after five and a half innings played, with the Mohawks "hustled out of town to avoid arrest for inciting a riot."[19]

Lloyd belted another pair of hits off of white pitching when the Lincolns split a dip with Earle Mack's All-Stars, 0–1 and 7–3. In the first game Williams and George Chalmers of the Phillies kept things close, with Mack's crew coming out on top. With the All-Stars up by one in the ninth inning, Earle Mack, son of Connie Mack, saved the game for his team when he cut off Lloyd at the plate from center field, preventing the score from being tied. Williams struck out 13 men in the game, Chalmers ten. In the second game the Lincolns got revenge, driving Chalmers from the box in the 7–3 win. Poles, Wiley and Williams got two hits each and Lloyd one.[20] Two weeks later the Lincolns finished this round of playing against white clubs, besting Chief Bender, a 21-game winner with the Athletics, by a score of 2–1. Williams, continuing to dominate "every pitching category" and all batters he faced, allowed a scant three hits in the game.[21]

In the winter of 1913-14, the Cuban League became known as the Liga Nacional de Base Ball de le República de Cuba. Historian Roberto Gonzalez-Echevarria speculates that the name change from "General" to "Nacional" reflected the fact that no Americans, white or black, were in the league that season. Whether due to a nationalistic impulse in Cuba or signs of war in Europe, Lloyd and his fellow Americans were not on the island that winter.[22]

*   *   *

Along with Jude Gans and Bill Francis, Lloyd returned to Chicago in 1914, rejoining his pal Bruce Petway, Frank Wickware and, of course, Rube Foster. In Harlem, as one might expect, the desertions caused quite a stir, with the baseball situation being "very much muddled." The McMahon brothers, now formerly of the Lincolns, were managing the Lincoln Stars, while Charles Harvey had secured control of the Lincolns and Olympic Field. The one asset that the Lincolns had managed to hang onto was "Smokey" Joe Williams, but even he was in the Northwest that spring barnstorming with Rube Foster's club.[23]

All was not wine and roses for Foster and his players that spring, however. One headline in the *Chicago Defender* read "Rube Foster's Team Starving in Oregon." The American Giants, the "World's Greatest Aggregation of Baseball Players and Chicago's Pride," were being forced to subsist on crackers and cheese, being turned down at every hotel and restaurant in Medford, Oregon. Only a non-segregated Japanese restaurant would offer meek amenities, at least until it opened. The cool reception had many of the players indignant, adding insult to injury in that a number of them, including Petway, were suffering various ailments. With the *Defender* assailing the color line in baseball, the American Giants played on, traveling to Portland and Lewiston, Idaho by the end of April.[24]

The presence of the American Giants on the west coast that winter created a great deal of consternation on the part of the white baseball establishment.

Pacific Coast League President Allan T. Baum, who had imposed the color line on the west coast, was not in accord with the fans, who wanted to see the Giants play. Fan desires did not help in Oakland and San Francisco, where the teams agreed with Baum and refused to play. This left the Giants to travel north where Manager Walter McCredie of Portland was of the same mindset as the fans, opting to play the Giants regardless of the competition they presented. While others may have been afraid to face them, he was not. The fans supported him for it, and the black press commended him, even as Williams tossed a no-hit shutout at them. The Giants celebrated Easter on the Pacific Coast, besting Portland twice more.[25]

The Giants then moved to Pullman, Washington, defeating the Washington State College baseball team, 4–0. Chicago's Lee Wade scattered five singles to hold the collegians in check. By April 23 the Giants had found their way to Lewiston, Idaho, where they topped the local nine, 8–1. Except for the ninth inning the Lewiston club played the Giants even, but before the frame closed, the Giants pushed eight runs across to win it. Three days later they were in Omaha where Rube Foster, looking ahead to the start of the regular season said, "We have played all along the line (that winter) and have met victory on every hand. Just tell them that my team will be in Chicago on Sunday to play ... and we will win."[26]

With the curtain rising on the 1914 baseball season, the *Defender* announced that the American Giants would play the Gunthers on Sunday, April 26 at the American Giants Baseball Park, 39th and Wentworth Streets. Because it was the first game of the season, it was announced that all rail cars would transfer to the park. Transfer they did, for never in the history of black baseball in the Windy City had a lid-lifter generated such excitement. The largest crowed to have attended any of the black baseball openings in that city jammed the 39th Street grounds despite the cool weather. Automobiles arrived hours before the game, and fans stormed the box office when it opened. Box seats were sold out, the grandstand taken, and the bleachers packed, many fans going out there to keep warm. They all gave a boisterous welcome to Lloyd, Petway, Pete Hill and the others as their Chicago American Giants took the field.[27]

The Giants began hot. After Jess Barbour made an out, Pete Hill doubled to left and went to third on Pete Duncan's out. With two down the crowd began calling for Lloyd to "bring home the bacon." Ahead in the count, with three balls and a strike, Lloyd fouled one back, bringing the count full at three and two. When Gunthers pitcher Bradshaw shook off a sign, Lloyd dug in and drove the pitch into left for a double, scoring Hill "while the crowd stood on their seats and screamed like maniacs." Lloyd immediately stole third, and the crowd grew louder when Gans followed with a single, scoring Lloyd. Lloyd was brilliant on defense as well, once going behind second for a "seemingly impossible drive," before tossing it to Barbour at first who booted it, unable to comprehend that Lloyd had made the play. For their part, the Gunthers could do little with Wade, who struck out eight in the 4–0 win.[28]

Over the next few weeks, as Lloyd continued his "classy work at short," the Giants kept winning, holding the champion independent team from St. Joe, Michigan, to "seven lousy hits" in a 13–6 win, followed by a 2–1 victory against the West Ends. Lloyd, Gans and Hill all had doubles against the West Ends. Their fans, however, growing restless at the lack of competition, prompted Foster to assert that he would soon bring the strong teams from the east to Chicago. He subsequently announced that the Cuban Stars would soon be arriving, with the Lincoln Giants, Lincoln Stars, Royal Giants and Mohawks all coming west as well.[29]

A day after beating the Chicago Giants on May 23, the American Giants took on the Cuban Stars, who had just arrived in Chicago, winning 8–0. With the day proving ideal weather-wise for baseball, the game brought out a "throng." Lee Wade was strong into the ninth inning, striking out seven and holding a 2–0 edge, but then Cristóbal Torriente, Manuel Villa and Bombín Pedroso all got hits, Mike Gonzalez drew a walk, and Gans booted one in left, rallying the Cubans to a 4–2 victory. According to Frank Young in the *Defender*, "the Giants were simply over-confident," leading to them losing again to the Cubans the following day.[30]

In early June, Rube Foster and Cy Young, the legendary hurler, staged a duel at the American Giants' park, with the Giants coming out on top, 5–4. Young, 47 years old and the winner of 511 major leagues games, had last played in the bigs with the Boston Braves in 1911 and was pitching for Benton Harbor, Michigan. After allowing four runs in the first inning, Young settled in and did not give up another run until the seventh when Pete Hill doubled and Lloyd singled him in. A great play by Francis stopped a Benton Harbor rally in the ninth. A week later the Giants routed the South Bend Independents, 13–5. They finished the month by whipping the French Lick Plutos, 6–0. Lloyd had two hits for Chicago, one a double, and Booker had three. Batting leadoff for the Plutos and belting a double was a flashy young second baseman named Bingo DeMoss.[31]

James Riley refers to Bingo DeMoss as "unquestionably the greatest second baseman in black baseball for the first quarter [of the twentieth] century." He was the "consummate ballplayer," excelling in all phases of the game. A natural athlete, DeMoss had a great glove, was quick in the field, and had speed to burn on the bases. Like Lloyd, DeMoss was a line drive hitter who could spray the ball all over the field. He would later join the Chicago American Giants, ultimately replacing Pete Hill as its captain, a position he maintained for six years.[32]

In mid–July, Frank Wickware, the Giants' best pitcher, topped the Royal Giants, 8–2.[33] During his career, the "Red Ant" was "noted for his velocity, mound presence, coolness under pressure and smooth delivery." The "angular" 26-year-old was in the prime of an amazing career that, had he not enjoyed the bottle so thoroughly, may have landed him in Cooperstown.[34]

With the "Guns of August" sounding in Europe, a conflagration of nations called to a great war, baseball continued to be played in a country choosing to stay out of the conflict. In mid–August the Giants took a pair of games at home, defeating the West Ends, 5–1, in the opening contest, and the University of Japan, 4–0, in the second. The first game was played amid breaks in a deluge that had the West Ends fumbling with their gloves, unable to make the plays when needed. Lee Wade posted nine strikeouts for Chicago. Jude Gans pitched the second game, shutting out the Japanese collegians, 4–0.[35]

The Cuban Stars arrived in town next for a series with the Giants beginning on August 15. The Giants lost the opener, 5–1. Lloyd, deceptively fast and intuitive on the bases, prevented Chicago from being shut out when he stole home in the eighth inning. The next day it took ten long innings but the Giants turned the tables, upending the Cubans, 2–1. The Giants won when the Cuban catcher (Morgan) kicked Petway's perfect bunt towards third in an anxious effort to get Lloyd, who scampered home with the winning run. Wickware struck out 11 in the game, compared to Pedroso's three. Torriente had a double for the Cubans.[36]

Bingo DeMoss was regarded as the greatest second baseman in black baseball for the first quarter of the 20th century.

The American Giants subsequently took aim on defending their national Negro championship against the Brooklyn Royal Giants, billed as the "Eastern Kings" despite a mediocre season. It was a set that the folks in Chicago would not soon forget. In a scene out of central casting, thousands descended on the

39th Street ball park, "from every direction, and in every style, on foot, by electric and by autos." Many patrons took the field seats, better known as the "circus seats," and were heard throughout the series. Drunks also made their presence felt, making "foul and insulting remarks" in front of "the fair sex" and toward patrons who sought police help in having them tossed out. The crowd was intense, as was the action.

The American Giants took the opener when Wickware scattered three hits and struck out 12. They scored all of their runs in the third inning on singles by Petway, Francis and Barbour, an error by Harvey, and an infield out. Barbour got two of Chicago's five hits, one a double. Frank Earle led the way for the Royals with two hits. Game two went to the Giants as well, Wade holding the Royals to two hits. The affair had been a pitching duel until the seventh inning, when Dizzy Dismukes weakened. With three men on base and two strikes on Monroe, Barbour tried to steal home and Dismukes, attempting to nail him at the plate, threw it past Webster, the catcher. Three errors, a pass, and six singles put the game on ice for Chicago in the eighth. Lloyd turned a double play for the Giants and picked up a hit, while Monroe, Gans, Duncan and Francis had two hits each. The third game nearly ended in a riot when the Giants scored the winning run with two outs in the last half of the ninth inning. With two on, Petway batted for Gans and hit a fly to short right field, near the foul line. Both Handy and Earle ran for the ball, with Handy grabbing it but dropping it after Earle ran into him, letting both runs score. The Royals then claimed that the ball was foul, physically attempting to get to Umpire Fitzpatrick, who had to be taken from the field under police escort. It was the Giants' third win in as many games as they were again perched on the precipice of greatness.[37]

A grieving American Giants squad made it a clean sweep in besting the listless Royals, 3–1. The Giants were saddened over the tragic loss of Bill Lindsay, one of their top pitchers, who had died the previous Tuesday. Frank Young of the *Defender* noted that "Lindsay was one of Rube's best men, and is mourned by men of both races for he was one of the best pitchers in the business." Cary Lewis, writing for the Indianapolis Freeman, called Lindsay "one of the five greatest baseball pitchers in America ... a spit-ball artist with a wonderful bat." Born to a baseball-loving family in Lexington, Missouri, Lindsay came to the American Giants following stints with Kansas City and the Lincoln Giants. "He was a gentleman, respected both by fan, player and manager." Rube Foster was quoted as saying that "I have lost a great ball player, a fine gentleman, and a noble friend." American Giants teammates Booker, Bruce Petway, Frank Wickware, Jess Barbour, Wade and Bill Monroe served as pallbearers at his funeral.[38]

As the season wound down, the *Chicago Defender* heralded the American Giants as the "best of their kind in the world." "They have played great ball and are equal to some of the best teams in the country, having defeated the best" and been ducked by the rest. Rube Foster was so confident in the club that he offered to play the champions of the Federal League, an outlaw league that proved to be the last major attempt to establish an independent major professional baseball league in the United States in direct competition with the established National and American Leagues, operating in 1914 and 1915, but received no response.[39] Lloyd led the team in hitting at .323 (Foster, with many fewer at-bats, hit .450). Lloyd was also named shortstop on the West All-Star team picked by John Holway. Horace Jenkins had the Giants' best won-lost record at 9–1, but it was 35-year-old Rube Foster with the most wins at 11. Foster had barely missed pitching a perfect game that season against the Cuban Stars, as Jude Gans misplayed a Cristobal Torriente fly ball to left that fell in.[40]

* * *

Lloyd had a nice year in Chicago, but per his bent he went where the money was, so a year later he was back in New York as player-manager for the Lincoln Stars, a sequel outfit to the old Lincoln Giants, owned by the McMahon brothers. On the roster with Lloyd were Spot Poles, Frank Harvey, Zach Pettus, Jude Gans, Louis Santop and Dick Redding. It was a formidable squad.

"Cannonball" Redding showed "splendid form" in his first game of the season, striking out 19, while allowing two hits and pitching the Stars to a 12–0 shutout of Phillipsburg at the Lenox Oval, located in Manhattan's Inwood section. Flashing the hard stuff, Redding kept the Phillipsburg players off balance, while Lloyd chipped in at the dish with two doubles in as many plate appearances. Poles, Harvey and Redding each added two hits. Harvey had bested a club from Yonkers in the opening contest, 12–4.[41]

The Long Branch Cubans, fresh from a victorious trip through the south, found a stiff jab awaiting them in Inwood on April 25 in the form of the Stars, who won, 9–3. Bill Pierce and Redding both hit home runs, while Poles slapped a triple, and Gans, Harvey and Lloyd each doubled. Lloyd had three hits on the day. The Long Branch game was the second half of a doubleheader, the first coming against Summerville, which the Stars won, 6–4. In the next week, the Stars beat the Cubans twice more before large home crowds, 3–2 and 4–1. Then, with Redding allowing four hits, they shut out Doc Scanlan's All-Stars in a Memorial Day tilt, 4–0.[42]

On June 6 the Stars won a pair from the Philadelphia Pros and the Bayonne Stars, 11–0 and 9–0 respectively. Harvey pitched the first game, allowing five hits to a Philadelphia squad that coughed up three errors. In game two, Redding went the distance, posting seven strikeouts and allowing seven hits. Poles and Redding led the way on offense with two hits each, followed by Lloyd with a hit and stolen base, and Santop with a triple. On June 13 Redding won his 12th straight game, besting "Turkey" Mike Donlin's All-Stars, 9–3. Lloyd had a hit and scored two runs, with Poles and Gans throwing in two hits apiece. Redding won two more the next week, his 13th and 14th in a row, the second coming against Almendares, 12–2. The Stars claimed 21 hits from the Cuban pitchers.[43]

Steaming toward the end of June the Stars, with Frank Harvey on the bump, topped Empire City, 13–6, and then "carried off the honors" in a twin bill against the St. Aloysius team, winning 6–2 and 1–0, the latter of which went five innings on account of rain. Redding scattered three hits in the shutout, claiming his 15th consecutive win, while Lloyd banged a double. Doc Sykes got the win for the Stars in the opener.[44]

July began much the same, with the Stars winning twice against negligible competition, beating the Fire Department team, 5–1, and Larry McLean's All-Stars, 6–5. While Doc Sykes cruised in the opener, it took late-game heroics for the Stars to beat McLean's club. With two down in the top of the ninth inning, Poles and Kindle singled, setting the plate for Lloyd who then doubled, sending in two runs and securing the win for Redding. The Stars then beat Bridgeport, 4–1, behind the "tryout" pitching of Cuban ace Mulo Padrón. Padrón scattered seven hits in the contest, hit a batter, and struck out three.[45]

"El Mulo" Padrón was a versatile athlete, excelling on the mound, at the plate and in the field. Reputed to have taught Hall of Famer Willie Foster the change-up, Padrón used his own off-speed pitch at two speeds —"slow and

Luis "El Mulo" Padrón was a versatile athlete excelling on the mound, at the plate and in the field. Reputed to have taught Hall of Famer Willie Foster the change-up, Padrón used his own off-speed pitch at two speeds: "slow and slower." He was at times dominant, carving a .629 winning percentage over his 19-year career.

slower." He was at times dominant, carving a .629 winning percentage over his 19-year career. Padrón is rightly considered among the three top Cuban pitchers of his era, along with José Méndez and Bombín Pedroso, while at the same time being among Cuba's greatest outfielders.[46]

Redding continued his domination of all things resembling competition, lifting the Stars against former big leaguer George Mullin and McLean's All-Stars, 4–3, for his 19th straight victory. Santop had three hits off Mullen, and Lloyd two. Redding got his 20th win a week later, besting "Turkey" Mike's All-Stars, 5–3. Lloyd had two hits, one a double, and Poles had four.[47]

Redding's sensational streak came to an end the following week in a tightly pitched Sunday afternoon affair in Indianapolis, losing, 2–1. He did not have time to worry about it though, as the Stars were en route to Chicago for a set with the American Giants. In Chicago, Lloyd, Santop, Redding, Gans and the others were treated like returning heroes, with a "storm of applause" greeting them. The Giants were not quite as inviting, besting the Stars, 2–1 in a 12-inning affair, before dropping a close one, 1–0. With Redding on the hill in game three and hungry to get another streak going, the Stars delivered the worst beating the American Giants had received in years, a 13–0 "trouncing." Redding fanned five in the game, allowing seven hits. Bill Gatewood of the Giants, however, was not quite as sharp, serving up 13 hits, three of them doubles and one a triple. Lloyd, brilliant on defense in turning three double plays, also lashed two hits, scoring once. The Giants won the series, however, taking three games to the Stars' two.[48]

The American Giants had just returned from Indianapolis, where a riot had nearly occurred in its game with the ABCs. In front of 3,500 "lusty fans" at Federal Park, Frank Wickware fired continuous fastballs at Indianapolis batters, looking to shut them down and shut them up. The Taylor brothers had bragged that they were going to take the game, regardless of who was up for Chicago. The contest went smoothly until the seventh inning, when with the score tied 2–2, Rube Foster sent Richard Whitworth in for Wickware, followed by Bill Gatewood. The bases drunk with "Hoosiers" and dust "blowing around the diamond" interrupting the game, an argument ensued at home plate over Foster's demands to sprinkle the field. The umpire became so upset that he promptly called four balls on the batter, walking in the lead run for the ABCs, and then forfeited the game to Indianapolis. Pete Hill, the Giants captain, came running out of the dugout to confront the man in blue, prompting both benches to clear, players grabbing bats and joining the melee. The umpire, angered by Hill, took out a pistol and hit him in the face, breaking Hill's nose. Several other players were hurt in the pileup as well. The *Defender*, chastising the actions taken in Indianapolis, called it a "bloody chapter," asserting that another such outburst would "kill Afro-American ball play-ing."[49]

Amazingly enough, the Giants and ABCs played the following day, but in the third inning, the Giants up by two runs and Indianapolis at bat, all hell broke loose again. Foster, by his own account, began walking out to the coaching box when a police sergeant, calling him "the dirtiest names" Foster had ever heard, ordered him back to the dugout. The sergeant demanded to know who it was that had started the argument the day before. When Foster questioned why, the sergeant responded, "If you open your mouth, I will blow your brains out." According to Foster, the police sergeant "stood there for at least five minutes" heaping abuse on the coach, calling him all kinds of names. Foster ultimately sent Bauchman in to coach third, but when Bauchman arrived there, he noted the base was a bit out of the line and so moved it back. That prompted C. I. Taylor onto the field, who pushed Bauchman aside and called for the police, who arrived and began beating Bauchman over the head. Foster blamed Tom Bowser, one of the ABCs owners, who was "in with the police and a bondsman," for allowing them onto the field. "No one else could have done it," Foster concluded. Foster then asserted that he and his team had been humiliated as never before.[50]

By the end of August the Lincoln Stars were home, "fresh from their tri-umphant trip through the Middle West." They immediately set about devour-ing the local competition, taking the Jefferson Athletic Club, 6–1, and Poughkeepsie, 4–2. The game with Poughkeepsie was a "hummer," one of the best seen at the Oval that season. Redding got the win for the Stars, striking out eight, but Poughkeepsie hung tough, the Stars not putting it away until scoring two in the eighth inning to win it. Doc Sykes then shut out the Long Branch Cubans in Camden, New Jersey, 4–0, while Harvey pitched a 8–1 victory over the Camden nine.[51]

Lloyd got a hit in the game with Poughkeepsie, his last of the season with the Stars, for within days he and Jude Gans had jumped back to Chicago with the American Giants. The summer trip through the Midwest may have rendered them nostalgic, or simply given Foster an opportunity to sway them back from the McMahons. Resentment over his salary had mounted on Lloyd's part, certainly since a doubleheader in Chicago when the Stars were not paid. As they lined up to receive their money, they learned that Jess McMahon had "drunk up" the payroll. Lloyd was so angered that he swore his strongest oath, "Dad gum it!" and made plans to head west. Lloyd, "the game's greatest short-stop, barring none," was looked upon to fill the American Giants' biggest need, while Gans would "plug the hole in left," giving Foster the "strongest team in the country."[52]

Lloyd immediately paid dividends with a hit and a run in a 7–3 win over the Cuban Stars. The Giants then bested St. Louis in both games of a twin bill, before dropping one to the Chicago Union Giants, 9–7. The Giants tried every way to win the latter contest, but could not get it done. They took the lead in the fifth inning on two bunts, two hits and three errors, but ceded the lead when the Union Giants posted five runs in the sixth. Foster's club got even the next week, however, beating the Union Giants, 4–0 on "Big" Richard Whitworth's no-hitter. "They have come into their own," wrote Frank Young in the *Defender*, and they had. Whitworth, a power pitcher with a filthy slider, allowed just three men to reach first, two on walks and one on an error by Lloyd. Lloyd's error of Jackson's grounder made had the crowd uneasy for a moment, especially as Whitworth passed Green and Clarkson sacrificed to move the runners up. Whitworth settled down, however, stranding the runners at second and third.[53]

The black press was full of reports that autumn that D. W. Griffith's controversial film, *Birth of a Nation*, was being pulled from theatres and, in certain cases, kicked out of entire states because of the violence it provoked. Riots broke out when the film was shown in Boston and Philadelphia. Chicago refused to show it, forcing an appellate court to enjoin the city from doing so. The film, notorious because of its flawed interpretation of history, portrayed the Reconstruction era following the Civil War as a debacle, arguing that blacks could never be integrated into white society. Its portrayal of the Ku Klux Klan as a redeemer of sorts, necessary to the reinstitution of honest government following Reconstruction, drew the most ire, particularly from scholars such as W. E. B. DuBois. More than anything, it again signaled the lingering ill will directed toward blacks by a large percentage of white society, a sign of the long walk still to come.[54]

With Chicago's fight against *Birth of a Nation* in Appellate Court, Rube Foster tried to lure Joe Tinker and his Chicago Federal League club into a series of games. Rube, insisting that he would postpone a planned west coast tour if necessary, suggested the games could be played for charity. Rube was ready to face white players, even if it cost him money. Tinker, however, while scheduling other white semiprofessional clubs, ignored Rube's bait. Foster, "much peeved" over Tinker's refusal to play him, commented that it was probably best if his club left town. "We are getting to be too much of a drawing card. Our park is too near to the White Sox and they figure that we are competitors. The local papers do not give us anywhere the space that out-of-town papers do when we are traveling.... We will give a fine account of ourselves in the winter league."[55]

The Giants' swing, a planned 25,000 miles in all, was said to have been "the longest jaunt" ever attempted by a professional club. The trip took them to Omaha and Denver, before arriving in Los Angeles to play in the California Winter League. After that, the Giants were scheduled to play in Hawaii before retuning to Chicago in April by way of Montana, Wyoming, the Dakotas and St. Louis. However, after the Hawaii trip was cancelled, Foster scheduled a trip to Cuba instead. Foster had also intended to travel south to New Orleans, but the ballpark was washed away by a hurricane, causing the games to be cancelled.[56]

The Giants won their opener on the coast, 10–0, amid published reports that José Figarola, one of Cuba's top catchers, had been killed when hit in the chest by a pitch from José Méndez, who was said to be "prostrate with grief." There was some concern that the incident would affect Méndez's career. Such alarm proved unnecessary as two weeks later it was revealed that Figarola had not been killed, only bruised, and that rumors of his death had been "spurred by his enemies."[57]

In the midst of the Giants' western trip came word that Booker T. Washington had died. Washington, the prototype of a rags to riches tale, had been born into slavery, yet through education, perseverance, and shrewd leadership had lifted himself to the pinnacle of African-American life in the United States, one where he was viewed — if only by white America — as a spokesman for all blacks in this country. It was Washington upon whom Presidents called for advice regarding the appointment of African Americans to federal offices. It was Washington to whom the philanthropists went seeking deserving recipients for their dollars. He wielded a mighty voice and an even greater legacy. He had critics, like W. E. B. DuBois, William Monroe Trotter and others who disagreed with him over his views on industrial education, or those like Ida B. Wells Barnett who believed black folk were better off leaving the South, while Washington encouraged them to stay. Through it all, however, he worked tirelessly toward the economic empowerment of African Americans, the acquisition of basic civil rights and the establishment of a more just nation, one where equal justice among the races was a given, not something solely to be earned. When he died the world wept, with 35,000 people attending his funeral at Tuskegee, Alabama, home of the college he built.[58]

Charlotte M. Bigelow of Chicago, exhibiting a prophetic sense of rhyme and a kinship with the biblical *Exodus* from Egypt, spoke for the masses in penning this "Requiem" to Booker T. Washington:

> On Pisgah's mount he stood,
> Far stretched the Promised Land,
> Beneath lay the vast camp,
> Of Israel's stricken band!

From the Nile-watered sands,
Red Egypt's grain-gold fields,
To Pharaoh's royal throne,
Vain agonized appeals.

Crushed spirit, darkened soul,
Stunted brain, the dower
From brutal servitude,
Weak regenerate power!

Back to Sinai's crest,
To that appalling night
When God spake from out cloud,
Hidden from mortal site!

The Wilderness, the years,
The struggle, the uplift,
Faith slowly wakening,
Through gloom — a rift!

As mists before his gaze
The years pass as a scroll,
In light Divine he sees
Futurity unroll!

With steadfast eye he views
The way he may not tread,
But knoweth well, another
Will follow where he led!

So, trustful lays him down
Upon that toilworn height,
There, with his God, alone,
He passeth from man's sight.[59]

In early November the Giants traveled to San Diego, taking one on the chin from a group of "western cracks" known at the Pantages, 7–4. The Pantages were fronted by Roy "Hippo" Hitt, a pitcher brought in from Ed Maier's Vernon Tigers in Los Angeles to face the Giants, and who dealt smoke and benders all day long. He was opposed by "Smokey Joe" Williams, who uncharacteristically allowed seven runs on 14 hits, while striking out a mere three. With Hitt dealing, the Giants plated two runs in the second inning on a walk to Gans, a double by Bauchman, and a single by Petway. With the Pantages up, 5–2, in the sixth, Hill beat out a bunt to first; Duncan advanced him by slamming a hard grounder to second. Lloyd then got one in his wheelhouse, driving a triple over Berger's head at shortstop and into the gap between left and center, scoring Hill. Tully McAdoo and Gans followed meekly, however, as the Pantages remained on top to stay.[60]

"Red Ant" Wickware got the Giants back on track the next week with a three-hit shutout of the Los Angeles Cline-Cline Nine, 4–0. In fact, one of the hits was a Texas Leaguer that "Lloyd could have gotten had he hustled a little faster." The hit came in the ninth inning when Bert Whaling, a catcher for the Boston Braves, hit a blooper which Lloyd took his time going after as it fell in safely. It was a rough day in the field for Lloyd, who also booted one in the third, but he fought back at the plate, getting two hits. Wickware, ignoring the errors and some early wildness, which he overcame by bearing down with men on base, was on his game, striking out six. The Giants followed this by besting a team from San Bernardino, 6–3, and again taking the Pantages, this time 3–2. Lloyd had four hits in the two games.[61]

A month later, the Giants clinched the California Winter League pennant, besting the Pantages on Christmas afternoon, 4–3. Wickware took the hill for the Giants, working "to perfection" against the Pantages' Roy Hitt, who was tough until the sixth. In that inning Pete Hill got it going with a leadoff single to left, followed by Duncan's infield hit advancing Hill to second. With two on and no outs, Lloyd picked up two quick strikes on "healthy swings." He then stepped out of the box, rubbed his hands in the dirt and climbed back in, determined to get a run in. As if "by magic," Lloyd drove Hitt's next pitch, a bender, over the center field wall for the longest home run of the winter, Hill and Duncan scoring ahead of him. Lloyd got to Hitt again in the eighth when the hurler, this time trying to walk Lloyd, tossed a mistake that Lloyd served down the left field line for a double. Lloyd's three hits paced the Giants in the pennant clincher.[62]

With the California Winter League adjourned, and horrific flooding taking place across the south in Kentucky, Mississippi and Louisiana, Lloyd and the Giants moved on to Cuba for more winter ball. Playing in what John Holway described as "huge" parks, the Giants compiled a 5–9 record. Bombín Pedroso led the league in batting at .413, while Cristobal Torriente led in steals, triples and home runs. Lloyd led all non–Cubans with a .393 average.[63]

In Havana on March 10, the Giants took a doubleheader from the Reds, winning a close pitching duel, 2–0, followed by a lopsided 14–3 affair. Wickware bested Palmero in the lid-lifter, allowing just two hits, one a triple by Marsans who also had three stolen bases, and striking out seven. The "Red Ant" was in trouble several times but managed to wiggle out behind stellar defense. In game two, the Giants played the Cubans "off their feet," collecting 14 runs on ten hits. Lloyd and Gans stole three bases each, and McAdoo two more. Lloyd was also sound in the field, turning a "lightning double-play" in the sixth to squelch Havana's only real threat. The two wins "shoved" the Giants past Havana into second place as they prepared to face Almendares, "the pride of the island."[64]

A week later, the Giants beat Almendares, 8–1, pounding 16 hits off the Cuban tandem of Tatica Campos and Pedroso. After scoring a pair of runs in the first inning, heavy hitting in the sixth, including a Lloyd triple and a double by McAdoo, gave the Giants three more runs to ice the victory. Lloyd had four hits in the game, while Jess Barbour had three, including a triple. At this point in the campaign, Lloyd was second in the league in batting at .454, following only Torriente at .432.[65]

By the end of the month the Giants were back in the states, stopping over for a Sunday afternoon game against the Indianapolis ABCs in New Orleans on their way back west. Aside from Bingo DeMoss, the ABCs featured William "Dizzy" Dismukes, a new superstar who would post 17 wins in 1915. They also had in center field a "tough, combative 21-year-old former soldier" named Oscar Charleston, who had played baseball while serving in the Philippines with the 24th Infantry.[66]

Oscar Charleston would become what many believe to be the greatest all-around baseball player in black baseball history. A slugger favorably compared with Babe Ruth, Charleston also had speed to burn, playing center field with reckless abandon, "robbing batters of sure hits." Jocko Conlan, a Hall of Fame umpire who saw him play, believed that Charleston was the greatest black player of his time, comparable in the field to the Cleveland Indians' Hall of Fame center fielder Tris Speaker. Others, like Ben Taylor, argued that Charleston was the greatest outfielder who ever lived — period. His unique blend of power, speed and defensive ability placed him on a rarefied plane seldom experienced by a ballplayer. Charleston was also hot-tempered, "not to be intimidated, and whose fights both on and off the field are as legendary as his playing skills."[67]

Oscar Charleston, a slugger favorably compared with Babe Ruth and with speed to burn, was arguably the greatest all-around player in black baseball history.

The game was a "hummer." The Giants, slow out of the box, faced an uphill battle when, down seven zip in the ninth inning, with fans "standing on their heads nearly screaming their lungs out," they rallied, coming up one run shy, losing 7–6. Having tallied six runs with two outs and runners on second and third, the Giants pushed ABCs starter Dizzy Dismukes to the clubhouse. A victory was in sight. One single would have scored two runs, but Gans grounded out to the pitcher, ending "the greatest game that Crescent City fans had ever witnessed."[68]

The game was not without some controversy, when in the midst of the ninth-inning rally Lloyd hit a home run that was subsequently overruled by an umpire who said that the bomb had landed two feet outside the flags marking the fence line. Lloyd was awarded a ground rule double instead. The Giants, feeling justly robbed, contested the call, arguing that Lloyd's hit had landed beyond the flags, but to no avail as crowds swarmed the field, causing a 30-minute delay. Foster, seeking to avoid a riot, opted to accept the ruling and play on.[69]

On the coast a week later in Sacramento, the Giants took a pair of games from the Portland Coasters, 11–6 and 5–2. Lloyd batted .500 in the dip, but it was the pitching of Ed Washington that stole the show. Washington, an 18-year-old phenom recently signed by Rube Foster in Los Angeles, used a deceptive underhanded delivery with an array of breaking pitches to thwart the highly regarded Coasters, rejecting them time and again. The Giants then traveled to Portland to take on Seattle at Rainier Valley Park, walloping the home team 11–3 in game one. The hot-hitting Lloyd led the Giants with three hits, including two doubles. In the second game, the Giants easily beat the Portland Baby Beavers of the Inter-City Baseball League, 13–1. The visitors slammed out 14 hits, while the "little ones" could manage only four. Again, Lloyd was the "Ty Cobb" of the matinee, getting four hits in six tries.[70]

The Giants finished their long winter trip by drubbing the University of Oregon, 11–0, besting Seattle, 4–2, and winning an uphill battle against the Tacoma Tigers, 10–8. Their only loss came in Bellingham, Washington, when facing Vancouver of the Northwest League, 8–5. The Giants made a run at things in the ninth inning, but fell short when Grant nubbed a roller that forced Hill at the plate. Gans followed by rolling out, and Clarkson Brazelton, who was catching, flied out to center to end things.[71]

It had been by all accounts a glorious tour for the Giants, the team winning 20 out of 24 games against Pacific Coast League teams alone, including three out of four against defending champion Portland. Rube Foster's Giants had "traveled farther" that winter "than any ball club in the world," winning the Winter League in California before jumping to Havana to face some of the top players in the game, and then jumping back to take on more west coast opponents. They also faced a myriad of other teams along the way, the ABCs and the Lincoln Giants to name two.

When the Giants finally arrived home just before the start of the 1916 regular season, they were welcomed with a banner headline pronouncing the return of "Rube Foster and His Famous American Giants." Most celebrated of all was Lloyd, the lynchpin at shortstop and the clean-up batter. But Lloyd had become more than that. He was a leader, someone whose innate decency and optimism could carry a club, even when his bat and glove might not. He was a player who personified the term "professional," and as the Giants traversed the map, Lloyd was there, his qualities in full bloom. John Henry Lloyd was becoming one of the game's great ambassadors. Along with Pete Hill, Frank Wickware, and Bruce Petway, he formed the core of one of the most remarkable baseball teams of the early twentieth century, Chicago's "Famous American Giants."[72]

FOUR

That's Jai Alai!

World War I began in Europe in August, 1914. "The Great War," as it became known, was a horrific conflict that ravaged the European countryside, and by 1916 had left millions dead. Over 700,000 casualties were incurred in one battle alone, Verdun, turning the *Plain of the Woevre*, once home to "peaceful fields, farms and villages," into a "strip of murdered nature." Americans waited anxiously.[1] President Woodrow Wilson campaigned for re-election that year on a slogan that he had "kept us out of war," yet preparations for involvement, based largely on the protection of America's commercial maritime interests, were being made even as he spoke. Should the United States be called into action, something that Wilson had little doubt of by this point, the armed forces had to be ready.

John Henry Lloyd was one of millions of American men ultimately called to register for military conscription — the draft. His registration, signed in 1918 when he was 34 years old and playing with the Brooklyn Royal Giants, was set to expire in September of that year. Listing his occupation as baseball player, Lloyd noted that he lived with his wife at 538 Lenox Avenue in Brooklyn, and was under the employ of Nat Strong.[2]

While Lloyd did not serve in the conflict, age surely an impediment, other black players did, most notably John Donaldson, Dick Redding, Louis Santop, and Oscar Charleston, who was already a veteran of the Philippines conflict. Charleston was said to have been so strong that he could tear a baseball in half with his bare hands.[3] Other players drafted included Jude Gans, Dizzy Dismukes, Frank Wickware, and Spottswood Poles.

These men were among the 367,000 African Americans to serve with distinction in the armed forces during World War I. The black 369th Division became the first Allied unit to reach the Rhine River. Upon their return, they were given a parade through Harlem where they were cheered by a million people. John Donaldson served with the 365th Infantry in France.[4] W. E. B. DuBois, editor of the *Crisis*, a monthly publication of the NAACP, which he had helped found, encouraged African Americans to do their part: "Let us not hesitate. Let us ... forget our special grievances and close our ranks shoulder to shoulder with our white citizens ... fighting for democracy."[5] But true democracy did not come, certainly not then, and compared to their white big league counterparts, the number of black players called to duty was greatly disproportionate. As John Holway succinctly put it, white big league teams did not lose nearly as many men to the service.[6]

This kind of disproportionate treatment prompted blacks to continue a collective refrain against the bias exhibited against them. This was especially true in the nation's black newspapers. The *Chicago Defender* printed one such statement, written by A. H. Lee; known simply as "Be Careful Mr. Prejudice," it was powerful in its simplicity:

> Be careful, Mr. Prejudice,
> The world shall always know
> You went to dark old Africa
> Some hundred years ago.
> You coaxed the native to the shore
> And brought him 'cross the bay,
> He still is here, you brought him here,
> And so he's here to stay...
>
> Be careful, Mr. Prejudice
> He cannot help his shade,
> God made him as he wanted to
> As other things He made.
> There's no use trying to squeeze him out,
> That only crowds the way,
> The black man's here, you brought him here
> And so he's here to stay...
>
> Be careful, Mr. Prejudice,
> Thy heel is rough and hard,
> Withal retribution is
> Oppression's great reward.
> You can't escape the reckoning;
> it's going to come some day.
> The black man's here, you brought him here,
> And so he's here to stay.[7]

Lloyd was still in Chicago in 1916, gearing up for what would be one of the great seasons of his career, a year in which he batted .373, was named to the West All-Star Team, and won John Holway's mythical Fleet Walker Award as the top player in the West. The *Chicago Defender* trumpeted the start of the Giants' 1916 season, noting that "Rube and Men in Good Condition Despite Long Trip." The Giants had left Chicago the previous autumn on

October 16, traveling nearly 25,000 miles, and by the time they returned had been on the road playing ball for "six months and fifteen days." Meanwhile, the *Defender* encouraged "all loyal race men and women" to welcome the team home for the opener, "for they advertised Chicago more than all other enterprises combined."[8]

On May 9, at Schorling' Park, in a game played on a gorgeous, sunny day, although one where a cool wind blew in during the later innings, Lloyd, Pete Hill and Leroy Grant proved "too much" for the West Ends, winning 5–2. The Giants received a rousing ovation as they emerged one by one onto the field, tossing the ball around before the early-arriving crowd. Rube Foster was "given an ovation seldom given a ballplayer," an especially boisterous welcome.

Tom "Schoolboy" Johnson took the mound for the Giants, quickly disposing of the visitors. In the bottom of the first inning Bruce Petway struck out, Hill beat out a bunt to third and stole second, and Pete Duncan was hit by a pitch. The inning died on the vine, however, when Hill was thrown out attempting to steal third, followed by a Lloyd walk and Grant grounding out. In the second Bill Francis started things with a sharp single. Francis' bad leg bothering him, Rube Foster, on agreement with the visitors, was forced into the game as a courtesy runner, bringing a roar of laughter from the crowd. The "huge manager," however, silenced those laughing by stealing second and then moving to third on the bad throw. Foster next attempted to steal home, but with the count two and two, Harry Bauchman struck out on a wide one and the West End catcher to doubled up Foster.

After the visitors scratched out a run in the third inning, Hill belted a one-out double and Duncan walked. With the fans clamoring for a run, Lloyd fouled off six pitches before flying out to center. Grant followed Lloyd, grounding out to short to end the inning. The West Ends looked to pull away in the fourth, loading the sacks, when with one out a sharp liner was mashed to Francis at third who dug it out of the dirt, shot it to Lloyd, who in turn whipped it to Grant for the double play. The deuce turned the Giants' fortunes because in the fifth Petway flared a single, Hill singled, Duncan sacrificed, and Lloyd shot a liner over second, scoring Petway and Hill. Grant singled, and he and Lloyd pulled a double steal, Lloyd hook-sliding safely into third. Following a commotion between the umpire and the visiting manager over what he believed was Lloyd's questionable theft, Jude Gans fanned and Francis ended the inning by flying out to center. In the seventh, Duncan belted a one-out double, Lloyd singled sharply, scoring Duncan, Grant tripled to the fence, scoring Lloyd, and Gans singled, scoring Grant. Two hits and an error at first gave the West Ends another run in the ninth, but it was not enough, the Giants closing it out.[9]

With Rube Foster on the bump, the Giants then whaled La Porte, 13–1. Laughter could be heard throughout Schorling Park from the 3,000 in attendance as the battery of Foster and Petway was announced, the fans clearly sensing that a joke was on in the form of Foster, whose appearances in the box were becoming increasingly rare. The joke was on La Porte, however, as the old man scattered six hits, struck out four, and allowed just a single pass, this in spite of a rain delay. Cary B. Lewis of the *Indianapolis Freeman* reported that the veteran hurler "still possesses some of the old-time punch and is able to fool the boys with that Foster curve." The *Defender* noted that Foster was "as good as ever." Lloyd led the offensive barrage with a double and single, while Hill, "as usual, got his hit."[10]

Three days later the Cuban Stars rolled into Chicago on the magnificent arms of Mulo Padrón, José Junco and Bombín Pedroso, and the slugging Cristóbal Torriente. It was the beginning of a season-long set between the two clubs, who seemed to play each other more often than not. The Giants, their staff well rested, countered with "Big" Richard Whitworth, a "classy" power pitcher with a sinking fastball, who in his second season with the club formed a stellar tandem with Frank Wickware. As expected, the pitching duel was sensational, the game described by Mr. Fan, a sportswriter with the *Defender*, as "[s]ome game, some game."[11]

Cristóbal Torriente resembled Oscar Charleston in that he was a power hitter with great instincts and deceptive speed in the field. The "muscular lefthander" was a notorious bad ball hitter, swinging and connecting on anything from nose to toes, with power to all fields. An accomplished base thief as well, Torriente was "a complete ballplayer with superb talent." C. I. Taylor once said of Torriente, "'there walks a ballclub.'" The New York Giants once scouted the light-skinned Torriente with designs on signing him, before ultimately taking a pass because of the "rough texture of his hair," which may have given away the scam.[12]

Having rained all that morning, the weather turned balmy, as the two teams gave the 3,000 fans in attendance their money's worth. Whitworth was tough, allowing the Cubans just two first-inning hits, one a clean single and the other a wind-aided floater from Pedroso falling just beyond Grant's reach. (Pedroso was hit in the head in the sixth inning and forced to leave the game.) Padrón was equally effective for the Cubans, serving up goose eggs until the sixth when Lloyd beat out a poor throw by Hooks Jiménez. Grant then rolled a slow one to short, and Lloyd, going into the bag standing up, blocked the throw to first, both runners safe. Then with two outs — Gans having fanned and Francis forcing Lloyd at third — Grant came all the way around on a ball that got away from catcher José Rodríguez for the game's first run. The Giants got another run in the seventh when Hill belted a "clean" two-out double, Duncan singled, and Lloyd doubled sharply over second. That was all it took, the Giants winning, 2–0.[13]

Coming that June to the Windy City was Tom Bowser's "Jewell's ABCs" of Indianapolis. Advertised as the original ABCs, this club had broken off from the team led by C. I. Taylor, the better known ABCs. The ABCs, named for the American Brewing Company, had originated in Birmingham, Alabama, under C. I. Taylor's tutelage, before moving to West Baden, Indiana. It possessed some of the best talent in the West with Elwood "Bingo" DeMoss at second, "Candy Jim" Taylor at third, Ben Taylor at first, Oscar Charleston in center field, and a staff led by Dizzy Dismukes and Dicta Johnson. In 1914 Taylor moved the club to Indianapolis, bringing in Tom Bowser as a part owner. Bowser held the lease on Washington Park, the ABCs' home field. By 1915, however, Taylor had ousted Bowser, gaining full control of the team and the lease on the park. With Taylor now in charge, Bowser took — for a time — Bingo DeMoss and others, forming "Jewell's ABCs." Clearly, this bunch was not up to par with the former squad, as Chicago stifled them, 6–3, on Tom Johnson's three-hitter.[14]

Bowser's crew was plagued by miscues, particularly at shortstop, with Pudge Hutchinson committing three errors, two of them on poor throws. Mr. Fan of the *Defender* surmised that perhaps Hutchinson, who had been discarded by the Giants a year earlier in favor of Lloyd, was a little nervous because of the delegation of fans that had turned out to welcome him. On the other side, Lloyd was flawless, and in the sixth inning dug a "hot grounder" from DeMoss out of the dirt, tossing him out at first.[15]

Cristobal Torriente was a power hitter with great instincts and deceptive speed in the field. The "muscular lefthander" was a notorious bad ball hitter, swinging and connecting on anything from nose to toes, with power to all fields. He was a complete ballplayer, of whom C. I. Taylor once said, "There walks a ballclub."

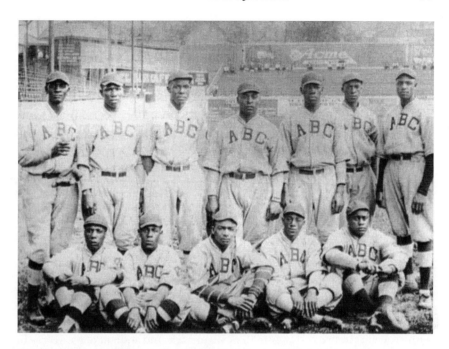

The 1921 ABCs. Under C. I. Taylor's leadership, the ABCs became charter members of the Negro National League, fielding talented ballclubs from 1920 to 1926. In this photograph: C.I. Taylor, back row, first on left; Oscar Charleston, back row, middle; Ben Taylor, back row, third from right; "Steel Arm" John Taylor, back row, third from left (courtesy Negro Leagues Baseball Museum).

The Giants continued winning into July, taking a hard fought holiday series with the Cubans at Schorling Park. Tom Johnson was again tough on the Cubans in game one, keeping it close for the 3–2 victory. Lloyd, clearly the top shortstop in the game, fielded everything that came near him, while picking up a hit in the decisive ninth inning. In game two, an 11-inning affair played before what was reported as the largest crowd "ever assembled to see a semi-pro game," Richard Whitworth bested Mulo Padrón, 3–2. Lloyd belted two doubles for the Giants. Game three, with "Red Ant" Wickware and Junco pitching, was knotted at 1–1 when it was called because of darkness in the seventh inning. Chicago's faithful did not have to wait long for redemption, however, as the Giants, paced at the plate by Lloyd and Francis, rallied in the eighth inning a day later to best the Cubans, 5–4.[16]

With the Giants up 3–0–1 in the series, they took the final game, 1–0, a walk-off victory coming with one out in the ninth inning. Until then, both pitchers had held serve, José Junco holding the Giants to five hits, and Wickware, his best stuff evident, allowing three meaningless singles. In the last of the ninth, Jess Barbour led off with a hit for the Giants and took second when Junco plunked Hill. Petway was then sent in run for Hill and Barbour "startled the crowd" by stealing third. With men on first and third and no outs, Duncan laid down a sloppy squeeze bunt. Barbour was out at the plate, with Petway advancing into scoring position. With one out and the crowd on its feet, Lloyd stepped to the plate. Hitless to that point in the game, the slugging shortstop did not disappoint, slashing a "sharp wallop" into right-center field that scored Petway from second with the winning run.[17]

After dropping one to Charlie Mills' St. Louis Giants, a game in which Tom Johnson was all over the place, errant in both his delivery to the plate and throws to first, Rube's bunch regrouped to beat St. Louis, 6–3 and 6–3. Foster used both games to rest his staff, with Jude Gans going the distance in game one and Foster himself taking the hill in the second, allowing nine hits but coming away with the win. The Giants then lost one to the Cubans, 4–0, Mulo Padrón earning the shutout, before topping the West Ends in a double bill, 2–1 and 4–1.[18]

By this point in the 1916 campaign, the Chicago American Giants were the best black baseball team in the West, bar none. Their record bore it out with crucial series victories over the Cuban Stars and Indianapolis ABCs. In fact, they had just beaten the Cubans again, 6–5, when the irrepressible Foster, always on the hunt for a gate, scheduled a game with a traveling team from Kokomo fronted by former Detroit Tigers ace George Mullin. The game was billed as Foster against Mullin in a match-up of yesterday's heroes. Lloyd, Petway and Hill had faced Mullin before, and with some success, battling the Tigers in Cuba during the winters of 1909 and 1910. Mullin had been on top of his game then, having pitched six complete World Series games between 1907 and 1909, allowing only 12 earned runs over 58 innings for a 1.86 ERA. In the 1909 World Series, played shortly before arriving in Cuba, Mullin won two games, including a five-hit, ten-strikeout, complete game shutout against Honus Wagner and the Pirates. He finished with 29 wins in 1909. But seven years had passed; did the old hurler have anything left? Was Rube up to it? Those were the questions on the mind of the season's largest crowd as it made its way to Schorling Park that Sunday afternoon.

It did not take Mullin long to answer. On a day in which he "simply had too much stuff on that little sphere," Mullin shut out the Giants, 5–0. He was great, allowing a mere three hits to Rube's sluggers, while smiling and enjoying himself as the game progressed. On the other end, Kokomo hitters took Foster all over the yard, gathering 12 hits. The lone highlight of the game for the Giants was a brilliant double play started by Lloyd in the second inning, when he dug a ball out of the dirt with one hand before sending it on to Bauchman at second, who turned it to Grant at first. The loss be damned, fans went home that day having enjoyed themselves, not a "sore-headed loser" in the bunch.[19]

As the Giants played for the gate against Kokomo, the McMahon brothers' Lincoln Stars, with Zach Pettus, Bubber Parks, and Louis Santop, were cleaning up the East. With their ascension to first place and subsequent eastern ball championship, it was announced that they would travel west later that fall to face the American Giants for the "championship of the world" (*Chicago Defender*, August 5, 1916).

Prior to the postseason, however, the Giants had unfinished business, namely the resumption of their seemingly endless campaign with the Cuban Stars, one that stretched into the middle of the series with New York. In late July the Cubans were again in Chicago to face the Giants. With Cristóbal Torriente pitching for the Cubans, Lloyd went on the attack, lacing three hits and providing "stellar work around short, pulling down a line drive with one hand" and getting to everything entering the hole behind second. He was easily the feature of the game, which the Giants won, 5–4. His defense had become nothing less than spectacular; in one game a fan was heard to shout, "That's not baseball, that's Jai Alai."[20]

The Giants followed up by sweeping a doubleheader from the Cubans in Chicago, 8–1 and 5–3, on a hot, 112° afternoon, before taking them again, this time in Gary, Indiana, by the score of 6–3. They finished the brief road stint by besting a white club in Joliet, 8–5. It was Lloyd's first-inning homer, a three-run clout plating Hill and Duncan, which proved "too much" for Joliet. The smash was said to have been "the longest ever seen" at the Joliet venue.[21]

Brilliant skies and a packed house greeted the Lincoln Stars when they arrived at Schorling Park for the twin bill start of their championship set with the Giants. The opening tilt pitted Doc Sykes against Whitworth, and everyone in Chicago east of the White Sox and Washington Senators game was paying attention. The strong gate was an indicator of the burgeoning popularity of Foster's Giants, particularly in that the first place White Sox, loaded with stars such as Shoeless Joe Jackson and Eddie Collins, were playing only five blocks away.[22]

Sykes was brilliant in spots for the Stars, putting "something" on his slow ball "that kept the slugging Giants baffled," but ultimately wilted, allowed 12 hits and losing, 6–5. Lloyd led the way with three hits for Chicago. For his part, Whitworth, the Giants stopper, pitched aggressively, staying inside on the Lincolns batters, but his chin music resulted in eight walks. That was something, Mr. Fan reminded, "that does not conform to the rules of the

playing book." Ad Langford brought the Stars back in the second game, holding the Giants to three runs on seven hits, winning it, 6–3. Besides pitching
a great game, Langford slammed a bases-loaded, three-run triple in the sixth
inning to seal the victory.[23]

Over the next week and prior to resumption of the series with the Lincoln
Stars, the Giants ventured to St. Louis for five games, and then to Jeffery's
Ball Park in Kenosha Wisconsin to face the Cuban Stars on what one scribe
reported was a "sea of mud." Playing hurt and worn out from travel, the
nomadic Giants dropped the affair, 5–3, before the largest crowd to ever witness a ballgame in Kenosha. Mulo Padrón scattered seven hits for the Cubans,
with Grant getting four of them. In the field, it was Lloyd's uncharacteristic
error in the first inning which led to the first of three Cubans runs scored in
the frame. The Cubans rallied again in the fourth when Pelayo Chacón singled,
Gervasio "Strike" González sacrificed him over, Cristóbal Torriente was
plunked, and Bobby Villa doubled, scoring two. Then Bombín Pedroso doubled, scoring Villa. Lloyd scored the Giants' only run in the third, singling
after Duncan had whiffed and moving to second when Francis walked. After
Gans struck out, Petway singled, bringing in Lloyd.[24]

The Giants left for Chicago immediately following the game to resume
their series with the Lincoln Stars, who had spent the week resting. That
week, the two clubs split a pair of games; the Giants lost the first one, 10–8,
their hurlers issuing six walks. The day's second game, the series' fourth, was
an extra-inning pitching dual between Sykes and Wickware and went to the
Giants, 1–0.

It was said that never in the history of baseball in Chicago had a "better
or cleaner game been played" as game four of the Giants–Stars series. As the
game progressed, featuring plenty of sensational plays, Wickware gained confidence while growing stronger, especially with the brilliant support of his
defense. In the fourth inning, with two runners on, Bubber Parks and Zach
Pettus attempted a double steal for the Stars. Petway whipped the ball to
Lloyd who promptly sent it back "like a bullet" and Parks was out at the plate.
On offense, Grant tallied four hits, while Lloyd went hitless, although he was
robbed on a great play by Red Miller at third base in the tenth. And as the
goose eggs mounted on both sides the game proceeded in suspenseful fashion.[25]

Chicago's defense was at its best in the top of the 11th inning. Parks led
off by scorching one that looked good for three bases, but Barbour at second
made a leap and stabbed it out of the air for the out. Pettus then grounded
sharply to Lloyd, who glided close to second base for the drive, whipping it
to Grant for out number two. With Bruce Hocker, the Stars' big first baseman

at the plate, "Red Ant" Wickware wasted little time, throwing one by him. Wickware then stepped off the mound, smiled, and came again, this time with a heater so fast that "Hocker couldn't see it." Strike two! Pausing to push some dirt into the pitchers' box, Wickware slowly rose, set, cocked and fired. It was gas, high and tight, a pitch that would have beaten the famous train "Twentieth Century Limited," said Mr. Fan. Hocker, with no chance, swung, trying to fight it off, but it was in Petway's glove by then. In the top of the climactic 12th inning, "Big Bertha" Santop led off for the Stars, belting a long high one to Gans in left for out number one. Francis killed Ashby Dunbar's grounder at third for the second out, while Grant got Ed Green's high foul in back of first to retire the side.[26]

With Chicago's fans on fire, Pete Hill walked to start the bottom half of the inning. Duncan then laid down a sacrifice that Sykes fielded, tossing to Pettus at first and moving Hill to second. Following an intentional walk to Lloyd, Francis busted, moving the runners up. Sykes had thought to throw to third, but Hill had him beat. With the winning run at third and the fans on their feet, LeRoy Grant, already with three hits on the day, came to the plate. Grant hit a "terrific smash" to Parks at shortstop, who, after smothering the ball, threw it over Pettus' head at first, Hill coming in with the winning score. It was Grant's fourth hit, "as he had the throw beaten."[27]

On August 20, having split another pair and knotted at three wins each, the Giants and Stars faced off in the climactic Friday afternoon championship round. Doc Sykes, having baffled the Giants the previous Sunday, was sent to the hill again to confront the Giants' Tom Johnson. Johnson got into trouble in the first inning when Dunbar singled and Parks shot one over second, which neither Bauchman nor Lloyd could get to, putting men on second and third. After Pettus popped up to Petway, Santop was purposely walked to load the bases. Grant Johnson fanned, but Bruce Hocker promptly belted a bases-clearing triple. The Giants slipped a run across in the second. Lloyd led off with a triple, but then held up when Gans rolled to Johnson at second for an out. Grant then singled to score Lloyd. The Giants threatened again in the third and might have scored two to tie it. With one out, Barbour tripled to right, and Hill hit one just sharply enough to Parks for the latter to fumble it. Hill was safe at first with Barbour holding at third. Bill Francis singled, one of his three hits in the game, scoring Barbour and advancing Hill to third. Lloyd followed, grounding to Johnson at second who threw Hill out at the plate. Lloyd, however, "lost his head" and started to second, with Francis taking a big turn at third. Halfway to home Francis turned back to the bag, but Santop's snap throw got him to end the rally.[28]

With one out in the sixth inning, Grant doubled, forcing Sykes from the mound. With "Gunboat" Thompson on in relief, Petway dropped a triple over Blocker's head, scoring Grant. Langford relieved Thompson, promptly fanning Bauchman, but walked Johnson, the pitcher, after reaching a 0–2 count. Barbour doubled, scoring Petway and moving Johnson to third. Pete Hill followed by hitting the ball under the scoreboard for three-run homer. The bases clear, Francis walked, as did Lloyd, before Gans doubled on a hit-and-run, scoring Francis and Lloyd. Grant's foul pop to Miller at third ended the bleeding. After getting another run in the seventh, the Giants rallied again in the eighth when Francis doubled, Lloyd drove him in with a single, and Gans scored Lloyd with a triple. Grant pushed Gans in with a single, then stole second, before Petway's bomb cleaned the bases. Bauchman followed with a single and a stolen base, moving to third on an error by Langford. Langford then got Wickware on strikes, but allowed Bauchman to score on Barbour's sacrifice. The Stars answered with two runs in the ninth, but it wasn't enough, the Giants taking the game, 15–7, and with it the series. For his part, Ad Langford, who was always tough on the Giants, won two of the Stars' three victories.[29]

Their victory was short-lived. A flat Giants squad dropped one the next day to the Cuban Stars, 9–6, but rebounded on Sunday, shutting out the Cubans, 3–0. Wickware was again "in grand form," allowing the Cubans no runs on three hits. The Giants plated one run in the second inning and two more in the seventh when Petway walked, Bauchman doubled and Wickware singled, scoring Petway. Barbour then sent a sacrifice fly to Torriente in center, scoring Bauchman to end it.[30]

With the Cubans on hold at least for another week, Foster's American Giants turned toward a "grudge match" with C. I. Taylor's Indianapolis ABCs. In Foster and Taylor, this series pitted two club owners who disliked and mistrusted one another. This was especially true of Taylor, who believed Foster to be a hypocrite who had unfairly taken too much credit for the success of black baseball. Foster jealously guarded his western domain, fearing that Taylor's business motives clashed with his own. He also loathed Taylor's aggressive tactics in lifting players from other teams, perhaps recognizing his own original sin at work.[31]

Taylor was bad for the game, Foster asserted, pointing to the many negative incidents involving the ABCs as proof. One such occurrence, which Foster alleged did "irreparable harm to blackball," took place in a 1915 affair between the ABCs and a white all-star team. The controversy arose late in the game on a disputed call at second base when the umpire called a white baserunner safe. Bingo DeMoss, the ABCs second baseman, became so mad that he charged the umpire, trying to punch him. While DeMoss missed,

Oscar Charleston, rushing in from center field, did not, landing a haymaker on the ump, knocking him to the ground. Fans stormed the field and it took 18 police officers to get things under control. For their troubles, Charleston and DeMoss were thrown in jail and charged with assault and battery, this during a time when if a black man went into jail for striking a white, he might not come out. The incident was indicative of what Foster believed was Taylor's problem; C. I. Taylor had lost his players' respect, turning them into "hoodlums."[32]

Although the two clubs had faced each other once earlier in the season, the Giants winning, 6–3, it has been written that this series was the first time the squads had faced off that year. The argument went that Taylor's perceived ducking of Foster's Giants was a major reason for the existing enmity.[33] One thing is clear; enmity existed on both sides and it charged the proceedings that took place in the coming days.

The *Defender* observed that the lid-lifter was played in front of the "largest throng that ever witnessed a ball game on a semi-pro lot." Many in the stands had ventured to Chicago from Indianapolis to cheer on their famed "Bull Moosers." The game itself, a 3–1 Giants win, proved a hard-scrabble affair, with Bingo DeMoss becoming so enraged over a ninth inning collision at the plate with Grant, who held onto the ball for the out, that he struck Goeckel, the umpire, and had the Giants not acted fast to defend the man in blue, all hell would have broken loose. As it was, the melee proved a spectacle. DeMoss, with only one hit on the day, was already stressed over a spectacular play Lloyd had turned on him in the fourth, when the former banged a hard bouncer to short and Lloyd, "making one of his great sensational plays," sent it to Grant at first for the putout.[34]

The game began with the Giants pushing a run across in the bottom of the first behind a walk to Hill, followed by Duncan's single, Lloyd's walk, and Clark's error at shortstop on Francis' grounder, scoring Hill. Grant then lashed one over second, scoring Lloyd and Francis. The ABCs made some noise in the sixth when DeMoss got on, then Brown sent a grounder to Grant at first and was safe on an error, advancing DeMoss to second. After Dismukes struck out, Shively lofted a high foul behind third base that Lloyd, Francis and Hill converged on, looking for a moment like a collision, before Lloyd called off the others, making the out. He then turned and threw out DeMoss who was trying to advance, receiving a nice ovation as he headed in.[35]

Indianapolis made a final push in the ninth, as Rabbit Shively got on with a sharp single to third, DeMoss singled over second, and "Candy Jim" Taylor sacrificed to Wickware, who fielded the bunt and tossed to Grant at first as the runners advanced. Angry over Taylor's sacrifice, Wickware banged the next batter, Ben Taylor, in the head to load the bases. With the "huge crowd" standing en masse, the umpire called Foster and C. I. Taylor to the plate to review the ground rules. The meeting adjourned, Mortie Clark grounded to Bauchman at second, "who with a double play in sight, messed up everything by falling, all hands were safe," Shively scoring on the play. With one out and Russell Powell up, the count 2–1, Wickware tossed one in the dirt that Petway briefly let by him before pouncing on it and firing to Lloyd at second to get Ben Taylor, who had drifted too far off base on the bobble. DeMoss then inexplicably started off third and Lloyd attempted to gun him down, fired to Francis just as DeMoss headed back to the bag. As Francis reached for the throw, DeMoss broke for the plate, prompting Francis to gun the ball to Grant, who was covering home. With both Grant and the umpire bracing for a collision, DeMoss came in spikes high, taking Grant down as the tag was applied. "You're out!" the umpired ruled, ending the game and prompting the fracas noted above.[36]

Foster's Giants did it again the next day, besting the ABCs, 4–2, even though they were out-hit, nine to four. On Tuesday, August 31, the ABCs rebounded, topping the Giants, 7–4. A misjudged fly ball in the ninth inning, followed by two "clouts," one an Oscar Charleston triple, did it for Indianapolis. The Giants had scored three runs in the first inning on Lloyd's single, Francis' double and Grant's single. They posted ten hits in the loss, Lloyd getting one and Barbour three. Jeffries got the win for the ABCs, with Dismukes hurling in relief. The Giants fought back the next day, beating Indianapolis, 5–2. In the set's final tilt, the Giants took an early 2–0 lead before the ABCs staged their "usual batting rally" in the eighth inning to score three runs. The Giants came back with one in the ninth, on Oscar Charleston's muff of Pete Duncan's easy fly to center field. With the game tied, the umpire called it in the tenth on account of darkness, thereby assuring a 3–1–1 Giants win in the series.[37]

The Cubans returned to Chicago the following Saturday for a split set at Schorling Park against the Giants and ABCs, first besting Indianapolis 7–5, and then absorbing a no-hitter by the Giants, 6–0. The "Bull Moosers," as Indy was called, played another tilt with the Giants the following Thursday, this one a 3–2 Giants win in which Lloyd got four hits. The no-hitter was a seven-inning tandem effort, pitched by Tom Johnson, who went the first five, and Richard Whitworth, who finished the last two. Great defense, however, particularly on the part of Hill, Duncan and Gans, was credited as much for the shutout as the pitching. Duncan especially received notice for pulling in a line drive just as it reached the fence. The Cubans fought back a day later, beating the Giants, 12–10, in a sloppily played contest.[38]

For their overall efforts, the Chicago *Defender* proclaimed the American Giants "World's Champions" for 1916. It was announced that Rube Foster's Giants would be presented with a championship flag on Sunday, September 12, by Edward R. Litzinger, candidate for Member of the Board of Review. The Giants, it was said, had earned "their spurs" by leading the Cuban Stars by ten games, and defeating the best teams in the country, including C. I. Taylor's ABCs and the Lincoln Stars of New York. Unfortunately for the Giants, in the Negro Leagues or otherwise, championships are not won in September, but October. Foster's team would have the opportunity to rightfully justify its claim the following month.[39]

Over the next month the Giants worked hard to pad their statistics, scoring wins against local white clubs such as the Gunthers, hailed as the city champs; avenging an early season loss to the Magnets — not to be confused with the All-Nations *Magnates* of Kansas City — a game in which a Lloyd triple drove in the winning tally in the eighth; and Henry's Greys. They also traveled to Kenosha, Wisconsin to play the Jeffery Automobile Club, a white team, winning 10–3. The win proved costly, however, as Bruce Petway, the team's stalwart catcher, suffered what was described as a severe leg injury when he was hit by a pitch. The Giants would need Petway if they were to compete with the "Big Magnates," J. L. Wilkinson's multiracial All-Nations club, featuring José Méndez, Cristóbal Torriente and sensational southpaw John Donaldson, considered at the time to be the best pitcher in black baseball. Wilkinson's All-Nations team was coming to town, fresh from drubbing the ABCs twice.[40]

John Donaldson, like Spot Poles, was a World War I veteran, having served with the 365th Infantry in France. The "poised" lefty was fearless on the mound, with exceptional command. Lloyd would later call him the "toughest" pitcher he ever faced. He was a battler! His out pitch was a devastating "hard, sharp-breaking curve," and he used it with demoralizing effectiveness. Donaldson was the "first great black left-hander" and is considered along with Willie Foster and Nip Winters as one of the great lefties in black ball history.[41]

The All-Nations' team, aside from "playing the ABCs off their feet," were in the process of demonstrating to world that it was possible for black and white professional ballplayers to participate side by side "in harmony" on one team. This factor, it was argued, "more than anything else has pleased the thousands of fans who turned out to see them play." The *Defender* went so far as to allege that had the Chicago White Sox been able to utilize the diversity enjoyed by the Magnates, they would certainly have won a pennant. There is no doubt, the *Defender* chided, "that the Sox could have used Petway when (Ray) Schalk was injured. Lloyd would have easily made good at short and Hill or Barber (*sic* Barbour) would have cavorted about the center garden like a calf in a pasture.... Whitworth or Donaldson is far better that any pitcher on either the north or south side.... Yet with all this, the fans go back to sit another winter to figure out why no world series came to Chicago. The truth is in a few words. Color of a man's skin did it."[42]

The *Defender* also scolded Cap Anson, who had said more than once that "the public objected" to black and white players participating together in professional baseball. "Far from it!" the *Defender* cried. "The All Nations make him out a candidate for the Ananias club." The Magnates were playing before crowded parks in every town, with many smaller communities suspending business during the afternoon of the game. People came out in large measure to witness the greatness of the team's players, particularly its pitching, with Donaldson and Méndez, neither of whom was white, fronting the staff. It failed to make sense, the *Defender* asserted, that the men with the money would not "break down the barriers" and let men such as these through, giving them "a chance to earn a living" while competing with white players on an even basis.[43]

On October 3, in front of record crowds at Schorling Park, the All-Nations club set out to show that their skill and diversity made it the best team in baseball, while the American Giants, defending their turf, were determined to prove otherwise. They both won, splitting the doubleheader; the Giants won the opener, 11–2, with Petway back behind the dish, and the Magnates, with Donaldson on the mound, took game two, 6–3.[44]

The first game started fast when in the bottom of the first inning Barbour singled, Hill sacrificed him to second, and Barbour stole third. After Duncan struck out, Lloyd grounded to Frank Bluekoi at second, who fumbled the ball long enough for Lloyd to reach first, scoring Barbour. Lloyd then stole second, advancing to third on Coleman's high throw. After Francis walked, Lloyd stole home, bringing the crowd to its feet. The Giants plated three more runs in the second, one in the fifth and five in the sixth to post an 11–0 lead. The fifth-inning rally began when Duncan beat out a bunt and Lloyd singled. The Magnates nailed Duncan at third, who cut down Evans, the third baseman, in the process, forcing a timeout in the action so that Evans' torn pant legs could be addressed. Francis then singled, bringing Lloyd home.[45]

The Magnates finally scored two in the seventh inning when with two outs Méndez singled, took second on a passed ball, and came home on Torriente's single to right. Coleman moved Torriente to third with a single of his own. Torriente scored on a wild pitch, making the score 11–2. The Magnates threatened again in the eighth, but were cut down by good defense. Wilkins led off by lining to Lloyd at short. Kennedy sent a long, high fly ball to Duncan for the second out. After Evans singled to left, Méndez hit a line drive toward the gap which looked good for two bases. As the crowd jumped to its feet, however, Barbour leapt, spearing the liner, a "spectacular catch" that sent everyone into "hysterics." Richard Whitworth was stellar throughout for the Giants, scattering nine hits, five of which went to the Cubans, Méndez and Torriente.[46]

Game two saw a masterful pitching performance by John Donaldson, who allowed two runs and struck out eight, including the side in the ninth inning, bringing Big Ed Walsh, the future Hall of Famer and former spitball ace of the White Sox, to his feet in appreciation. Ed Walsh knew good pitching when he saw it. In 1908 Walsh won 40 games in 49 starts, 42 of which were complete games. That same year, he tossed 11 shutouts with 269 strikeouts. In both 1911 and 1912 Walsh won 27 games, tossing 33 and 32 complete games respectively. Sam Crawford of the Tigers remarked that when Walsh threw his "devastating" spitter, it disintegrated on the way to the plate. "Just the spit passed by," Wahoo Sam recalled.[47]

The Magnates scored one run in the first inning and three in the fourth on Clarence Coleman's bases-clearing double to break it open against Wickware. They scored two more in the top of the sixth when Donaldson helped himself by slamming a triple to start the inning. After Wilkins grounded out to Lloyd, who held Donaldson at third, Kennedy tripled to right, scoring Donaldson. Kennedy came around on a sacrifice fly by Evans. The *Defender*, a bit apologetic, noted that the "champions" had bowed only "to the PROWESS and the CUNNINGNESS of John Donaldson the great," nothing more. The *Indianapolis Freeman* went further, arguing that while the Magnates seldom played teams the caliber of the Giants or the ABCs, with Donaldson on the mound, they could beat anyone.[48]

Foster's Giants finished their schedule the following week against the local Magnets, champions of the city league. It was the final game played by the Giants at Schorling Park that season and preceded a western swing taking them to Kansas City for three games with the All-Nations and then to Indianapolis for a climactic tilt with the ABCs. The game with the local Magnets was not a contest as the Giants "walked all over Artie Lieb's men to the tune of a 12 to 6 score," chasing Zarser, the starter, in the third. All 12 of the Giants runs were scored in the first two innings, after which they played listlessly, looking for the train. The visitors created some excitement when they scored four runs in the seventh, but Richard Whitworth, given the near insurmountable lead he had to work with, had been coasting. Gans and Francis led the way for the Giants with three hits each, while Eddie Lavin played a fine game in the field for the locals, getting a hit as well.[49]

As noted, it had been announced that the Giants would be traveling to Indianapolis, following the series with the All-Nations, leaving both the Giants and ABCs "on edge." The *Defender* reported that the two teams were expected to draw record crowds in what again was being touted as a World's Championship match. According to C. I. Taylor, four umpires were to be used in the series, virtually unprecedented in black ball play. Wagers were flying as well, with thousands of dollars bet on each club. While most of the bets were at even odds, many wagered 2 to 1 and even 5 to 3 for the Giants. Few gave odds on the home team, but it was a sucker's bet, for while the Giants played their way west, the ABCs practiced and got in much needed rest, especially at shortstop where Mortie Clark had been slowed by injury for a few weeks. The ABCs laid in wait, hoping to get the Giants on the run early, "then slaughter them."[50]

Before that epic series could begin in Naptown, Chicago had to dispense with the All-Nations. The American Giants arrived in Kansas City. on Saturday morning, October 13, ready to play that afternoon. In game one, the Giants came from behind in the eighth inning against Maples, a white pitcher, scoring two runs, and added another in the ninth for the win. Tom Johnson pitched for the visitors, allowing five hits. On Sunday, John Donaldson pitched for the ABCs in a game Kansas City had to have. Because of the victory Donaldson tossed in Chicago, Kansas City fans figured it would be a walkover. But this game was played on a muddy field, and although the Giants were again held to four hits they won the game, 5–2. Richard Whitworth started for the Giants, giving way to Frank Wickware in the ninth inning to close it out. The third game, finally, went to the All-Nations, a ten-inning, 8–7 "fray." Donaldson, playing left field, stole home in the sixth, adding to the excitement. The Giants, however, cared little for the loss, happy as they were to get out of town with a series win. Following a $400 payday resulting from a 14–7 victory over a team called the Beavers at Laporte, Indiana, the American Giants headed to Indianapolis to meet the ABCs.[51]

It was again billed as the unofficial "Colored World Series" of 1916 and has been described by one historian as the "closest that any of these competitions ever came to a gang war."[52] Yet five days before the series began, real life violence again found its way into the headlines of the black press, this time with the lynching of two black men in Paducah, Kentucky. Brick Finley, 35 years old, was accused of attacking Mrs. George Rose, a white woman, while Asa Thornton, 20, was charged with merely having applauded Finley's crime. Upon learning that Finley had been taken into custody, an angry mob of whites gathered outside the city jail, demanding that he be turned over. As city officials stood aside, Finley was taken from his cell and to Mrs. Rose's home to be identified. Along the way the mob apprehended Thornton. Once positively identified by Mrs. Rose, the two men, one after the other, with Thornton pleading for his life, were bound and strung about the neck to a tree at one end and a car on the other and hanged. A number of shots were then fired into their bodies, after which the mob, "quietly and methodically," gathered wood, built a fire and burned both bodies. It was reported that 6,000 people witnessed the murders before finally dispersing.[53]

While mob violence continued as the preferred mode of justice directed at blacks, particularly in the south, pockets of opposition were being forged. A week after the Kentucky lynching, a Tennessee mob bent on lynching a black man was foiled when black "members of the race" showed the courage to prevent it. In Jackson, Tennessee, a mob of 100 or more whites gathered to lynch Walter Elkins, a black man who had allegedly struck a white fellow worker on the head with an iron bar. Both men were employed by the Illinois Central shop. "Spurred on by their wives," a number of black men armed themselves with Winchesters and revolvers, buckled up their belts, and went to Elkins' home to guard him throughout the night.[54]

It was said that the Paducah lynching, carried out by similar workers of the Illinois Central shops, had "put the same bee in the bonnets of these men," but conditions proved different in Jackson. When the mob started toward Elkins' home and were told of the reception that awaited them, they meekly turned back. It was a brave stand, a "do or die" position likened to that of Crispus Attucks, which saved Elkins. "The south knows no law when it comes to the black man," the *Defender* boldly asserted. "The officers of the law don't try to prevent lynching, BUT AROUND THE WORLD WILL LIVE THE DEED OF THIS SMALL NOBLE BODY OF MEN WHO BRAVELY DEFENDED ONE OF THEIR KIND AND REFUSED TO SEE HIM DIE LIKE A DOG."[55]

The fact that black men were being killed like dogs at a time when American boys, black and white, were readying for a Great War in Europe renders such actions beyond the pale of horrific or illegal. They were vile, treasonous, and against the very notion of the Republic. But racism reigned over the land, had so since the nation's inception, and in spite of declaratory language to the contrary, or a bloody civil conflict claiming 600,000 lives, nothing had yet stamped it out. Professional baseball, as it stood, was indicative of the pandemic. It would ultimately take actions such as this, fought one at a time, waged by men and women with little or no notoriety, citizens seeking a better life and basic civil rights to exorcise such legislated hatred. The ignorance that fostered such behavior, separating as it did working class whites and blacks, was not eradicated in 1916, but efforts to do so were under way and would remain in place for generations to follow.[56]

On a cold, wet day in Indianapolis, a less than expected crowd of 2,300 braced to watch the American Giants take the field against the host ABCs for the start of a scheduled five-game championship set. Tom Johnson went to the hill for Chicago to face Dicta Johnson for Indianapolis. In the first inning, with two outs and Pete Hill on first, Hill broke for second base, advancing all the way to third on a fumbled catch by Clark covering second followed by "Candy Jim" Taylor's drop at third. Lloyd drew a walk, and while Dicta Johnson held the ball, he broke for second. Dave Malarcher, in for Bingo DeMoss at second and covering the bag, let the throw go through him, allowing Hill and Lloyd to score the game's first two runs.

The ABCs got on the board in the bottom of the third inning when George Brown walked, Bingo DeMoss, having entered the game in the top of the inning for Malarcher, bunted safely moving Brown to third, and Rabbit Shively bunted him home. In the top of the fourth, Lloyd came to bat and set the crowd buzzing. After taking the first pitch for a strike, he fouled off two before taking the next two balls. Lloyd then fouled one over the grand-stand before fanning on a high pitch up around his neck. It was noted that this was the first time that Lloyd, "the world's greatest colored shortstop," had ever struck out against the ABCs "and the crowd got on him about it." After the Giants failed to score in their half of the frame, the ABCs took the lead, scoring two runs on an error by Bauchman at second, hits by Candy Jim and Ben Taylor, and long flies by Oscar Charleston and Russ Powell. DeMoss also had a hit in the inning.

The Giants fought back in the fifth inning when Jude Gans singled to center, Bauchman forced Gans with a fielder's choice, Tom Johnson walked, and Barbour singled, scoring Bauchman, with Johnson out at the plate on the throw, Charleston to Clark to Powell, 8–6–2. Barbour advanced to second on the throw and Hill singled to left, scoring Barbour, again giving the Giants the lead. The Giants scored one more run in the seventh on a Jess Barbour double that plated Gans, securing the 5–3 win.[57]

The ABCs turned the tables the next day, besting the Giants, 1–0, behind Dizzy Dismukes' three-hit pitching. Dismukes walked three men in the second inning, but Francis and Petway were both picked off and Gans was caught stealing. After this, the record gets sketchy. According to the *Indianapolis Freeman*, in the eighth, Mortie Clark singled but was caught off base by a quick throw from Wickware. Singles by the Taylor brothers and Oscar Charleston loaded the bases, bringing right fielder Jim Jeffries to the plate. Jeffries hit a sharp one to Lloyd, "who muffed it," allowing Ben Taylor to score the winning run. The *Defender*, however, reported a different scenario, asserting that after Clark was picked off, "Candy Jim" Taylor singled and moved to second on his brother Ben's single. With two on, Oscar Charleston flew out to Duncan in right, bringing up Jeffries, who drove in the winning tally with a single, not an error by Lloyd. Interestingly, neither paper credited Lloyd with an error in the line score. John Holway, in his recap of the series in *The Complete Book of Baseball's Negro Leagues*, summarized the record found in the *Defender*. Regardless, the ABCs took the game, knotting the series at one each.[58]

Game three, played on October 24, proved to be another three-hit, 1–0 shutout for Indianapolis, this time with Dicta Johnson serving up the goose eggs. The weather, again dismal, forced an equally poor turnout of just 500 people. In the bottom of the third inning, Mortie Clark drove in the ABCs' only run, one of five hits on the day for Indianapolis, including a triple by DeMoss. The game came to a halt, however, in the seventh when Rube Foster was ejected and refused to leave the diamond until police were summoned, at which point he pulled his team off the field, forfeiting the game to the ABCs.[59] "Young" Elwood Knox of the *Freeman* ironically chastised Foster's "bulldozing actions," asserting that his behavior was humiliating to C. I. Taylor, who had done much to bring good, credible baseball to the community. "He should have left without a word," Knox wrote.[60]

Foster later defended his actions, stating that he merely had gone over to the first base line, picked up a glove that had been lying in the coaching box and put it on his hand. Ben Taylor, captain of the ABCs, asked the umpire to make Foster put the glove down. The umpire in turn told Foster that Taylor objected to his wearing the glove and that he would have to remove it. Foster refused, telling the umpire that if he was disobeying any of the playing rules he would remove it, but as he was not, he would not. Foster then asked for, and got, the support of the umpire in chief, who agreed that no rules were being violated. The base umpire, however, did not budge, ordering Foster to remove the glove. When Foster refused, he was ejected from the game. Believing that he was being treated in an unfair manner, he drew the team from the field "in a quiet and gentlemanly manner." Foster claimed that in the game played the following Sunday, one officiated by big league umpires, he was allowed to wear the glove, thus vindicating his position.[61] In game four, Oscar Charleston went 4-for-4, staking the ABCs to an 8–2 victory and a 3–1 lead in the set.

The 1916 season's final game between the Chicago American Giants and the Indianapolis ABCs, played on October 29, came down to hitting and defense, or a lack thereof. The pitching, at the start, was done by Dismukes and Ruby Tyree, but would necessitate relievers on both sides. Dismukes was wild, allowing the Giants a quick two runs. Barbour, Hill and Duncan singled, scoring Barbour, before Lloyd walked to load the bases. After Francis flew out to Charleston in center, Grant "got hold of one," sending it deep to Shively, scoring Hill on the tag. The ABCs got one back in their half on Charleston's single, which scored Clark.

The Giants came right back on a triple to left by Gans, who scored on Barbour's fielder's choice to third, making it a 3–1 lead. The lead was short-lived, however, as the ABCs rallied for three runs in the third inning to move ahead. Clark walked to start the inning. Jim Taylor singled to center, and when Hill air-mailed it over third base trying to catch Clark, Clark scored, with Taylor coming around to third. After Ben Taylor was put out, Charleston blasted a triple to left, scoring Candy Jim. It was Charleston's sixth consecutive hit in the series. Powell singled Charleston home, sending Tyree to the showers, replaced by Wickware. After striking out DeMoss, Wickware walked Jeffries, moving Powell to second. Wickware loaded the bases by walking Dismukes, but got Shively to fly out to Gans ending the inning.

The scored held at 4–3 until the sixth inning, when the ABCs busted things wide open, pushing seven runs across on five errors, three from the usually indomitable Lloyd. Jeffries led off with a grounder to Lloyd, whose wild throw sent Jeffries to second. A wild pitch from Wickware sent Jeffries to third; he scored two batters later when Shively's hit to center got away from Pete Hill. With Shively on second, Clark sent one to Francis at third, who threw to Lloyd to catch Shively. The throw was late, however, and Lloyd's relay to first was wild, moving Shively to third and Clark to second. Jim Taylor walked, loading the bases for Ben Taylor, who singled, scoring Shively and Clark, pushing Jim Taylor to third. Oscar Charleston beat out an infield hit to Barbour, with Taylor holding at third. After Powell struck out, DeMoss banged one at Lloyd, who kicked it for his third error of the inning, scoring Taylor and Charleston, DeMoss holding at second. Jeffries' single to center scored DeMoss. Dismukes fol-

Ben Taylor, the smooth-fielding, sharp-hitting member of the famous Taylor family, was one of the greatest first basemen in black baseball history (courtesy Negro Leagues Baseball Museum).

lowed with a single, but Jeffries, attempting to score, stumbled over the third base bag and was tagged for the final out. "The crowd was frantic. Seven runs, five hits, five errors."[62]

The ABCs scored once more in the seventh, and the Giants brought home four runs in the eighth and one in the ninth, but fell short, 12–8. The *Defender's* headline blared that the "Season's Series" had been knotted at four wins each, while the *Freeman* declared outright victory for its home team. The *Defender* refused to take into account Foster's game three forfeit, which was under protest. For its part, the *Freeman* demanded that the forfeit be counted. The forfeit, rightfully taken into account, measured with the final game played in Indianapolis correctly awarded the season series to the ABCs at 5–4–1.[63]

With both sides claiming victory, the *Associated Press* went forward, spreading the word throughout the land that Indianapolis had taken down the mighty American Giants. Foster, for his part, did not initially refute it, claiming while on the train back to Chicago that "it was a battle of youth and speed against old age, and the A's are just too good for me, that's all." He then locked himself in his stateroom and said, "Don't anyone bother me until we get to Chicago."[64]

Back in the Windy City, however, Foster's tune changed, asserting that the game three forfeit arising from his vindicated actions was under protest, and that the second game of a scheduled doubleheader on October 22 had been cancelled because C. I. Taylor feared losing again. According to Foster, the season contract between the two clubs called for 12 games, which had not been "fulfilled," and therefore the ABCs had not rightfully won the championship. As noted, taking into account the forfeit, the record stood against Chicago at 4–5–1, with potentially another game to go. It was not played. Taylor, for his part, argued that the missing game made no difference to the ultimate outcome, that being an ABCs championship. As is perhaps understandable, the *Defender* stood with its man, while the *Freeman* endorsed Taylor. In an editorial cartoon by J. R. Warren published in the *Freeman* on December 12, Foster was presented as a masked bandit, demanding that Taylor hand over the championship, to which Taylor replied, "I will not, it's mine.... We won it fair."[65] The consensus went to the ABCs, for reasons of right, fairness and perhaps Foster's fatigue, for his teams had won all other recorded western championships between 1910 and 1922.[66]

With the debate still hot, both clubs moved on, the ABCs taking on the Bicknell Braves at Bicknell, Indiana, while the American Giants set steam for Schofield Barracks in Hawaii to play the Wreckers, the 25th Infantry's "crack baseball team." There was some speculation as to whether Lloyd would accom-

The 1915 Breakers Team. Back row: Unknown, Dick Redding, John Henry Lloyd, Jude Gans, Louis Santop, Leroy Grant. Middle row: Unknown, Dicta Johnson, Joe Williams, Zack Pettus, Bill Francis. Front row: Pete Hill, Unknown, Dick Wallace, Spottswood Poles.

pany the Giants on the trip. The *Freeman* had gone so far as to question whether Lloyd's playing days might be done "as he was thinking of devoting his time to his property in Florida." The *Freeman*, remembering Lloyd as "a wonder in his day," commended him for stepping aside "to give the youngsters a chance to play." Wishful thinking or otherwise, the claim had no merit as Lloyd was still at the top of his game despite batting a meager .188 at Indianapolis that October. Lloyd batted .373 that season, was named by John Holway to the western all-star team, won Holway's mythical Fleet Walker Award for most outstanding player in the West, and was still considered the class of the field at shortstop. The youngsters, it seemed, would have to wait, for at 32 years old there was still "too much Lloyd."[67]

FIVE

The American Giants

Rube Foster took his Giants south that winter, playing and working at the Royal Poinciana Hotel in Palm Beach, Florida. Foster had been urged to bring his Giants to Palm Beach in response to the "runaway" wins being posted by members of the Lincoln Giants, Brooklyn Stars and Brooklyn Royal Giants, who were playing for the Breakers against a Poinciana squad made up mainly of ABCs players. Better competition from the west was being sought, and Foster was happy to oblige.[1]

One of the reasons Lloyd was not in Cuba that winter involved Almendares' objection to Havana's use of African-American ballplayers. Almendares, which had narrowly lost the 1908-09 championship to Havana, demanded that the league ban foreign players. Lloyd, Pete Hill and Bruce Petway had played for Havana the previous fall, leading the club against the Detroit Tigers and a major league all-star team. After being notified that their continued play with Havana was being contested, and then waiting for some resolution, they gave up, joining Foster in Palm Beach. Before leaving town, Lloyd commented to *La Lucha*, a Cuban newspaper, that "[i]t is a poor rule that will not work both ways." The Cubans ultimately agreed — although not in time to help Lloyd — Almendares lifting its demands, and the league got underway in early February.[2]

In their first game in Palm Beach, Foster's Giants, with Lloyd at short, Oscar Charleston in center field, and the Cuban Mulo Padrón on the mound, battled the Breakers and "Smoky Joe" Williams to a ten-inning, 1–1 tie, darkness ending things. At that moment, nowhere in the world was better baseball being played.[3]

In front of a big crowd, Williams and Padrón dueled into the tenth, Williams allowing three hits for the Breakers while Padrón allowed a mere five for Foster's bunch. The Giants threatened in the second inning before running themselves out of the frame. After Lloyd walked, Francis moved him to second on a muffed grounder by Joe Hewitt at shortstop. When Grant grounded out, both runners advanced into scoring position at second and third. But Foster, taking an early hand in the game, ordered a squeeze play that was botched, ending with Lloyd out at home and Francis at third. The Breakers scored the next inning when Spot Poles doubled and scored on Hewitt's double to right. The score held into the ninth when Jess Barbour singled to center and moved to second on Pete Duncan's fielder's choice. After Charleston struck out, Lloyd lined a double into the left field corner, scoring Barbour to tie the game, just before the night beckoned.[4]

The Breakers bounced back the following afternoon, posting an 8–2 drubbing of the Giants behind the mound work of Andrew "String Bean" Williams, the quiet, elongated ace of the Brooklyn Royal Giants. Williams, a "cold weather pitcher" with a lively curveball, scattered four hits. The Breakers jumped to a two-run lead in the first inning when Poles walked and advanced on Hewitt's single. Santop then singled to score Poles and Hewitt. The Breakers added runs in both the third and fifth innings. Foster's men got their runs in the fifth when Barbour reached on Hewitt's error, Duncan sacrificed him to second. Charleston bunted and was hit by the throw while running to first, scoring Barbour. Lloyd beat out a bunt to first, advancing Charleston, who came home on Todd Allen's fielder's choice.[5]

On February 6, Tom Johnson held the Breakers hitless into the ninth inning, when the easterners pushed one across, falling, 4–1. Johnson had a no-hitter "in his mitt" before walking Bill Handy, who went to second on Jimmy Lyons' out at first and moved to third on Zach Pettus' out. Blainey Hall, batting for pitcher Williams, then singled over third to bust up the no-no, bringing Handy in for the lone tally. Poinciana had opened the scoring in the first inning against Dick Redding, who started for the Breakers but failed to "get into the box score," when Charleston walked, stole second, and moved to third on Pete Hill's fly out. Lloyd then sent a long fly to Jules Thomas in center field, scoring Charleston. After Grant and DeMoss walked to lead off the second, Redding was yanked in favor of Joe Williams, who went the rest of the way for the Breakers, allowing just two hits.[6]

As with any pitching gem, Foster's club played stellar defense behind Johnson, with Lloyd, DeMoss and Charleston up the middle all contributing. Oscar Charleston, who because of his weak arm played a shallow center field, was said to have been capable of catching anything between the foul lines. Dave Malarcher, a teammate of Charleston's with the ABCs, once recalled Charleston running down a deep blast to center, one hit "way over [his] head." Charleston ran so fast to get the ball that he overran it and had to turn back at the last second to make the catch before it hit the ground. "It was marvelous. Marvelous."[7]

With the hyperbolic news of Jack Johnson, the "American world's champion pugilist," having single-handedly captured an Austrian submarine while en route to Barcelona, Spain, and having drifted at sea for three days, Foster's team dropped one to the Royal Poincianas, 3–1. It was a "comedy of errors," five in all, that forced Mulo Padrón to the showers and allowed the New Yorkers to take a lead in the fifth inning, never looking back. "Smokey Joe" Williams, again tough on the Giants, held the "Windy City lads" to eight hits, prompting the Chicago press to wonder aloud whether Rube would sign him for the coming season[8]

The New York team broke through when Williams bunted, advanced to third on a hit-and-run play from Poles, who also bunted safely, and then stole second. With runners on second and third, Louis Santop "came through with one of those nasty infield hits which was mean to handle and two runs went across." They scored one more in the seventh when Pettus doubled to left and Williams drove him in with a hit to right-center. The Giants' lone run came in the eighth when Duncan "shot a hot one over third," Lloyd forced him at second, Barbour advanced Lloyd to third with a single, and Dan Kennard, batting for Grant, grounded out, but not before scoring Lloyd.[9]

After the two clubs battled to another stalemate, one reminding fans of "[T]he charges and counter charges of the German and French troops" along the European front, Padrón, in "mid-season form," got the better of the New Yorkers, hurling a masterful one-hit shutout in a 7–0 victory. The Breakers' only hit came on an eighth-inning blast to center by Pettus, which was almost caught by Duncan, who laid out in a vain attempt to preserve the no-hitter.

The Giants got things going early when Duncan singled in the first inning and Hewitt kicked a DeMoss grounder at short, sending Duncan to second. Duncan came around on a wild pitch by Williams. In the sixth inning, Duncan got to Williams for another single, was sacrificed to second by DeMoss, and came home on Pete Hill's double. Lloyd singled Hill home, but was cut down "deader un a door nail" trying to make second base on the play. Foster's team pushed four more runs across in their half of the eighth when Padrón singled, advanced to third base on Duncan's third single of the day, and came home on a wild pitch that sent Duncan to third. After DeMoss walked and stole second, Hill singled, scoring Duncan and moving DeMoss to third. Lloyd skied to Wallace at third, Charleston walked to load the sacks, and Allen sent a long one to Poles in right field, scoring DeMoss. Grant doubled, scoring Hill.[10]

Rube Foster was enjoying Florida and seemed quite satisfied with the way his men were "working their way into shape" (as if they ever stopped playing long enough to fall out of shape). Speaking to a reporter, Foster anticipated that fans in Chicago would "be wild" to see their team in the summer, particularly the young "pony battery" of catcher George Dixon and pitcher Ruby Tyree. (Tyree, nephew of local Bishop Tyree, failed to pan out when, after being "showcased in the first game of the season and winning his first two decisions, his performance dropped off, prompting a trade to St. Louis in early May.)[11]

Over the next week, Foster's crew played three more games against the Lincolns. In game one, showing "no mercy whatever" for "Smokey Joe" Williams, they drove him from the box, only to watch as "Cannonball" Redding was summoned into the game. A comparable scenario might have had Grover Cleveland Alexander sent to the showers, replaced by Lefty Grove, or Christy Mathewson knocked out of the game in favor of Walter Johnson; in other words, an all-star game setting. Yet here it was, and the Giants, undeterred, kept pounding, gathering ten hits in all, three by Lloyd and two each by Hill and Allen. With Mulo Padrón on the mound for the Giants, "doing as he pleased," the Lincolns had little chance. Padrón was on again a few days later, this time shutting out the Lincolns, 6–0. The offense came when Grant tripled in the sixth inning, driving in Barbour and Allen, and then was doubled home by Hill. Two more runs came when DeMoss walked, stole second, and scored on Pete Hill's second double. Hill came around when Lloyd doubled. The Chicago gang was simply too formidable.[12]

As winter drew near an end, Foster began circling the wagons, preparing for the coming season. His first move was to sign Dick Redding, C. I. Taylor's ace hurler, who had won three of the five games in the 1916 series. He followed that up with another theft, this time signing Bingo DeMoss, black baseball's finest second baseman. A year later, Foster grabbed Oscar Charleston and Taylor's own brother, "Candy Jim." Foster would also sign José Méndez from J. L. Wilkinson's All-Nations team, Jimmy Lyons from St. Louis and Floyd "Jelly" Gardner from the Detroit Stars. When it came to raiding rosters, no one was better at it than Ol' Rube.[13]

Making their way north, the Giants beat a team from Mobile, Alabama, 8–0, and trimmed Wiley University, 6–3. They moved on to New Orleans where, with Redding on the mound, they topped the Cubans, 4–3, before tying a New Orleans club, 2–2, in a five-inning contest. In New Orleans, Lloyd and the other players were treated like kings, escorted around town in automobiles by Butcher Hill, captain of the local Red Sox, treated to a creole dinner hosted by Joe Geddes, an undertaker, and lavished at the Iroquois Club, the oldest and most exclusive venture of its kind in the south. When Sunday morning came, the team, en masse, gave thanks at the St. James A.M.E. Church. The Giants, and Foster in particular, felt at home in the

Crescent City, and the people of New Orleans were "crazy" for them, calling them "their boys." It was expected that with Lloyd playing his best baseball in five years, Hill still "knocking them out," Petway as good as ever, and Redding and DeMoss in the mix, the Giants could not falter.[14]

In spite of the forecast regarding Lloyd's readiness, his batting average dropped over 100 points, to .266, in 1917, but his defense remained stellar, and now paired with DeMoss up the middle, the Giants fielded perhaps the best double-play combination in all of baseball. In fact, pitching and defense proved the benchmark for Foster's club that summer, with Redding, Tom Williams and, for a time, "Red Ant" Wickware on the bump, combining for a 1.59 earned run average. Lloyd, DeMoss, LeRoy Grant and Bill Francis rounded out a strong infield, George Dixon and Petway bore the tools behind the dish, while Duncan, Hill and Jess Barbour patrolled the outfield. It was a club built for Chicago's "huge" American League Park, also home to Chicago's White Sox. Foster's inside game — one of pitching and defense, bunts, steals, and hit-and-runs — fit the joint perfectly.[15]

Not to be overshadowed by New Orleans, and with the season a day away, Chicago feted "their boys" with a soiree of its own, hosting the Giants at the Elite Café No. 2 in a "rousing send off" to the coming season. After a sumptuous dinner, speeches were made by the *Defender's* Frank Young; Lieutenant F. L. McFarland of the Eighth Regiment; Julius Taylor of the Broad Ax; Pete Hill, Dick Redding, and Rube Foster. Lloyd, who preferred the background at such an affair, was called on for a speech, but "begged" out of it. B. F. Moseley, toastmaster for the evening, "glowed" in his tribute to the team, and was in return acknowledged by Foster as having been responsible for the fact that members of the Race in Chicago had a ball team within walking distance of their homes. The evening proved a worthy tribute.[16]

Five thousand fans jammed Schorling Park on opening day, yelling themselves "hoarse" as the Giants won the season opener, 5–3. The game, played against Jake Stahl's City Leaguers, a white team, was the first chance for Chicago fans to see Foster's young battery, Tyree and Dixon. Tyree, showing good form early, fanned 11 over the first seven innings before giving way to Dick Redding. Redding subsequently struck out four, got one batter to foul out and the other to fly out to Duncan in left. Lloyd, who got on twice with a "hot" single and an error, was masterful in the field, turning an unassisted double play in the fourth and anchoring another deuce in the fourth.[17]

Two weeks later the Giants, amid a weak stretch of games against local teams, took on Chicago's West Ends, winning a close one, 3–2. Tom Johnson, coasting until the seventh inning when his arm tired, allowed six hits to the visitors, and was rescued by Redding, who entered amid wild applause to stop the bleeding. Brown, the West End's pitcher, held the Giants to just four hits in a "corking good" show, good enough to win. Only DeMoss, Hill, Grant and Lloyd managed anything off him, Lloyd singling while meekly popping out in the fifth and seventh. Foster was not in uniform, and at no time was seen on the field. Meanwhile, his nemesis, C. I. Taylor and the Indianapolis ABCs, with Dismukes on the mound, fared little better that day, surviving an eleven-inning tie against the Kokomo Red Sox, a local squad paced by former Tiger George Mullin. While Brooklyn's Royal Giants were tearing off wins in the east, it was clear that neither of the western stalwarts had found mid-season form, at least not in early May.[18]

Race issues continually found the headlines that May as D. W. Griffith's *Birth of a Nation* and "all pictures or plays tending to incite race hatred" were banned in Cleveland. In Memphis, a brutal lynching was reported, while another took place in Lloyd's hometown, Jacksonville, Florida. An African-American man named Walter Robinson was killed by a white mob seeking to help a man beat his rent. Robinson's troubles began when the white man who owed Robinson rent moved out without paying and then roundly abused the latter when he called to collect, to the point of having Robinson arrested for disorderly conduct. A short time later, while Robinson was riding in the "Crow Section" or rear of a street car with his brother, they were both insulted by "several rough necks," the brother getting off the car to avoid trouble. One of the aggressors was later identified as the police officer who had earlier arrested Robinson. After leaving the car, Robinson was followed and further bullied, but made it home. About an hour later, after leaving his home to run some minor errands, Robinson was confronted by the former tenant and several others, who had a car standing nearby. Seeking to elude trouble, Robinson moved up the street, but was pursued, knocked down, kicked and beaten cold. While he lay unconscious, the gang of murderers shot him to death and drove away.[19]

After picking up wins against two more local teams, the Roseland Eclipse and Chicago Heights, Foster's team readied for a tougher tilt with the veteran-laden Chicago Giants, featuring John Beckwith, Walter Ball, and former teammate "Red Ant" Wickware.[20] In the top of the first inning, "playing in unseasonably foul weather," American Giants hurler Tom Williams got Jude Gans to fly to center, starting things off. On the next play, however, Bobby Winston grounded to the stalwart Lloyd, who promptly "chucked the ball over Grant's head" at first base into the stands, sending Winston to second. Jennings worked the count to three and two before doubling to center, scoring Winston. Pettus sacrificed Jennings to third, but Beckwith flied to Hill in center, closing out the top half of the inning.[21]

Wickware took the mound to great cheers which only grew louder as he put the first pitch across on Duncan, but after waiting out two balls and another strike, Duncan doubled. For the "Red Ant," it was downhill from there. DeMoss banged a hot one for a single, sending Duncan to third; Hill sent a long one to Gans in center, scoring Duncan. Lloyd then doubled on what should have been a single, but taking advantage of lackluster play by the infield, stretched it out with a great slide, "Jennings tagging at him twice, but missing." He then stole third as Barbour swung at a high one, and came home on Barbour's subsequent roller to short. Lloyd was on his game, and Foster's bunch was up by one.[22]

After the Giants went down in order to start the second, Wickware went back out for what became his last inning of work as Dixon walked and Duncan singled, getting Walter Ball up and throwing with men on first and second. DeMoss also walked, filling the bases and sending Wickware to the showers, replaced by Ball. Hill walked, bringing Dixon home. Ball, frustrated with the umpire Goeckel's strike zone, let it be known before settling in to get Lloyd to pop up, and Barbour to ground to third. Meanwhile, Tom Williams was cruising. By the sixth inning he had faced a scant 18 batters and allowed two runs, one unearned. He got Ball, Gans, and Winston in order in the fifth — on three pitches! But after he plunked Booker to start the seventh, his defense rallied. With Booker on first, Joe Green hit one over second, but Lloyd, still smarting from the earlier error, got to it, fell down, but regained his feet in time to slide into second just ahead of Booker for the force. Ball lined to Lloyd, who quickly doubled off Green at first to kill the inning and effectively the game as the Giants failed to threaten in the eighth or ninth, Foster's team winning it, 4–2.[23]

The *Defender's* Mr. Fan wrote that one thing the game had proved, "Lloyd is still without peer at shortstop. ... [h]is play in the seventh was a dream." But was he the best? That same day a young shortstop playing in Atlantic City, New Jersey — Dick Lundy — was drawing raves for his play with the Bacharach Giants, a club formerly known as the Duval Giants, having migrated north from Jacksonville a year earlier. Lundy, "of whom great things are always expected," would later be hailed as the shortstop of the twenties in black baseball, one who bridged the gap between Lloyd and Willie Wells, to form an all-time trifecta at the position. He would also endure a mixed bag of emotions regarding Lloyd, who was at once an idol, mentor, manager and rival to the younger player. As for Lloyd, he was anything but through, serving notice that his play still set the tone for the American Giants, who would need him the following week with Mulo Padrón and the Cuban Stars coming to town to face Dick Redding, held back by Foster for the occasion.[24]

With the Cubans in town, the American Giants won the first game, 2–1. Lloyd collected two hits in the contest, with Tom Johnson getting the win. The following Sunday the two clubs went at it again, this time in a pitchers duel featuring Redding and Padrón, the "Cannonball" prevailing, 1–0. Redding allowed the Cubans just five hits in the game, but was nearly outdone by Padrón, who gave up three hits to the Chicagoans, one to Lloyd. It was ultimately dumb luck that won it for the Giants, the deciding tally coming in the fifth inning, without a hit. Jess Barbour opened the frame with a walk, and then distracted Padrón to the point of his snapping off several throws to first in an attempt to hold Barbour on. Bill Francis bunted toward third where the charging Bartolo Portuondo fielded it but threw wide of first, pulling Striké Gonzalez off the bag. Gonzalez, recovering to find Barbour flying around second, fired the ball to third, but the base was uncovered, the ball rolling to the fence and allowing Barbour to "tango" home untouched. Gonzalez, it turned out, in his haste thought Rube Foster, coaching third, *was* the third baseman, prompting the throw. Baseball games can be like that — nine innings of crisis, resolved by an errant glance.[25]

That Sunday Chappie Johnson brought his Dayton Giants to town, where they were afforded a lesson in "first class pitching" and strong hitting by Lloyd, Chicago prevailing, 9–2. Lloyd started the "fireworks" in the second with a double, and followed in the third with a bases-loaded triple over Charles Wilson's head in right-center. Two innings later Lloyd got on with an error, then showed his prowess on the basepaths by pilfering second and third. He had home "stolen clean" but Francis grounded out back to the pitcher. Lloyd finished his assault with a single in the eighth. The only time Lloyd failed to reach that day came in the seventh when Williams made a great one-handed stab of Lloyd's line drive to shortstop.[26]

Lloyd continued to mash the ball the next week, blasting a triple in the 12th inning to beat C. I. Taylor's Indianapolis crew, 3–2, on a Tuesday afternoon before 7,000 at Schorling Park. The win, coming as it did, took Lloyd off the hook for a Sunday afternoon loss two days earlier in which the shortstop threw one into the stands, allowing the ABCs and Bill Gatewood to steal one. This time, Lloyd's hit brought Pete Hill home from first with the winning run. Tom Johnson allowed four hits that Monday in beating the ABCs and Dismukes, 3–1. A week later, the Giants topped the ABCs and Gatewood, 6–4, before trimming them again, this time on a 1–0 shutout by Redding. In the latter contest, Lloyd was removed in the seventh inning after suffering a minor injury. With Barbour on for Lloyd at shortstop, Foster's men finished up the week with a twin-bill assault of the Chicago Giants, winning both ends, 11–1 and 2–1.[27]

The Fourth of July weekend at Schorling began with a charity event played for Harry Moore, a 42-year-old former ballplayer who was sick at his home, 14820 5th Avenue in Chicago, with the last stages of consumption.[28] Moore had been one of the top outfielders of his era, playing with the Chicago Union Giants, Philadelphia Giants, Leland Giants, New York Lincoln Giants and others. A man with an "impeccable reputation," Moore was a highly regarded ballplayer and one of the most popular in Chicago. The game was organized by Rube Foster and Pat Dougherty of the Union Giants, with all proceeds going to Moore. The two squads consisted of American Giants and Union Giants players and were managed by Lloyd and Pete Hill respectively. The game was played in front of an overflow crowd, many tickets sold to out-of-towners who mailed their contribution in. The game, an afterthought under the circumstances, saw Dick Redding get the win for Lloyd's crew, 2–1. Contributors included Charles A. Comiskey, owner of the Chicago White Sox, who sent $25 for the cause; C. I. Taylor from Indianapolis, and other players and managers from around the country. Within days, Moore, "the great ball hawk," was dead.[29]

On Saturday, at Hammond, Indiana, Foster's club topped Bombín Pedroso and the Cuban Stars, 1–0. Tom Johnson went the distance for the winners, allowing the Cubans four hits, while the Giants scratched out their only run in the eighth inning. A day later, with the two teams back at Schorling Park, Lloyd came off the bench to win it in the eighth, driving in the go-ahead runs. In the frame, Tom Williams singled before being forced at second on Pete Duncan's ground ball. Bingo DeMoss singled, moving Duncan to third. Pete Hill was then intentionally passed, setting up the potential double play with Petway coming to the plate. It was Lloyd instead who stepped in, still nursing an injury but on as a pinch hitter and bringing the crowd to its feet. The sacks loaded and down a run, Lloyd sat on Padrón's offering and with a "crack" smoked it like a bullet into right field, giving the Giants a 3–2 lead. The margin held as Tom Williams, winner of 12 games in 1917, got Juan Guerra to ground back to the mound, José Rodriguez to fly out to center, and Herman Rios to pop to DeMoss for the final out.[30]

Tom Johnson was in rare form the following Sunday, holding Jewell's ABCs to two hits in a 4–0 shutout. The Giants had just returned to Chicago from Cincinnati where they had played a set of games against Taylor's ABCs, winning all five and convincing Taylor that perhaps this was the finest club yet fielded by Foster, one certainly to be reckoned with. The *Defender* agreed, plastering the team photo all over the sports page that morning. Rube Foster sat front and center, dapper in a light-colored suit and trim straw hat tilted slightly back; the venerable Pete Hill sat on one side of him, Bill Francis on the other, Duncan and Williams on the ends. Lloyd stood with arms crossed at the end of the second row, hat smartly pulled down, eyes fixed on the camera, a slight smile; next to him, in his catching gear, stood his pal Petway, then Redding, Barbour and Whitworth. Redding looked imposing. In the rear were Johnson, DeMoss, Grant and Dixon, the other catcher who at that point in the season led the team in batting. This team, *THE AMERICAN GIANTS*, boasted three future Hall of Famers (including Foster), and others deserving of strong consideration.[31]

The Giants spent the next week playing a series of games against a club billed as the Texas All-Stars, winning 7–5, 7–6 and 16–2. The last game, with Foster on the slab, was a comedy as far as the Giants were concerned, "for they hit and ran at will."[32] The series proved a needed respite, for the following week Taylor's ABCs were back in town for a scheduled Sunday doubleheader, followed by a pair to be played at Detroit. In the opener, the ABCs, with the recently acquired "String Bean" Williams on the mound, "slipped one over" on the Giants, winning it, 8–4. The Giants tied it up in the seventh inning when Whitworth singled and was forced at second by DeMoss. DeMoss promptly stole second and Mortie Clark erred on Pete Hill's roller, sending DeMoss to third. Hill stole second, leaving men on second and third for Lloyd, whose two-run triple knotted the score at 4–4. The game stayed tied

The 1915 Chicago American Giants. Top row, left to right; Bill Gatewood, Jess Barber, Leroy Grant, John Henry Lloyd, Jude Gans. Bottom row, left to right; Dick Whitworth, Pete Hill, Rube Foster, Bruce Petway, Pete Booker, unknown (courtesy of the John Henry "Pop" Lloyd Committee).

into the 11th inning when Candy Jim Taylor belted a triple of his own that was just fair, and scored when his brother Ben Taylor grounded out to the right side. Whitworth then plunked Russ Powell, Frank Warfield singled and Mortie Clarke doubled, scoring two to put the ABCs up for good. The following day the Giants took advantage of two bad innings from Bill Gatewood, plating seven runs in the span and winning, 8–2. Dick Redding held the "Taylorites" to five scattered hits.[33]

At Detroit, a large crowd was thrilled to watch the American Giants and ABCs again battle in a close affair, this one tied up 2–2 and called by darkness following "fifteen brilliant inning of baseball." The game was a pitching duel between the crafty String Bean Williams and Cannonball Redding, "the smoke artist of the Giants." According to the *Defender*, the only thing that marred the game was the umpires, who allowed C. I. Taylor, who was not in the game, to exceed his rights by going out in the middle of the field to hold conferences with his men. It was noted that "big league umpires" would not have tolerated it. As with any good pitching match-up, the game featured strong defense on both sides. While Lloyd, DeMoss, Ben Taylor and Charlie Blackwell all had their moments in the field, the play of the game was turned in by Dave Malarcher, who robbed Bruce Petway of a triple, going back and pulling down Petway's long drive with one hand. According to some of the local scribes, it was "the most sensational bit of fielding ever seen" there.[34]

With Lloyd and the Giants in Detroit, news out of Florida would have certainly piqued their interest. For the first time in the history of the state, a black man had been acquitted by a jury for the confessed killing of a white man. The story involved Edmund Murch, a white man from Bangor, Maine, who was caught in the home of George Thompson, the black man who fatally shot him. A Miami editor pronounced the case a valuable

The versatile, smooth-fielding Dave Malarcher was a speedy switch-hitter who could bunt and run the bases in the inside style of baseball that Rube Foster preferred. He was also adept at working pitchers deep into the count by fouling off pitch after pitch until finding something to his liking (courtesy Negro Leagues Baseball Museum).

precedent for Florida. "It should prove to every Negro that he has the same right to defend his home against the white man" as a white man would. While that claim was somewhat of a stretch, the case did represent some progress, especially as Thompson had not been taken out and lynched.[35]

The Giants and ABCs met one last time in Detroit "before the largest crowd" that had ever witnessed a non–Tigers game in the city, the Chicagoans prevailing, 3–2. With Tom Williams and Tom Johnson (not to be confused with the Giants' Tom Johnson) pitching for their respective sides, neither team got a hit until the sixth inning, when Duncan misjudged Jim Taylor's long fly. Ben Taylor followed with a single of his own, and Warfield singled in "Candy Jim," who was back with the ABCs. Down a run with one out in the eighth, the Giants got on the board as Barbour doubled and DeMoss singled him in. Hill doubled, scoring DeMoss, and took third on Lloyd's out and scored on a passed ball. The "Taylorites" got one back in the bottom of the frame, but that was it as Dick Redding, whom the Detroit papers favorably compared to Walter Johnson, came on to save it. The "white players could have learned many a trick and a good lesson from these boys," opined the Detroit papers."[36]

Back in Chicago a week later, the Giants took on the Cuban Stars in what witnesses regarded as a pitching battle of big league proportions. Tom Williams pitched for Chicago, opposed by Mulo Padrón for the Cubans. Williams, who like Tom Johnson had attended Morris Brown College, was a very smart pitcher with an array of crafty pitches thrown at different speeds from varied angles. He was also tough on base runners, effectively using a snap throw to first or second base.[37]

On this afternoon, Williams had "everything on the ball that could be put on it, curve, drop, spitter, fast, floater and some we didn't know about." In doing so, he held the Cubans to two "lonely" hits, one of which was an inside-the-park round-tripper by Juan Guerra, who might have been thrown out at the plate were it not for the offline relay from Hill to Lloyd to Dixon. Guerra was the only Cuban to pass first base, and one of only four to reach it. The Giants scored both of their runs in the first inning when with one out, DeMoss singled to left, Hill sent him to third with a hit-and-run single, Lloyd singled to left scoring DeMoss, Duncan was plunked and Francis walked, forcing in the deciding run. After that, Padrón settled in, allowing just three hits the rest of the way, but Williams was more effective, allowing only Guerra's eighth inning bomb and winning, 2–1.[38]

The Cubans fought back two days later, besting the Giants, 3–2. It was another pitching duel, this time between Wickware and José Junco, with the Cuban prevailing. Both pitchers were so dominating that neither team was able to score until the eighth inning, when two errors by Leroy Grant, combined with a walk and a double, lifted the Cubans to a "trio of tallies." The Giants rallied in the eighth as well, scoring two runs, but came up a run short.[39]

The Giants left town the following Saturday for Indianapolis to play a return engagement with the ABCs. The two clubs had already met 20 times that season, Taylor's team managing just five wins, two games resulting in a tie. The teams were very familiar with one another. It was also announced that the Giants would play a three-game set with the Cubans at Redland Field in Cincinnati, before traveling to Pittsburgh for a set at Forbes Field.[40]

On a "great day" at Washington Park in Indianapolis, during which C. I. Taylor "got sick," the American Giants took both games of the Sunday doubleheader, 4–1 and 8–3. In the *Defender*, columnist "Mr. Fan" noted that "7,000 rooters went home very, very sad, just like mourners to a funeral." Jess Barbour led the way in the first affair with three hits, while Lloyd added a pair and Redding struck out five. For his part, Rube Foster was only too happy to let the Giants win without his aid, so he remained in street clothes near the gate for much of the game, rarely going near the bench. Lloyd stayed hot in game two with a fourth-inning triple and a double in the seventh, driving in two runs.[41]

The bats cooled a week later, however, as Mulo Padrón and the Cuban Stars shut down the Giants at Forbes Field, 5–0. The game was a scoreless affair into the 11th inning with Padrón and Dick Redding going at it, before Redding "blew up" allowing the Cubans to pound "several long ones." Bernardo Baro, the Cubans' brilliant hot dog of an outfielder, launched a long triple to center field, bringing in the deciding run. The Giants gathered seven hits, including a triple by Pete Hill, but left eight men on base.[42]

Fresh from the west, the American Giants "blew into" Atlantic City for a three-game set against Dick Lundy and the Bacharach Giants. It was a match-up featuring Lloyd, the game's best shortstop, against Lundy, thought by some to have surpassed Lloyd at this point in his career. The Bacharachs also featured "Chance" Cummings, an excellent defensive first baseman and one whom Lloyd had known since their days in Jacksonville.[43]

Dick Lundy was "the greatest shortstop anybody ever saw." Known as "King" or "Sir Richard," Lundy was black baseball royalty, and was favorably compared to Lloyd, Willie Wells, and Hall of Fame major leaguers Joe Cronin and Honus Wagner.

Jess Barbour laced a single through the middle to open game one. DeMoss walked, both men advanced on a passed ball, and Barbour scored on Pete Hill's bunt. Lloyd drove De Moss home with a single to center, advancing to third on a dropped ball by Pettus, who compounded things with an errant throw to Lundy who could not hang on. Duncan drew a walk and Francis was hit to load the bases, before Grant's long sacrifice fly to center scored Lloyd. Dixon bounced one into right field to score Duncan, giving the Giants an early four-run lead. The Bacharachs came back with three runs in the bottom of the frame, due in no small part to shoddy defense on the part of Chicago. The scored stayed tied into the eighth inning, when Lundy doubled to left and came home on Tomm's long sacrifice to left field, but that was all the Bacharachs could muster, leaving a door open for Chicago in the ninth.[44]

Bill Francis led off the ninth with a double to left. After an error and a quick out put runners at second and third, Dick Redding, batting for Tom Johnson, walloped a long fly into left field, scoring Francis and giving the Giants a 5–4 lead. In the bottom of the frame, Redding walked the leadoff batter before rolling a double play; DeMoss to Lloyd to Grant. Redding then struck out Downs to seal the Giants victory. The Giants won again the following day with "Cyclone" Tom Williams blanking his old team, the Bacharachs, 4–0. Williams held the Atlantic City squad to four scattered singles, while Bingo DeMoss led the way with three singles for the Giants.[45]

As the Giants marched on, news from Memphis, Tennessee, again showed that regardless of the heroism on display by blacks in the armed forces, their long struggle against racism would not end soon. In Memphis, Eli Person was lynched "in broad daylight" for transgressions perceived by an angry white mob as intolerable. He was burned to death his ears and lips cut off, and his head decapitated and thrown onto Beale Street, "the district occupied by the businesses making their money off the earnings of the Race." All of this transpired while a throng of passersby watched and did nothing. Photographs of Person's head were taken and sold only to whites for a quarter apiece, yet the *Defender* was able to get one and publish it under the headline "Not Belgium — America."[46]

With the summer at an end, the Giants traveled to Navin Field in Detroit and pasted a Labor Day spanking on the Cubans, winning both games of a doubleheader, 4–2 and 2–0. They turned on the ABCs next, crushing the "Taylorites" 7–0 and 6–3. Foster's club was cruising, and with the fall upon them it seemed that no one could stop the juggernaut. Even when they did manage to drop one, the score was generally close, such as the one-run, 12–

inning loss — caused by a "bonehead play" — to All-Nations, or Jess Barbour's tenth-inning error giving a game to the Cubans. But this team always bounced back, besting All-Nations a week later and the Cubans in the latter half of the same doubleheader. The American Giants were a team on a mission to prove that they were the best group of ballplayers in the world, or least against those who would face them.[47]

In September Foster challenged the Eastern champions, the Lincoln Stars, beating them three games to two, to claim the 1917 black baseball championship. The Giants then wrapped things up with a set of games against two white squads, one named Ragan's Colts and featuring Ed Corry, a young hurler recently signed by the St. Louis Browns, the other against an All Star collection of major leaguers. Ed Corry got the best of the Giants in the first game, topping Dick Redding in a "fast 2–1 battle." Foster's men rebounded the next day, however, humiliating the "white lads," 11–4. Finally, before a good autumn crowd, the Giants ended their "brilliant season" with a 9–3 victory over the "All Stars." Playing heads-up baseball, the Giants took the lead in the fourth inning, adding a few more an inning later to pull away. The Giants pitching was solid with Tom Johnson getting the start, then giving way to "String Bean" Williams who in the seventh passed the baton to "Cannonball" Redding. Bob O'Farrell, Charlie Pechous, and Morrie Schick of the Chicago Cubs and others played for the All Stars who managed only seven hits. Lloyd, who was stellar at shortstop, taking everything within reach, had a double for the winners.[48]

It had been one of the greatest campaigns in the history of black baseball, but there was little rest on this circuit. A week later the *Defender* announced that the Giants would soon head to West Palm Beach, Florida, to work and play at the Royal Poinciana, facing their rivals, the Breakers, comprised mostly of New York and Brooklyn standouts. They did so, however, without one of their star hurlers, Tom Johnson, who was drafted into the military, and without Lloyd, who opted to stay in Chicago to work at the United States Army Quartermaster Depot. Foster, having already lost Johnson, became so "miffed" at Lloyd that he found another shortstop, a "slick fielder" named Bobby Williams. Undeterred, Lloyd moved on, landing the player-manager job in Brooklyn with the Royal Giants, and for good measure taking Dick Redding with him.[49]

Regardless of his having lifted Redding, Lloyd and his old mentor parted amicably. Foster might have seen Lloyd as having lost a step, as his batting average that season, .266, reflected. Lloyd, now 34, may have agreed to an extent, for when he arrived in Brooklyn he placed himself at first base rather than shortstop, deferring to Joe Hewitt, an exceptionally fast base runner with wide range in the field. For the remainder of his career, Lloyd moved between shortstop, first and second, wherever he felt best able to help his team. Those in 1918, however, who thought that Lloyd was too old to be effective were making a mistake, and "the old man" proved it, slugging everything within reach for another 13 seasons.[50]

SIX

Second Wind

In 1918, John Henry Lloyd was hired by Nat Strong to manage and play for the Brooklyn Royal Giants. He was 34, young for a manager but getting on for a shortstop. Perhaps with that in mind Lloyd slid over to first, deferring to Joe Hewitt, a fast, able middle infielder who enjoyed a great deal of range. Aside from Redding, whom Lloyd had brought with him from Chicago, Lloyd had on his staff Irvin Brooks and, for a time, John Donaldson and Tom Williams. Louis Santop was penciled in behind the plate, and would bat .368 while there.[1]

Santop was a big man, 6'4", 240 pounds, with a powerful bat and gun to go with it. It was said that he could stand at home plate and throw the ball over the center field fence, and could hit it farther still. His tape measure homers during the dead ball era were legendary. These bombs went so astonishingly far that they earned him the moniker "Big Bertha," after the Germans' World War I long-range artillery weapon.[2] In his prime, Santop was the black game's top draw, and he was paid like it, earning up to $500 a month. Compared often to Babe Ruth, Santop enjoyed but a single chance at head-to-head competition with the "Bambino," collecting three hits, including a double, while Ruth wore the collar. Having played with Santop earlier in his career, Lloyd hoped the catcher would anchor his lineup, but it did not happen, as Santop was drafted, spending most of 1918 and 1919 in the Navy.[3]

The team was owned by Nat Strong, an aggressive white businessman, unliked by a majority of owners and players because of the tactics he exercised in booking most black games in the east, demanding an additional 10% of the gate for his services. Strong presided as an officer with both the Royal Giants and the later New York Black Yankees, controlling black baseball in New York City. He also invested in strong white semipro teams such as the Brooklyn Bushwicks, the Bay Parkways, and the Cuban Stars, providing ready competition for the Royals and Black Yankees in the process.[4]

Such a contest took place in late May, 1918, with the Royal Giants besting the Bushwicks at Dexter Park in Brooklyn, 3–2. On a Sunday afternoon, before a large crowd, the Royals posted two runs in the first inning and another in the sixth to hold off the Bushwicks. Tom Williams, over from Chicago, got the win for the Royals. The itinerant Williams pitched for four teams in 1918 — Chicago, Brooklyn, Hilldale and the Lincoln Giants, posting a combined 10–0 record for the season.[5]

Lloyd recalled years later that Sunday afternoon games had been illegal, so to see a game, a fan had to buy a club membership ticket. While it might seem a bit much by today's standards, it proved the doggedness of such fans, who Lloyd believed were more informed and less "pampered" than modern fans. "Even the fans are different," Lloyd said. "Many of them [today] hardly know what's happening unless the ball is knocked out of the park. Our followers were dyed-in-the-wool fans who knew the game."[6]

Two weeks later, on another guilty Sunday, more of these "dyed-in-the-wool" fans jammed Olympic Field to see the Royals sweep a double dip from the Lincoln Giants, 4–3 and 7–3. In the first game, an 11-inning affair in which both Lloyd and Joe Williams were hurt, Tom Williams was strong again, allowing the three runs in the fourth inning before settling in. The Royals pushed the deciding tally across in the top half of the 11th, then turned things over to Redding who finished it off. Williams and Redding were back at it again in game two, holding the Lincolns to three runs, this time one coming in the fifth, the other two in the seventh, while the Royals pushed six runs across in the top of the ninth for the victory.[7]

By the middle of

Left: John Henry Lloyd, Brooklyn Royal Giants. In 1918, Lloyd was hired by Nat Strong to manage and play for the Brooklyn Royal Giants. He was 34, young for a manager, but getting on for a shortstop. *Right:* Louis Santop used a big, heavy bat and was noted for his tape-measure home runs during baseball's deadball era, earning him the nickname "Big Bertha" after the Germans' World War I long-range artillery piece.

June, Lloyd had the Royals cruising, besting the Bushwicks in "two well played games," the second of which went 11 innings, 2–1 and 8–6. Tom Williams won game one, allowing seven hits, as Lloyd sat out, Ed Douglass filling in for him at first base. By July 4, however, the club's offense had hit the skids, compliments of the Lincoln Giants. In a pitching duel for the books, "Smokey Joe" Williams and John Donaldson, fresh from the west, having just signed with the Royals, hooked up at Olympic Field, making spectators of everyone else. Williams was masterful, tossing a four-hit shutout, Lloyd getting one and Santop none. Donaldson was a horse, too, allowing seven hits and a single tally. Anticipating a close, low-scoring game, Lloyd played shortstop. The Royals, with Irvin Brooks on the mound, bounced back in the second game, 4–1. Lloyd's club picked up all of its runs in the first three innings as Brooks settled in, allowing the Lincolns a lone score in the fifth.[8]

Irvin Brooks, of Nassau, Bahamas, would become one of the best all-around players in the league over the next decade, yet also one of its least publicized. Easing away from the slab after injuring his arm, Brooks became known as the best utility man in the east. And in a rarity, Brooks played his entire 16-year career in Brooklyn with the Royal Giants.[9]

The following Sunday Joe Williams and John Donaldson engaged in another pitching duel at Olympic Field, the Lincolns' ace prevailing once more, 3–2. Lloyd again played short, flagging everything within reach, while also contributing a hit. With Santop out of the lineup, the offense was led by Donaldson's three hits and Tom Fiall's two. The Royals rebounded later in the week, taking two from the Bushwicks, 6–1 and 6–1. Lloyd, Douglass, Fiall and Hewitt had two hits apiece in the first contest, while the second was called in the sixth inning on account of rain. The Cubans, however, on a recent tear having topped Williams and the Lincolns, 5–4, brought the Royals back to earth, beating them, 6–3.[10]

Following a circuitous schedule, the Royals again took on the Lincolns in a Sunday afternoon pair at Olympic Field, losing the first but winning the second. In game one Joe Williams allowed two runs on six hits to the Royals, with John Donaldson, playing outfield, getting two of them. Irvin Brooks was nearly as effective, holding the Lincolns to four runs on seven hits. In game two, Donaldson, this time clear of Williams, got the win behind eight runs of support against the Lincolns' two. Donaldson went to the mound again the following week to face a white team led by Hank Thormahlen, former pitcher of the New York Yankees. Donaldson took the loss, 5–2, as Bodie, also formerly of the Yankees, led the way with two hits. José Figarola, a highly regarded but light-hitting Cuban catcher, playing out of position at first base, got two hits for the Royals. His brief appearance with the Royals would be his last in black baseball.[11]

With the season winding down, a few more games were played locally against white all-star teams. One such affair pitted a watered-down Lincolns squad against an all–National League club fronted by Rube Marquard, former ace hurler of the New York Giants. Marquard, a hard drinker and even harder thrower, was "treated badly" by the Lincolns, who touched him for 16 hits, winning 8–0. At the same time, the "All Nationals" could do very little with Joe Williams, who struck out six in the shutout. Williams won three more games against big leaguers that fall, not including one that was forfeited to him when pitcher Bullet Joe Bush of the Boston Red Sox purposely cut a ball with his spikes and refused to let the umpire look at it, therefore drawing the forfeit.[12]

These games indicated the high level of competition presented by black teams when afforded an opportunity to face their white counterparts. Over the better part of the next three decades, players such as Satchel Paige, Josh Gibson, and Hilton Smith toured the country playing baseball against white major leaguers like Dizzy Dean and Bob Feller. And their talent level was up to it! To hear Lloyd say it, "We had whole teams of top notchers ... Rube Foster, Cyclone Joe Williams, Dick Redding ... Oscar Charleston ... Bingo DeMoss, Oliver Marcelle ... Lundy. They were 'big league' all the way.... Tell me today who rates with Johnny Beckwith? The same year (1927) Babe Ruth hit 60 home runs, Johnny hit 72.... I could go on naming great ball players.... In my book, they were not only great, they were the best."[13]

John Beckwith. "Tell me today who rates with Johnny Beckwith? The same year (1927) Babe Ruth hit 60 home runs, Johnny hit 72," said Lloyd of his longtime teammate.

Al Fennar, who had a cup of coffee in black baseball from 1931 to 1934, once described Beckwith as "devastating." "He was awful (to hit against)!" Fennar said. He explained how as a rookie with the Harlem Stars and not knowing who Beckwith was, he once positioned himself to play Beckwith straight away. Seeing the depth at which the rookie was playing, Oliver Marcelle at third base told him to back up. "I was way out," Fenner recalled. "I was back — Beckwith hit the ball and I jumped and the ball hit in the glove and took the glove and everything and headed for left field." Beckwith could play anywhere, shortstop, catcher, outfield, but according to Fenner, "all they wanted was to get his stick in there."[14]

While Lloyd acknowledged that not all black players were the caliber of Beckwith — "we had many ordinary men" — the majors had "ordinary" players as well, many of whom would not have smelled the show were it not for black competition being locked out. Of course, this was a concern to the white power structure fighting to keep blacks out — as it was in defense plants and elsewhere — but this head-to-head competition ultimately came to soften the nation — somewhat — to the idea of blacks and whites playing together, thereby laying the groundwork for the game's desegregation, which came in 1946 with the Brooklyn Dodgers' signing of Jackie Robinson.[15]

* * *

With American doughboys returning from the Great War in Europe, Lloyd began the 1919 season managing and playing for the Royal Giants. By mid–June, however, after having played at least three games, he jumped the Royals, leaving for Atlantic City, New Jersey, to become player-manager of the Bacharach Giants. The fresh start must have done him good because he fared well on the season, batting .310 while managing and playing shortstop throughout. While there was no mention in the press as to why Lloyd left, one can surmise that it must have been the money. It always had been — and would be. It was most certainly the reason for Redding, who was just back from the war and who within a month joined Lloyd on the South Jersey shore with the Bacharachs.[16]

Redding had signaled his return earlier in the season when on May 8, he faced off with "Smokey Joe" Williams and the Lincoln Giants before a large crowd at Olympic Park in Harlem. Tossing a two-hitter, "Cannonball" gave everything he had yet came up short as the Lincolns pushed the game's only run across with one out in the bottom of the ninth to support Williams' winning no-hitter. "Smokey Joe" called it "the greatest game I ever pitched."[17]

The Bacharachs, formerly known as the Duval Giants, were comprised largely of players recruited from Jacksonville. "We all went to school in Jacksonville," recalled Napoleon "Chance" Cummings:

> (Dick) Lundy, Willis Crump, McKinley (Bunny) Downs, Shang Johnson ... and ... a left-handed catcher called Willy White.... [W]e played at least three times a week. Saturday was the big game; we always made $25 a man.... In 1916 this man came down to Jacksonville to look the ball clubs over and bring us up to Atlantic City. They had a mayor at that time named Bacharach, and we were named the Bacharach Giants.... When we first came here (Atlantic City), they had seven or eight teams here, but we put 'em all out of baseball, because nobody could play with us.[18]

Lloyd's and Redding's arrival made John W. Connors and Barron D. Wilkins, owners of the Bacharachs, the "two happiest mortals" in baseball, especially after their team, with Lloyd and Redding in place, trounced the Treat 'Em Roughs in a doubleheader at the Dyckman Oval in upper Manhattan, 6–0 and 8–4. The Treat 'Em Roughs, a local semi-professional club, was organized by Guy Empey, who along with many of his players had recently seen service overseas during World War I. With the Treat 'Em Roughs dispatching most of their competition that summer and the Bacharachs greatly improved, the contests were eagerly anticipated.[19]

Games they may have been, but contests they were not. In the first tilt "Cannonball" Redding was his usual self, striking out 13 while setting them down scoreless. His breaking pitches had Empey's Roughs "swinging like a gate." At the same time, the Bacharachs bunched their hits off Clinton, the Roughs' pitcher, scoring five runs in the sixth inning and one in the eighth. Ben Taylor, in from the west, got two hits, one a bomb, with Ernest Gatewood, Spot Poles and Redding chiming in with one each. The second game was

John Henry Lloyd with the Bacharach Giants. In 1919, he batted .310 while managing and playing shortstop for the Atlantic City Bacharach Giants (courtesy the John Henry "Pop" Lloyd Committee).

more of the same with the Bacharachs' "Big Boy" Roberts and Jess Hubbard holding the Roughs to four runs on four hits.[20]

The tables turned a week later as Jeff Tesreau, a former New York Giants pitcher now with the Roughs, matched up with "Red Ant" Wickware before a capacity crowd of 4,500 at Dyckman Oval, earning a close 2–1 win. Tesreau, who possessed a hard, "devastating spitball," earned a 115–72 (.615) mark and 2.43 ERA in seven seasons with John McGraw's Giants, allowing opponents a slim .223 career average. His best years came in 1914 when he was 26–10, and the year prior going 22–13. A horse at 6'2", 225 pounds, Tesreau ate innings, starting 41 games in 1914, completing 26 of them, and getting the decision all but five times. On this day, Tesreau's spitter danced all over the place; he allowed a single run with 11 strike outs. Wickware, who gave up eight hits in the loss, had 11 strikeouts as well, but walked five. The Bacharachs fought back in the second game, easily defeating the Roughs, 8–2.[21]

Lloyd's men continued their rough treatment of Empey's squad two weeks later, winning 5–1 and 6–2. Wickware and Redding split the bill for the Bacharachs, with the "Red Ant" also on in relief for Redding in game two. Wickware scattered five hits in the lid-lifter, the Roughs' lone tally coming in the third inning. Ben Taylor led the way on offense with a homer and two singles; Poles hit a bomb, and Lloyd doubled and singled. The second game, despite the 6–2 score, was another pitching duel with Tesreau striking out ten before tiring, allowing two runs in the ninth inning and four in the 11th. Redding struck out six prior to giving way to Wickware, who got two more in relief. Spot Poles belted two doubles for the Bacharachs.[22]

The Bacharachs finished the season behind only the Lincolns in the east, posting a .545 winning percentage. As the campaign wound down, they took on the best in the west — the American Giants and the Hilldale Daisies, losing two out of three to each. They also went up against another squad of white all-stars, this one led by major league hurler Carl Mays, who was 16–14 on the year. In the game, the former Red Sox ace bested Wickware and Redding in 14 innings. Mays, a solid pitcher traded in midsummer by Boston to the New York Yankees, gained unwanted notoriety the following season when a fastball thrown by him struck and killed Ray Chapman of the Cleveland Indians. This incident, more than any, directly led to baseball officially outlawing "trick pitches, including the spitball."[23]

*　*　*

By the next spring, 1920, and with the Bacharachs readying for a trip south to Jacksonville, Lloyd was gone, jumping back to Brooklyn with the Royals. The Bacharachs announced that "holding down" shortstop in the coming season would not be Lloyd but rather "Richard Lundy," with Oliver Marcelle at third, the Cuban Julio Rojo both catching and playing outfield, Ernest Gatewood behind the dish, and a stellar rotation consisting of Redding, Wickware, and "String Bean" Williams. Marcelle was a great third baseman, and according to Cummings, "the meanest ... I ever saw on earth.... They called him 'the Ghost.' And he could hit!" As for Lundy, who had batted .351 the previous season with Hilldale, he was "the greatest shortstop anybody ever saw." Cummings favorably compared Lundy to Lloyd and Willie Wells, and even Hall of Fame major leaguers Joe Cronin and Honus Wagner, concluding that "I've seen shortstops come and go, but Dick Lundy" was the best.[24]

The budding Lloyd/Lundy rivalry was pushed in the papers as much as possible. "Lloyd has been the kingpin around short for about 12 years," wrote

Ted Hooks in the *Age*. "At last, Lloyd has a rival who will make him speed up or lose his exalted position.... Lloyd at his best was no better than Lundy is right now.... Only one thing keeps Lundy from being rated over Lloyd now and that is his youth."[25]

Lundy may have been the best ever seen by Cummings, or considered a "second Lloyd" by the *Age*, but it was the veteran Lloyd, now 36 years old and for the first time being referred to as "Pop," a moniker that would tag him henceforth, who manned shortstop for the eastern all-stars that season, batting .333 and leading his team to the Eastern League championship series where they fell short, losing to Hilldale in an awkward set, two games to none, with two ties.[26]

With much taking place outside the lines that year: the Great War's aftermath; the passage of women's suffrage; a prohibition against alcoholic beverages; and the rise of Marcus Garvey's Universal Negro Improvement Association, the black press, to some extent, lost interest in covering baseball. Not even the teams could keep track of who was where in the standings; multiple clubs disputed the season's outcome. As noted, Ed Bolden's Hilldale Daisies and Lloyd's Brooklyn Royal Giants opted to settle the eastern championship on the field, with the Bacharachs the odd club out.[27]

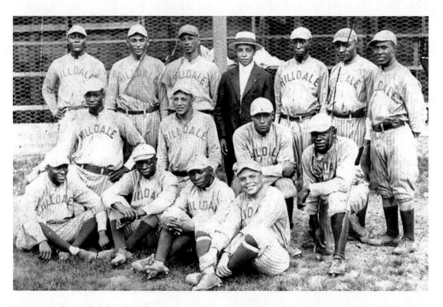

In 1923, the Hilldale Club became a charter member of the Eastern Colored League, winning the first of three pennants with a record of 32–17. In this photo are Ed Bolden, in center with suit, Spot Poles and Bill Francis (courtesy Negro Leagues Baseball Museum).

Shortly after the season, the Washington Senators, who placed a distant sixth to Cleveland in the American League that year, but who would play in two World Series by the middle of the decade, took on the Royal Giants in a best of three set. The Senators featured sluggers Sam Rice and Joe Judge, but did not bring their ace hurler, Walter Johnson, going rather with the Cuban rookie, José Acosta, followed by Jim Shaw and Harry Courtney. In game one Roy "Big Boy" Roberts of the Royals struck out 12 batters but fell to Acosta, 2–1, on infielder Buck Ridgely's error. A ninth-inning error foiled the Senators in game two, the Royals winning this time, 5–4. With Juan Padrón on the mound in game three, the Royals bunched four runs in the fourth inning to win it, 4–1. In spite of the win, Lloyd was not himself at the plate, gathering just two hits in 13 at-bats for a .154 average.[28]

The one baseball-related event that did bring about coverage in the black press during 1920 was the Chicago indictment, trial, acquittal, and ultimate banishment for life of the "Chicago Black Sox," eight players of Chicago's White Sox accused of conspiring with gamblers to throw the 1919 World Series. Ted Hooks, of the *Age*, saw the "Big Fix" and its upshot as an opportunity, arguing that with the "recent upheaval," Negro fans should begin a campaign to get black players into the major leagues. "Write now!" he demanded.[29]

Hooks rightly pointed out that major league baseball was in trouble. Americans had been stunned by this "murderous blow" to the national pastime, one which had played with the "faith of fifty million people" (Fitzgerald 67–68). The game, many believed, might not recover. Interest might well be inspired by the insertion of black ballplayers, many of whom had already proven themselves worthy through their service during the war, their gentlemanly conduct on the field, and the talent they conveyed. "White sportswriters," he felt, constantly praised the talents of black ball stars, and yet always ended with the refrain: "If he were not colored, etc., etc." Surely now, at such a desperate time, organized baseball would recognize this for its own sake. For Hooks, now was the moment. He would, of course, be disappointed, for regardless of need, talent, service, and amenability, racism's filthy hand still played a dogged role in this nation's pastime.[30]

* * *

In 1921, Lloyd was on the move again. Rube Foster had founded the Negro National League, the first organized black league. The league was heading into its second season, having been organized in the winter of 1919-1920 by Foster, J. L. Wilkinson of the Kansas City Monarchs, and others. Foster asked Lloyd to take over as player-manager in Columbus, Ohio. Sol White, the venerable black ball pioneer and one of Lloyd's earliest mentors, was brought on board as the business manager. "Pop loved it in Columbus," Nan Lloyd recalled, but the stint was short-lived. The Buckeyes were not very good, going a dismal 30–39 before disbanding. Lloyd, however, did not let up, batting .340 with 18 doubles and 20 stolen bases, earning a spot on the West All-Star team.[31]

After dropping the season opener to Indianapolis, 8–2, the Buckeyes stumbled along, losing a game for every game they won. On May 23 they took a close, 6–5 victory from the Kansas City Monarchs, rallying in the ninth inning for the winning tally. Lloyd, playing shortstop, got two hits, scoring once. But the following Sunday, they dumped a 13-inning affair to Dick Redding and the Bacharachs, 7–4. Redding went the distance, allowing seven hits, one a fifth-inning bomb by Robert "Highpockets" Hudspeth which got the Buckeyes on the board. The Buckeyes followed that by taking a beating at the hands of Toledo, 17–1, before losing again to the Bacharachs, 13–4. The indomitable Lloyd went 2-for-4 in the latter contest, boosting his average to .320. The Buckeyes finished out the week "falling into a trap" at Chicago, losing 2–0.[32]

The season played out that way for the Buckeyes, who, next to the Chicago Giants, were the weakest team in the circuit. Lloyd, however, had a great season, going four 4-for-4 in one game against the Cubans and ending up the year with a .337 batting average. He also finished third in stolen bases behind Charleston and Torriente, both of whom were much younger than he. But while Lloyd may have enjoyed his time in Columbus, he certainly could not have been enamored with the losing. Nor were the club owners, who pulled out their funding once the Buckeyes hit the skids, leaving this as the lone Columbus campaign on record in the Negro National League. For Lloyd, it was on to the next paycheck, and there was one waiting on him in New York.[33]

John W. Connors, owner of the Bacharach Giants, wanted to replace Dick Redding as manager of his squad. While the Bacharachs had finished first in the east with a record of 34–28, Connors decided he wanted Redding to focus on pitching, and with Lloyd on the market the call was simple. Connors had taken the team from Atlantic City to New York and was set to play their games at the New York Oval, 150th and River Avenue. Meanwhile, Dick Lundy and another version of the Bacharach Giants continued to play in Atlantic City.[34]

In front of 10,000 eager fans, the New York Bacharachs opened the 1922 season on Sunday, June 4, at the Oval, losing both games of a doubleheader to Hilldale. With Redding on the bump they dropped the first game, 8–6, and were "overwhelmingly" outclassed in game two, 19–4. It was a game in which Lloyd "used every pitcher on his staff in a vain effort to stop the heavy-hitting" Daisies. Later that week the Bacharachs bested Hoboken, 8–5, before being washed out while up 7–1 against the Madison Stars. It was noted that in spite of two months of preparation, the Bacharachs would need several more weeks of training before they would be able to succeed against the New York clubs.[35]

The New York black ball scene was awakened that week to allegations that gambling was rampant on the semi-professional lots of New York. Hugh S. Fullerton, writing in the *Evening Mail*, commented that:

> Open gambling, exhibitions of players thrusting money through the screens making bets with spectators during games, mobbing of umpires, and generally rotten conditions exist in many places. There are swarms of piker gamblers following the strong semi-pro clubs, wagering large sums on the results, and the evil is made worse by the fact that most of it happens on Sunday. At a recent game between two colored teams on a park which seemed perfectly safeguarded, members of one team went around the grounds, sticking money through the screen, betting and taking all the money in sight. The opposing team was best, but the umpire rushed, abused, threatened, and they finally weakened and the bets were saved. The thing was one of the most disgraceful in the history of baseball, but they got away with it.[36]

W. E. Clark, in the *Age*, professed ignorance as to whether the above occurred as Fullerton alleged, but did acknowledge that there was "entirely too much gambling at these games." He wrote that conditions at both the Bronx Catholic Protectory Oval, home of the Lincoln Giants, and the New York Oval, home to the Bacharachs, were so rife with gambling, bad language and fights that it had become "unwise for women to go" to these parks on Sunday for ballgames. "Unless some system is devised whereby the players of these teams and the gamblers who infest these parks may be controlled, the management cannot expect to receive the support of respectable people of the community."[37]

It is remarkable that at a time when columnists in the black press were insisting that organized baseball's best interest would be served by desegregating — especially in light of high-profile gambling scandals — that black players and owners would shoot themselves in the foot by continuing to operate and play under suspect conditions. It is understood that some of the owners and team officials came from the numbers rackets, Alejandro Pompéz and Gus Greenlee to name two, but that should not have guaranteed that past practice would spill into the park, or certainly to the level it did. The fact that gambling at the park was not prohibited tainted the competition and, to an extent, ran off decent patrons.

Yet not all ballplayers were gamblers; Lloyd most certainly was not. The fact that Lloyd, a professed Christian, could play through the vice on display around him shows just how competitive he was. Nothing would get in the way of his performing to his capabilities, which seemed to flower with age. New York was hardly the only town where gambling at ballgames was rampant. In cities and small towns alike, sports gambling was wide open. In Tampa, players would bet with spectators — fresh from the billiards hall — a pitch at a time. Does he get a hit or strike out? Where will he hit it? Will it be a single or double? What pitch is going to be thrown next? "They would bet money on every pitch and every batter and everything," said "Bitsy" Mott, a one-time shortstop for the Philadelphia Phillies who spent time with the Tampa Smokers. Being widespread did not excuse the behavior, however, nor could it have helped the game's reputation or the cause of desegregation. At a moment when organized baseball did not need a reason to bar blacks from the game, black ballplayers, owners, and hangers-on gave them an excuse to continue do just that.[38]

On June 20, the Bacharachs "swamped" the Bronx Yankees in the opening game of a twin bill at the Oval, 11–0. The second game, played against a team from south Philadelphia, was halted by rain with the Bacharachs down, 8–0. "Big Boy" Roberts got the shutout in the first affair, allowing five hits while striking out eight. Pete Duncan, playing left field, went 4-for-4, scoring three times to pace the Bacharachs. Two days earlier, Lundy's "Original" Bacharach Giants, with Nate Johnson on the mound, had defeated the Bronx Giants at the Oval, 5–2. Four days later, Lloyd's Bacharachs bested a local team at the Oval, 4–0. The following day they took both ends of a split bill, first against the "fast South Philly" Hebrews, 6–2, followed by a 6–5 win against a team from Phillipsburg, New York. Lloyd had reason to be content with the way his club was playing, particularly with the favored Hilldale coming to town for a doubleheader the next week.[39]

In two hotly contested affairs, games that had the large Oval crowd standing throughout, Lloyd's bunch bested Hilldale in both, 4–2 and 4–3. Redding faced off with Pud Flournoy, the Daisies' "heavyset lefthander," in game one, the Bacharachs surprising many with the win. With Henry Gillespie and Nip Winters on for the respective clubs, game two furnished as many thrills as the first. Gillespie, an "iron man" whose career covered parts of three decades, lasted longer than the lefty Winters, who was yanked in the eighth inning following two walks, but Harold Treadwell, an underhand control artist, came on to settle things down. The Bacharachs went ahead for good in the eighth on Pete Duncan's pinch-hit single scoring "Country" Brown.[40]

Lloyd, accompanied by team owner John Connors, then took his club west to face both the Kansas City Monarchs and Rube Foster's American Giants. In Kansas City, the Bacharachs, after starting hot, stumbled to split a four-game set. On Saturday, August 5, "Big Boy" Roberts was stellar for the Bacharachs as they took the first affair, 4–1. Nip Winters continued the assault a day later, besting "Bullet Joe" Rogan, 4–1. With ace Dick Redding on the mound, however, the Bacharachs dropped a close game three encounter, 3–2, before getting completely wiped out in the finale, 11–0. Rube Currie and Bill Drake did the honors for Kansas City in the final two tilts.[41]

The Bacharachs' five-game set with the American Giants at Schorling Park, which began on August 12, was billed as a "must win" series for Foster's squad.[42] Yet it was the Giants who stumbled out of the gate, coming up "on the short end of the score" two days in a row for the first time all season. In game one, "String Bean" Williams and Nip Winters, behind some "classy fielding," allowed 11 hits for the 5–4 win, while Mulo Padrón, with eight strikeouts, took the loss. The Bacharachs had been up by two runs in the ninth inning when "Jelly" Gardner singled for the Giants, driving in two runs to knot things. In the 11th, with a man on, Julio Rojo, with three hits on the day, doubled for the Bacharachs, driving in the winning run when Cristóbal Torriente's throw was mishandled at home by Jim Brown, the Giants catcher.[43]

In the second game, the Bacharachs were up 2–1 in the seventh inning when Chicago's Johnny Beckwith tied things on an error by Dick Jackson at second base. In the ninth, "Young" Aubrey Owens got Lloyd, who had already singled and scored twice, on strikes, before "Highpockets" Hudspeth doubled and Rojo singled him in for the 3–2 win. Harold Treadwell went the distance, getting the win for the Bacharachs. Lloyd scored two of his team's three runs, with one hit and a stolen base. With two victories in the barn, Lloyd's crew needed just one more in the remaining three games to win the series.[44]

A day later, the Bacharachs broke a scoreless tie in the top of the sixth inning against Dave Brown when Jackson beat out a hit, Rabbit Shively doubled and Oliver Marcelle grounded through Bingo DeMoss' wickets at second, scoring two. In the bottom of the inning, however, with two gone, Bobby Williams doubled. Beckwith walked and subsequently stole second, bringing Dave Malarcher to the plate. Malarcher, who batted .363 in the series, grounded to Lloyd, who was late getting to second, loading the bases. Jim Brown singled, scoring two to tie it. With Redding pitching for the Bacharachs and Brown solid for the Giants, the game stayed knotted into the eighth, when a Torriente single and an error by outfielder Romo Ramirez put the go-ahead run at second. Torriente came around on a dropped throw by Marcelle at third as the Giants took the lead. In the top of the ninth, Dave Brown got

Lloyd to pop up to Williams at shortstop, then struck out Hudspeth and Rojo to win it, 3–2.[45]

On Tuesday, Foster's Giants, down two games to one, came from behind to knot the series at two games apiece. The Bacharachs started things in the first inning when Rabbit Shively walked, Marcelle singled, and Lloyd's grounder forced Marcelle at second, sending Shively, "a desperate base runner" and "one of the fastest in the game," to third. With runners on first and third, Giants pitcher Richard Whitworth threw over to first, trapping Lloyd in a rundown, but Leroy Grant, playing first base, threw the ball into center field, scoring Shively. Down 2–1 in the fifth, Grant and Torriente worked "Big Boy" Roberts for walks. Nip Winters, on for Roberts, promptly allowed a pinch-hit infield single to Johnny Reese to load the bases. "Jelly" Gardner walked, forcing in Grant to tie things. Bingo DeMoss dragged a squeeze down the first base line that Winters fielded, scoring Grant and Torriente and giving the Giants a 4–2 lead. Jimmy Lyons "pulled the same stunt," bunting Reese in with another run. After the Bacharachs scored once in the sixth, the Giants answered in the seventh with DeMoss bunting home two more runs, Torriente and Gardner, giving the Giants five runners on three bunts and a 7–3 win.[46]

With the series tied at two games each, the Bacharach Giants of New York took on Chicago's American Giants in a 20-inning marathon, one in which the Giants were able to convert a walk, sacrifice and single into the winning tally. Harold Treadwell, three days removed from going the distance in game two, and in what became "one of the great iron-man performances in baseball history," again went the distance for the Bacharachs, all 20 frames, striking out 12 and allowing just nine hits in a "heady" effort. Dave Brown, relieving Huck Rile in the fifth inning, and not to be outdone, struck out ten batters over 16 innings for Chicago.[47]

For 19 innings neither side could get a run. "[B]rilliant fielding"—eight double plays and catches after long runs — thrilled the crowd, especially Hudspeth's one-handed stab of Dave Brown's liner in the 13th and Marcelle's running barehanded catch off his shoes of Williams' foul in the second. But it was a game of mental and physical endurance, and the club that could withstand the stress while maintaining its composure was going to win it.[48]

Huck Rile, a big, promising pitcher who later became a hard-hitting first baseman, started badly for the Giants when in the top of the first inning he plunked the speedster Shively. Rile was bailed out, however, when Lloyd signaled Marcelle to sacrifice Shively to second rather than sending the "Rabbit" on a straight steal. With one out Lloyd grounded to Williams at shortstop, followed by "Country" Brown's fly to Lyons, and the threat ended with Shively stranded at second. Lloyd's team missed another opportunity an inning later when Hudspeth singled, Rojo flied to Torriente in center, Duncan singled, and Jackson fouled out to the catcher, making it two outs, two on, Hudspeth at second. Treadwell singled to center, sending "Highpockets" lumbering around third toward an apparent score. But after going halfway home, he inexplicably pulled up and, trying to get back to third, was cut down on a great throw from Torriente. The score remained tied at 0 to 0.[49]

After Pete Duncan singled to start the fifth, Rube Foster lifted Rile, going to Dave Brown, who had pitched a nine-inning victory just two days before. Brown promptly got Jackson to force Duncan at second on a fielder's choice back to the box, Treadwell to lift a foul pop near third, and Shively on strikes, ending the inning. In the home fifth, Treadwell allowed a single to Grant before Brown forced him at second. With one down and one on, Marcelle kicked a grounder by Gardner, moving Brown over to third. Bingo DeMoss walked, and with runners on first and third, Jimmie Lyons flied to "Country" Brown in left, who threw Dave Brown out at home trying to score on the catch. Treadwell and Brown pitched scoreless baseball for the next 14 innings, breezing through innings, neither hurler giving an inch.[50]

When Pete Duncan again singled to start an inning, this time the tenth, Lloyd made a move that was questioned by many at the park and in the press during the game's aftermath, sending Romo Ramirez in to run for Duncan. Ramirez was promptly forced at second, and Treadwell hit into a double play to end the inning and negate the substitution. But the move lingered, like stench. Ramirez, whose throwing arm Foster considered suspect, went into right field for the more reliable Duncan. Foster's men would bide their time, waiting for an opportunity to test Ramirez, if a test presented itself.[51]

The Bacharachs threatened again in the 18th, with Hudspeth led off with a single to left and Rojo was hit by a pitch, putting runners on first and second. When Ramirez grounded back to the box, however, Brown made a fine play on Hudspeth at third. Jackson flied out, leaving men on first and second with two outs. Treadwell, considered a good-hitting pitcher, "dumped a bunt in front of the plate" for a base hit, loading the bases for Shively, who fanned to end the threat.[52]

In the bottom half of the 20th, Foster's advance knowledge of Ramirez bore fruit. Treadwell, who would never again pitch like he did that day, walked Torriente to start things, and Williams sacrificed him over to second. With a runner in scoring position, Foster signaled the switch-hitting Malarcher, batting left-handed against the right-handed Treadwell, to pull one into right, which he did, coming "through with a nice single." Ramirez, making a "desperate attempt," was unable to get the hard-charging Torriente, who beat the throw "by five feet" at the plate to win it. Many in attendance questioned

Lloyd, arguing that if Duncan had stayed in the game, Torriente would have never scored and the clubs would have battled on until darkness. But Lloyd made the switch, the game was "won fairly," the series went to Chicago, and the crowd went home "well satisfied." On the season, and indicative of the equal footing of the two clubs and perhaps their managers, the Bacharachs and the American Giants split ten contests. No quarter was given.[53]

Lloyd's Bacharachs returned to New York. On Sunday, August 20, playing their first game in the east in over two months against a local club in Orange, New Jersey, the Bacharachs began a stretch in which they reeled off wins in 18 of 22 games. Two of the losses came against the Chester, Pa., team, with one each to Plainfield and the ABCs. On Sunday, September 10, they won a doubleheader from the Farmer's nine of Brooklyn, and the following day topped the Sunbury, Pa., team on the road. Looking ahead to games in Baltimore, Norfolk and Richmond, Lloyd expressed optimism that his team would continue to play well.[54]

Two weeks later, on September 24, the Bacharachs took two games against the Bronx Giants, 4–0 and 11–8. Redding pitched the first game for the Bacharachs, breezing his way to a four-hit shutout. "Big Boy" Roberts was not as sharp in the game two win, allowing nine hits in what turned into a slugfest. Lloyd's team then traveled to Dover, New Jersey, where it beat back another squad of white ballplayers, this one an all-star team comprised of players from the World Champion New York Giants such as Heinie Groh, Rosy Ryan and Irish Meusel. Treadwell posted the win in game one, 5–4, allowing seven hits, while Dick Redding, "at his best," went the distance in the second game, winning 3–1.[55]

Across town, "Smokey Joe" Williams was busy fronting his Lincoln Giants to a pair of wins against the Cuban Stars, the first game of which he won on a long home run. The Cuban Stars boasted one of the great outfields of all-time with Pablo "Champion" Mesa, Bernardo Baró and Alejandro Oms. It also featured a lanky 16-year-old rookie phenom named Martín Dihigo.[56]

Martín Dihigo, a multifaceted player nicknamed "El Inmortál," has been called the "most versatile man ever to play the game of baseball."[57] Max Manning, who later pitched for a winter team that Dihigo managed in Cienfuegos, Cuba, commented that he "was a marvelous physical specimen — height, weight, broad shoulders. You could see the power that this man had."[58] A gifted five-tool player, Dihigo began his career at second base, gradually moving over to field the corners, then to the outfield, before going to the mound, where he became an exceptional pitcher. James Riley wrote, "Whether playing the outfield, the infield or pitching, he was awesome." Dihigo had a sensational arm, great range in the field, very good speed, and could hit with power. He did it all! In 1937, while playing in the Santo Domingo Winter League, he finished second in the league standings in both pitching and hitting, losing out to Satchel Paige in victories and Josh Gibson in batting average, nothing to spit at.[59]

The two victories over the Cubans were marred by "excessive betting" done openly during the second game. The Catholic Protectory Oval management had ironically been chastised for its failure to check betting at the park, and it had stopped, for a time, but the betting had resumed and was as bad as ever. The *Age* opined that betting at the park "could be wiped out if the professional gamblers who infest this park were barred" or if security was brought in to maintain order, and "enforce the law against betting."[60] As noted above, the entire scene, and others like it, continued to weaken any argument black baseball organizers had for using gambling scandals such as the one in Chicago to justify the game's desegregation.

SEVEN

Just Give Him a Bat

The 1923 season proved to be no different for Lloyd than the prior one had been. It began in turmoil, when Hilldale's "diminutive owner" Ed Bolden formed the rival Eastern Colored League, subsequently prompting a "baseball war" in which well-known players such as Clint Thomas and Frank Warfield left Detroit to sign with Hilldale, as did Biz Mackey and George Scales, who jumped from Indianapolis and St. Louis respectively. To manage his crew, Bolden convinced Lloyd to leave the Bacharachs for Hilldale.[1]

The squad Bolden pieced together was a powerful one. Louis Santop, a holdover from the previous year, did the catching, along with Mackey. Between the two powerful sluggers, they belted 16 home runs that season, equating to 48 over a 500-at-bat season.[2] The pitching staff was made up of forkballer Red Ryan, Phil Cockrell, and Nip Winters, who led the league in wins with ten, while the infield, with Lloyd and Warfield up the middle, "Judy" Johnson at third and "Tank" Carr at first, "was formidable."[3]

As he had with Brooklyn and the Bacharachs, Lloyd proved to be a patient mentor in developing young talent. "He was like a father to me," rookie shortstop Bill Yancey later recalled. "I was just a kid and he was the great Lloyd I'd heard so much about, and he's the one who taught me to play shortstop." Yancey remembered facing "Smokey Joe" Williams for the first time and being so nervous that he had the shakes, until Lloyd "gently reminded him that Williams had to get the ball over the plate just like any other pitcher." It worked, calming the rookie "considerably."[4]

At the end of March, 1923, Bolden sent out notices to each of his players to report to the Daily Grounds in Philadelphia for spring training on Monday, April 9. There were to be two weeks of "intensive drilling, including several practice games," before the opening of the league season. Tank Carr, coming over from Kansas City, had reported early, as had Mackey and Warfield, both of whom expected big seasons in their new digs.[5]

Their big seasons were rolling by late May when Baltimore's Black Sox came into town for a three-game set. In the first game, "Lloyd's Larruppers" lit up Doc Sykes for three bombs, "jarring all of the fillings out of the elongated dentist's teeth," winning 8–1. These homers did not include Lloyd's bid for a round-tripper in the first inning when his blast to deep center forced Harry Raggs to the wall, where he "leaped three or five feet" into the air to bring it back. Nip Winters, on the mound for Hilldale, came close to tossing a no-hitter in the affair, losing it in the seventh when Raggs' single got past "ole man Lloyd" at short. The Black Sox rebounded in the next two games, winning 8–2 and 4–3, closing within ten percentage points of Hilldale and the league lead.[6]

The next week, Hilldale split a pair of games with Brooklyn, winning the first game, 5–4. They then swept a non-league twin bill against a team from Elizabeth, New Jersey, 7–5 and 9–8, allegedly "the first double defeat for Elizabeth ever." After dropping two to the Bacharachs, Hilldale "swamped" Atlantic City, 10–2, getting to "Big Boy" Roberts in the sixth inning on three singles, a walk, an error and a double steal. They bested the Bacharachs again a week later, 7–

Rookie shortstop Bill Yancey later recalled, "[Lloyd] was like a father to me. I was just a kid and he was the great Lloyd I'd heard so much about, and he's the one who taught me to play shortstop."

5, before topping the Lincoln Giants, 5–2. By the middle of June, Lloyd's men stood alone in first place with an overall record of 26–10–1. George Johnson, Hilldale's speedy outfielder, led the league in home runs, stolen bases, and batting at .456, closely followed by Lloyd at .452.[7]

On June 21, and before an estimated 7,000 fans at Hilldale Park in Darby, Pennsylvania, "the murderous bludgeons of Captain John Henry Lloyd and 'Biz' Mackey, coupled with the air-tight relief pitching of 'Red' Ryan, gave Hilldale a hard fought 3–2 victory over the Lincoln Giants." Lloyd scored two of Hilldale's three runs, Mackey driving him in both times, with Briggs scoring the other on a Lloyd double. The Lincolns tied things at two-all in the eighth on a "Highpockets" Hudspeth triple before Lloyd went to his pen, bringing on Ryan who summarily ended the inning. In the bottom of the ninth, Hilldale won it when Lloyd doubled and came home on Mackey's sharp single to left center.[8]

Hilldale then took three from the Baltimore Black Sox, the last a 16–2 shellacking which prompted fans of the losing team to pour out in disgust over their club's "indifferent playing." Lloyd, "playing the true role of a leader," had been delivering in the clutch, turning apparent losses into wins, ably assisted by Biz Mackey, Tank Carr, George Johnson, Otto Briggs and Clint Thomas. The win kept Hilldale in first place with a league record of 15–7, just ahead of the hard-charging Cuban Stars, who were 11–5.[9]

While Hilldale kept a "dizzy pace" during the season's early stanza, it was the Cubans who were being viewed as the league's "sensation," playing all of their games on the road yet stringing together wins, including consecutive sweeps against Baltimore and the Bacharachs. With a lineup featuring Pelayo Chacon, Champion Mesa, Alejandro Oms, Bernardo Baró, a young Martín Dihigo, and pitchers Juanelo Mirabal and "spitball demon" Oscar Levis, Alex Pompéz's team, with clutch hitting and good pitching, was "intent upon packing the laurels of the new league back to the islands." Juanelo Mirabal, a hard-throwing right-hander who was born in Tampa of Cuban parentage yet was raised in Havana, proved effective against Hilldale throughout his career.[10]

On July 4, and with eastern team owners Ed Bolden, Alejandro Pompéz, Nat Strong and others meeting for the first time since the season got under way, Hilldale touched the Lincoln Giants for another close win, 2–1. At the meeting, the club owners all enthusiastically celebrated what had taken place in the league so far, with only minimal changes offered, such as finding more games for the Cubans, Bacharachs, and Royal Giants, each of whom had not played as many games to that point in the season. On the diamond, Hilldale rallied in the ninth inning for the win, again largely on the bats of Lloyd and Mackey. This time, however, it was "fleet" centerfielder George Johnson who saved the day, making a "sensational one-handed catch" of a deep Red Singer line drive to left center field that would have put the Lincolns up. It was the second long blast of the day for Singer, the clean-up-hitting second baseman who had belted a homer in the second inning. The Lincolns dispatched, Lloyd's pacesetters looked toward a pending showdown with Pompéz's Cuban Stars.[11]

With an estimated 7,000 fans jamming Darby Park on Saturday, July 12, Hilldale retained first place, checking the "Sensational Islanders," 6–4, rallying from a 4–0 deficit. The Cubans started things in the first inning when Mesa beat out a swinging bunt and advanced to second on Santop's drop of a called third strike on Baró. Oms next beat out a high grounder to Lloyd, followed by Chacon's grounder to first that he beat out when Winters dropped Allen's throw, allowing Mesa to score. In the fourth, Chacon led off with a double and was still on second when, with two outs, José Maria Fernandez laced a sharp single to center field, scoring him. Bartolo Portuondo then walked, and Oscar Levis banged one off the center field fence, clearing the bases, before being cut down on an aggressive play at third base. With a four-run lead, Levis had played the percentages, attempting to stretch the double into a triple, and it took a perfect relay from George Johnson to Clint Thomas to Judy Johnson to get him.[12]

With three and a half innings in the book, Hilldale got to the previously untouchable Levis, who as *Pittsburgh Courier* columnist Rollo Wilson remarked, may have left his best stuff on the basepaths. Frank Warfield led off with a single, advancing to second when Lloyd's attempted sacrifice was botched for a hit when no one covered first. With two men on, Mackey grounded to second, where Recurvon Teran fumbled the ball as Lloyd slid hard into the bag, severely wrenching his knee in the process. Lloyd had to be carried from the field; Phil Cockrell went in to run for him. With the bases drunk, however, Levis bore down, forcing Warfield at the plate on a come-backer from Thomas. The "Havana Cigarro" then struck out both George and Judy Johnson to get back in the dugout.[13]

Down by four runs, and with Lloyd in the clubhouse, the faithful were restless. The outcome looked dire for Hilldale. In the fifth, Levis weakened; Nip Winters doubled, Warfield tripled, and Mackey singled, narrowing the Cubans lead to a pair. That is where it stayed until the bottom of the eighth when "clean hits" by Mackey, George Johnson, Judy Johnson, Tom Allen, Winters and Briggs brought four "big runs" home to give Hilldale the lead, 6–4. The Cubans made a "desperate" push in the ninth, but were closed out by Nip Winters for the win. It had been a great game, one signaling Hilldale's resiliency to the rest of the league and to the Cubans in particular.[14]

With Lloyd on the bench "taking things easy" for the next month, Hill-dale played consistent ball, the "reserves keeping them out front" to the extent that by August 11, having just dropped a double dip to the Lincoln Giants, they still led the league at 28–13.[15] With the August heat beating down, Hill-dale swept four games from the Bacharachs, driving their old nemesis, "Rats" Henderson, from the box in three of the affairs. Lloyd's only concern to that point in the campaign was his pitching, which had been weakened by injuries. With Red Ryan returning from the injured list, however, and with Sam Ross, who had been driven to the hospital by an errant liner, back any day, Lloyd had "high hopes" that his team's pitching worries would soon be over.[16]

To help Lloyd with his pitching, Ed Bolden secured the use of Doc

Sykes, on loan from Baltimore, to shore things up. A week later, however, the pitching still looked ragged as the Brooklyn Royal Giants came in and pasted the Daisies, 11–6. Hilldale then lost another close one, this time to a team of all-stars from the Philadelphia Baseball Association, 2–1. The game with Brooklyn developed into a "free-hitting affair" with Scrip Lee taking most of the punishment. The Royals pounded him for 15 hits, Jacksonville's Bunny Downs leading the way with three singles. In need of offense, Lloyd finally came off the bench for the light-hitting Stevens, and quickly picked up two hits.[17]

Lloyd was still in the lineup a few days later when the Royal Giants again bested Hilldale, this time a ten-inning affair, 4–2. It was the pitching and hitting of Dick Redding, described by Rollo Wilson in the *Courier* as the "Bronze Behemoth of Brooklyn ... back from the baseball grave," who won it for the Royals with a two-run tenth-inning clout. "Cannonball" was the man that day and as Wilson aptly stated, "nobody could have beaten the Royals on Saturday."[18]

In front of a paltry 2,000 fans, one of the smallest gates of the year, and with the Royals up by one in the fifth inning, Lloyd singled to right, driving in Warfield from second to square things. In the eighth inning, though, with none on, Redding "rode one out of the park" for the lead. Hilldale scratched back in the ninth when Clint Thomas stuck his hand in front of one of Redding's fastballs "and it took five minutes to pry his fingers apart." Cockrell, running for Thomas at first, advanced to third on George Johnson's infield single, and following a walk to Mackey came home on Wade Hampton's "desperate shot" to right center field, this time knotting the game at 2–2. Into the tenth they went, each team battling to win what Rollo Wilson called "the best game of the year." With one out in the top of the frame, William Woods, just over from the Washington Potomacs, singled, again bringing Redding to the plate. Claiming he "had a date in Frankford" Redding won it with another long drive over the wall for a two-run homer. Redding's shot brought Hilldale half a game closer to the pack, if only for a moment.[19]

With summer cascading to fall, Hilldale remained in first place, ten games up in the win column, finally clinching things by the end of September.[20] Biz Mackey, winner of that season's mythical Fleet Walker Award, was hailed as the "Babe Ruth of the Eastern League," batting .440. "Pop" Lloyd, continuing to show everyone that the old man could still hit, finished second at .410.[21] But not all was cordial in Darby. On September 29, a "discreet paragraph in the white newspapers" announced that "to keep down dissension and correct matters which had crept into the situation, Ed Bolden had reorganized the Hilldale team for the P.B.A. (Philadelphia Baseball Association) championships and the five-game series with the Athletics" by suspending manager John Henry Lloyd with pay for ten days. Philadelphia fans were said to have been "up in arms" over what they considered to be an injustice to their "Miracle Man," the guy who had taken their team to the top. Under Lloyd's tutelage, Hilldale had won 137 games, lost 43 and tied 6 of 186 games played during the campaign.[22]

The dissension noted in the *Courier* may have involved Clint Thomas, the outfielder brought over from Detroit who, after batting .305, figured he deserved a raise. When he approached Bolden for one, choosing to go around Lloyd, the owner was said to have granted it. Lloyd, however, reportedly blocked the raise, angering Thomas, who later recalled, "Lloyd thought he owned me ... I never had much use for him from that time on." Pitcher Holsey "Scrip" Lee believed the issue was economics, asserting that Bolden could simply get Warfield as player-manager for half of what he had been paying Lloyd. Jake Stephens felt it was a performance issue, arguing that Hilldale had brought Lloyd over to replace him a shortstop, but "the old man couldn't do it. He was washed up. He could hit that ball, but you've got to cover territory. He didn't replace me; they retired *him!*"[23]

A week later Lloyd told Rollo Wilson that the ten days' suspension had in fact been extended "to include the balance of the season and forever." Lloyd said that he had been paid to the end of the season and informed by Bolden that his services were no longer required. The press release from Hilldale stated that Warfield would take over for Lloyd as manager. Rollo Wilson noted that Warfield had managerial designs and had become "a little messenger, sub rosa, from the club house to the office." Wilson also complained that fans, the ones who paid "the freight," were being kept in the dark as to the reasons for the changes. "[I]t was the strong hand of Lloyd which kept the temperamental (new) stars in line," Wilson asserted. "His

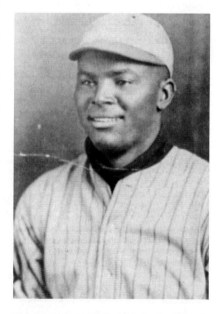

Raleigh "Biz" Mackey, a physical, hard-hitting catcher, exhibited defensive skills which were unsurpassed in the history of black baseball. Hall of Famer Roy Campanella credited Mackey with teaching him the finer points of catching.

diplomacy made them play the game. His fielding and hitting were features day by day." "Need anyone wonder," Wilson concluded, "that the fans are not satisfied?"[24]

By October 20, Lloyd and his wife Lizzie, along with Mack Eggleston and his wife, had safely arrived in Cuba, where they wrote Rollo Wilson at the *Courier*, explaining that things were good and that they were readying for the start of the Cuban winter league. The circuit was expected to have four teams: Marianao, Havana, Almendares and Santa Clara. Lloyd was named captain and shortstop of the Havana *Leones* or Reds, with Eggleston the catcher and Adolfo Luque the team's manager. Ironically, Clint Thomas and Nip Winters of Hilldale were both expected to join Lloyd and Havana in time for the season.[25] If Thomas and Lloyd had problems with each other, as was alluded to in the *Courier*, it did not show early as Thomas, playing center field for the Reds got four hits in his first game, becoming "a popular hero overnight." For his part, Lloyd played first base, continuing to grind out his "daily hits" when they counted most, such as against Almendares when Lloyd grounded one through Mike Herrera's wickets at second, was sacrificed to second, and scored on Hooks Jimenez's single to win it.[26]

As the season commenced, Santa Clara, boasting Oscar Charleston, Alejandro Oms, and Frank Warfield, got off to a fast start, with an .857 winning percentage by November 22. Lloyd's Reds, however, were dogged, pursuing the Leopards until during one stretch in late November they swept five consecutive games from Santa Clara, pulling within two games of the league lead. Lloyd and Clint Thomas were playing "wonderful baseball." On November 24, with Oscar Levis pitching for the Reds, Havana took the measure of Santa Clara, 9–5. A day later, with Luque on the hill, Thomas got two hits, while Lloyd, back at shortstop, scratched out one in leading the Reds to another win over the Leopards, this time 6–2. Levis came on in relief the next day, securing another win for the Reds, 9–6, while Andy Cooper shut the Leopards down three days later, 5–1.[27]

As word came of a second meeting of "Eastern Colored League Magnates," one in which it was determined that eight teams would be set to play in 1924, Havana topped Marianao, 7–3. It was the strong pitching of Oscar Levis and overall play of both Thomas and Lloyd that proved to be too much for Mariano. Lloyd, Thomas and Hooks Jimenez each had two hits for the Reds, while Levis scattered five hits over nine innings. The next afternoon, with Juanelo Mirabal pitching, the Reds shut out Marianao, 9–0. Marianao finally broke through against the Reds two days later, winning 3–1. That game, played at Almendares Park, was sewn up by Marianao in the fifth inning when D. Brown singled to right, Cooney singled over second, and Branon walked, loading the bases. With Luque on in relief for Red Ryan, Jimenez made a "spectacular catch" of E. Brown's liner over second, doubling Cooney up at second. Charlie Dressen walked and Beschoff threw to third trying to catch Brown napping, but Brown dashed home safely when Jimenez's throw went wide of the plate. Schreiber popped out to Lloyd to end the inning. Jess Petty held the Reds to five lone hits, three by Jacinto Calvo, Havana's center fielder.[28]

By the end of December, Santa Clara was still setting a "rapid pace" for the league with a .750 winning percentage, followed by Havana at .548, Almendares at .414 and Marianao at .300. Eugenio Morin, one of the finest infielders to come out of Cuba in the early twentieth century, now a catcher for Almendares, led the league in batting at .615, closely trailed by Dick Lundy, who had just arrived in Cuba and was batting .500 for Almendares. Of those with at least 100 at bats, Paito (Cpeto) was batting .374 for Almendares, with Oliver Marcelle hitting .373 and Oscar Charleston .363 for Santa Clara. In close to 120 at-bats, Lloyd was hitting over .280, while Thomas was at .282.[29]

On December 29, Havana bunched their hits in the second inning, scoring six runs to drive Nip Winters from the box, routing Almendares, 11–5. Lloyd's all-around play led the way for the Reds, with Juanelo Mirabal getting the win. Nip Winters and Almendares fought back a day later, however, besting Red Ryan, 7–5. The Alcranes then topped Santa Clara, 8–6, in a hard-fought contest. It was Winters again, this time pinch-hitting in the eighth inning, who made the difference, driving in two runs with a single.[30]

Oliver Marcelle, nicknamed "the Ghost," was an incredible defensive third baseman, whose glove wizardry at the hot corner earned him a legion of fans and a great deal of respect.

Though all four teams playing in Cuba that winter featured outstanding lineups, it was Santa Clara that ruled Cuban baseball in 1923–24, fielding one of the greatest teams in the island's history. With a team batting average of .331 and a stellar outfield consisting of Oscar Charleston, Champion Mesa, and Alejandro Oms, the Leopards were difficult to face under most circumstances. When mixing in an infield of Frank Warfield, Dobie Moore, Oliver Marcelle and Heavy Johnson, and the pitching of Dave Brown, Bill Holland, and Rube Currie, the club was simply unbeatable.[31]

Having been purged at Hilldale, it made sense that when Lloyd returned from Cuba, he would rejoin the Bacharach Giants; a club playing in what had become Lloyd's adopted hometown of Atlantic City. With the Bacharachs, Lloyd again performed the duties of player-manager, but this time, having the "acrobatic young shortstop," Dick Lundy, in place, Lloyd moved over to second base, marking the first time he had done so in 20 years. While some, such as Chance Cummings, later insisted that Lundy, also a native of Jacksonville, was as good as or better than Lloyd at shortstop, Lloyd could still outhit him, batting .427 in 1924 compared to Lundy's .365.[32]

*   *   *

By 1924, an unprecedented outburst of creativity among African Americans had flowered in all fields of art, including sports. What began as a series of literary discussions in Greenwich Village and Harlem evolved into an African-American cultural movement known as the Harlem Renaissance. The Harlem Renaissance carried the unique culture experiences of African America to Main Street, encouraging black folk to celebrate their heritage, becoming, as social critic Alain LeRoy Locke proclaimed, "The New Negro." At a time when white supremacist groups such as the Ku Klux Klan professed to have between six and ten million members nationwide, including elected officials, this was a remarkable departure.[33]

One of the factors contributing to the rise of the Harlem Renaissance was the great migration of African Americans to northern cities between 1919 and 1926. In his influential book *The New Negro*, Locke described the northward migration of blacks as more than a search for economic opportunity, but as a "spiritual emancipation." Black urban migration, combined with the rise of radical black intellectuals — including Locke, Marcus Garvey, and W. E. B. DuBois, editor of *The Crisis* magazine — all contributed to the styles and unprecedented success of black artists during the period.[34]

Renaissance writers such as Langston Hughes, James Weldon Johnson, Zora Neale Hurston, and Ida B. Wells-Barnett exemplified a new cultural pluralism, claiming their identity as Americans while articulating the culture and experiences of African Americans. Many of their works contained antiracist political messages and uplifting tones.

The music of black America proved to be such an important maker of the era that it provided the 1920s with its most lasting moniker, *The Jazz Age*. Rising not from Harlem but from New Orleans, Chicago, and St. Louis, jazz was central to the black arts movement and the emerging national culture. Through recordings and radio, jazz musicians such as Duke Ellington, Louis Armstrong, Fletcher Henderson and Jelly Roll Morton reached a wide audience, primarily among blacks but increasingly among whites who embraced the new style as their own. The blues, a style of music reflecting themes of working-class protest and resistance to racism, also found its way north, appealing to wider audiences.[35]

At the time, few people outside the black community took the Harlem Renaissance seriously as a major artistic movement. Nevertheless, the black community's cultural vitality in the 1920s contributed to the creation of a national culture, one in which sports played an increasing role. It was not out of the ordinary for columnists in the black press, caught up in the energy of the moment, to look for a time in the near future when black ballplayers could prove their worth as players and men on a field with the best ballplayers that white baseball offered. The dream proved premature, for in spite of the Harlem Renaissance, African Americans continued to face segregation and lynching as well as limited political and economic opportunities.[36]

With Lloyd set to play in Atlantic City that season, Rollo Wilson glibly let slip that Lloyd would have a surprise in store for his teammates on the Bacharachs when he arrived:

> The fact that *John Hennery* is bringing an alligator back from Cuba with him as a mascot and bat boy for the Atlantic City Bacharachs is arousing a good bit of interest here in the East. A specially prepared tank is being built for him. And it will be mounted on a flivver chassis. A standing order has been filed with the various steamship companies for a barrel of Cuban water to be delivered on each trip. This will be used to replenish the water in the tank. Mr. Lloyd, which is slang for John Henry, cables us that his pet alligator is learning a little more day by day. He says that he puts it in the refrigerator for a few minutes every day in order to accustom it to the colder climate of Atlantic City. There is some talk of listing "Money" as a player so he may be sent in as a pinch runner for old man Cummings on those hot days to come when his "dogs" will be yelping and snapping at the heat. The veteran first baseman says OK if it is for the good of the team.[37]

Lloyd's Bacharachs, minus the gator, jumped to an early lead in 1924, landing atop the standings at 5–1 by late May. A June swoon, however, combined with Hilldale's resurgence, dropped the Bacharachs from contention, and by Independence Day they were in fourth place with a record of 13–12.[38]

At the same time, black baseball was taking care of one of its own by raising money for Bill Pettus, formerly a first baseman for the Lincoln Giants, who was at the Sea View Hospital on Staten Island suffering from tuberculosis. In a game between the Lincolns and the Bronx Royal Giants played on June 29 at the Catholic Protectory Oval in the Bronx, $255.50 was raised to assist in Pettus' care. James J. Keenan, owner of the Lincolns, pitched in $25 himself. Another $125.75 was raised a week later, but by August 22, after a "game fight" with the disease, the 42-year-old Pettus was dead.[39]

In mid–July the Bacharachs took a pair from the slumping Lincoln Giants, 7–5 and 3–1. In the first affair, Hubert Lockhart scattered ten hits and five runs, while his offense collected seven runs on 11 hits. Dick Lundy led the way with two hits, and Lloyd had one. Lundy gathered two more hits in game two, but a combination of Dave Brown and Fred Daniels held Lloyd hitless. This was no small feat in that from June 29 to July 4, Lloyd had made 11 straight hits, tying the white baseball record held by Tris Speaker (later set at 12 by Pinky Higgins and Walt Dropo). In the span, Lloyd went 8-for-8 in two games against the Potomacs, and then got three more hits against Harrisburg before finally being set down, once, by Daltie Cooper of Harrisburg. Lloyd added three more knocks, giving him hits in 14 of 15 at-bats. Also in the streak, Lloyd had 26 total bases, including a double, a triple and three home runs. By mid–July, Lloyd was batting .407, enough for fourth place in the Eastern League trailing only Charleston, Santop and Lundy.[40]

With Lundy continuing at short and Lloyd at second, the Bacharachs dropped a 13–9 barnburner to Hilldale on July 20. The loss pushed Lloyd's club further into the pack and by late August it stood in fifth place at 22–22. At the same time, however, Lloyd was third in the league in batting with a .457 average. The Bacharachs remained in the middle of the pack for the rest of the year, closing things out in fifth place, just above .500 at 34–30. As Hilldale and the Kansas City Monarchs prepared for the first series where the winners of the western and the eastern leagues met, Lloyd once again traveled to Cuba, where as usual he raked with the best of them, batting .372 in 196 at bats.[41]

In Cuba for the 1924-25 season, Lloyd signed on with Almendares, joining Adolfo Luque, who was back pitching after a stint as manager, Manuel Cueto, and Oscar Charleston, over from Santa Clara, to form a potent lineup. With Santa Clara, minus Charleston, not what it was a year earlier, and facing financial hardship, Havana, with Martin Dihigo, Pelayo Chacon, Torriente and Mike Gonzalez, was thought to be Almendares' toughest competition. It did not play out that way, however, as the Alcranes sprinted to an 81/2 game league by early January, and were so dominating that when taken with the league's overall financial difficulties, forced management into declaring Almendares the champions and canceling the remaining games.[42]

*   *   *

With Lloyd in Cuba, nearly a "full quota" of commissioners from the Eastern Colored League gathered on January 24, 1925, at the Christian Street Y.M.C.A in Philadelphia to discuss pending issues for the coming season. Those in attendance included Nat Strong, Alex Pompéz, Jim Keenan, Ed Bolden and George W. Robinson, each with the task of drawing up a temporary schedule for the coming season, one that would be ratified at a later meeting. In doing so, the commissioners agreed to adopt a 70-game schedule, just as they had in 1924, but recognizing that unplayed games the year before had left a sour taste in the mouth of many fans, they determined to do a better job of balancing the schedule, this time insisting that the clubs play out their allotted ballgames. They also addressed "the umpire situation," namely agreeing to secure an efficient corps of rotating umpires to officiate league games, rather than assigning "homer" umpires to each of the individual parks.[43]

At the same time the Negro National League, or Western League, was being reorganized, while the Detroit Stars were brought under the management of new team owner George Hutchinson. On February 2, 1925, at its annual meeting, it was decided that the circuit would be reorganized with the following clubs, all of which had to qualify financially within 30 days: Chicago, St. Louis, Kansas City, Birmingham, Memphis, Indianapolis, Detroit and the Cuban Stars of Chicago. To that point, the only clubs to have qualified with paid-up memberships in the association were the Chicago American Giants, Kansas City Monarchs, St. Louis Stars and Cuban Stars. By the time the owners met again in early March, most of the arrangements for qualifying Detroit, Indianapolis, Birmingham and Memphis had been made.[44]

An estimated 5,000 people also turned out that February to say goodbye to Marcus Garvey as he entered federal prison in Atlanta. Garvey, the controversial leader of the Universal Negro Improvement Association, had been convicted of mail fraud two years earlier, and with his appeals now exhausted was set to enter prison. While many rightly pointed to the fact that it was Garvey's politics that were on trial, the charges of mail fraud stuck, and with it came a five-year sentence, one which was ultimately commuted by President Calvin Coolidge. Upon release, Garvey was deported to Jamaica, forcing him to lead his crusade from foreign shores for the remainder of his life. "Look for me in the whirlwind of the storm," he said, "for with God's grace, I shall come ... to aid you in the fight for Liberty, Freedom and Life."[45]

Alex Pompéz's Negro National League entry, the Cuban Stars, was an interesting club to watch in 1925. It was said that with the "ides of March," Pompéz would board his "rattler" for the Florida Keys where he would embark to his native "Queen of the Antilles," Cuba, in search of new talent to bolster his club. On paper at least, his team hardly needed bolstering, with a lineup featuring a young Martín Dihigo, Pelayo Chacón, Alejandro Oms, Champion Mesa and Juanelo Mirabal. And with Oscar Levis, Dihigo, Mirabal and Bernardo Baró in tow, the rotation was stalwart. While not yet *El Inmortal*, Dihigo pitched and played second base for the Stars that season, batting .299 with a 4–7 record. Pompéz, who refused to sign African Americans, prowled Cuba, Puerto Rico, Santo Domingo, and even the smallish St. Kitts and St. Thomas in search of more "apple busters."[46]

Lloyd Thompson of the *Age* anticipated that many of the "purveyors of baseball in the east" would be in top condition when the season rolled in. "Many of the players have worked through the winter among the Cuban and Florida palms," Thompson wrote, "and are in good physical shape already." The Bacharachs, he said, "down Atlantic City way," did not look to offer any major changes from the previous year. As the "field general of the seashore contingent," Lloyd looked to pencil in Yump Jones and Ernie Gatewood behind the plate, "Rats" Henderson, Johnny Harper, Red Grier and Hubert Lockhart on the mound, "Chance" Cummings, Lloyd, Lundy and Johnny George across the infield, and Charlie Mason, Chaney White and Ambrose Reid in the outfield. By June, third base was anchored by Oliver "Ghost" Marcelle, coming over in a trade from the Lincoln Giants for Mason, Tom Finley and Harper, giving the Bacharachs what historian Lawrence Hogan described as one of the "finest defensive infields of all time."[47]

Alex Pompez. A sports promoter, numbers banker, and influential owner, he helped negotiate the first Negro World Series, in 1924 (courtesy Negro Leagues Baseball Museum).

Some of the biggest news of the early season involved personnel moves. In a singular act of bargaining defiance,

Gerard Williams, the lively shortstop of the Lincoln Giants, held himself out of the March 29 season opener. Williams, who had spent the winter playing in Palm Beach and was rumored to be in great shape, had wired the Lincolns' owner, Jim Keenan, for his railroad fare. The money was sent and there was no indication that the shortstop was not going to play until shortly before the game when Williams, perhaps disgruntled over his salary, asserted that it was "too cold to play baseball" and sat out. Two weeks later, on Easter, the "peppy shortstop" was released from his contract along with team manager "Smokey Joe" Williams and Cleo Smith, to play in Pittsburgh for Cum Posey and his Homestead Grays.[48]

With George Scales now at shortstop for the Lincolns and Oliver Marcelle at third, the third season of the Eastern Colored League opened at the Catholic Protectory Oval with New York taking a doubleheader from the Bacharachs, 6–1 and 4–3. In the first affair, "Rats" Henderson opposed Dave Brown in what was said to have been a "pitching duel" but hardly fit the bill with the Lincolns, led by "Highpocket" Hudspeth, driving six runs across on Henderson, who was "a bit wild." The Bacharachs' lone run came on a "Pop" Lloyd single in the third, bringing Lundy around to score.[49]

The Gee brothers — Rich and Tom — were the stars of game two, the former stepping in for "Steel Arm Johnny" Taylor, after Taylor had set down the Bacharachs' heavy hitters — Young, Lundy and Lloyd — in the ninth inning. In the tenth, center fielder Tom Fial delivered a one-out single for the Lincolns, followed by Tom Gee's single, which advanced Fial to third. Following a brief discussion between Jude Gans, the Lincolns' manager, and Oliver Marcelle, Gans sent Rich Gee up to pinch-hit for "Steel" Taylor. Gee delivered a long single into right, breaking up the game and giving the Lincolns the victory. By the end of the week, Lloyd's crew was 2–2 and in third place.[50]

The following week the biggest trade of the Eastern League season was announced, with the Lincolns' Jim Keenan sending Oliver Marcelle, the "stormy petrel" of a third baseman, to the Bacharachs for three pitchers, Leroy Roberts, John Harper and Savage, a lefty. The trade, if approved, would reunite Marcelle with Lloyd, who along with Lundy would man a stellar infield. Within a month, however, the trade was skewed as John Harper refused to go along with things. Marcelle was returned to New York. Keenan, though, desperate for the arms that this trade would provide his club, pushed through and by June 27, Marcelle was on his way back to the Bacharachs, this time for Mason, Finley and Harper, who had acquiesced, at least for the moment. By July 4, however, the *Age* reported that Harper still had not shown up in New York.[51]

On May 21 the Bacharachs pushed three runs across in the top of the tenth inning to best Hilldale, 8–6. With the scored tied at five in the ninth, Hilldale booted things away as Lundy, credited with a double, nubbed a roller through Warfield's wickets at second, and was followed by Lloyd who eked out a "cheap" single when he grounded to Carr at first base and no one came over to cover the bag. Young's single scored Lundy; Lloyd came around on a fielder's choice and Young on a double steal. "Rats" Henderson, on for Gillespie, held the Daisies to a lone run in the bottom of the frame to save it.[52]

With talk of Ed Bolden breaking up Hilldale to save the Eastern League, Bolden's Daisies hung one on the Bacharachs, 11–4. The idea was that by dealing some of his veteran stars, Bolden would preserve the competition necessary to bring out fans in other Eastern League hubs, fans growing weary of the constant beatings inflicted on their clubs.[53] As proof positive, the Daisies took "Rats" Henderson for "13 solid blows" including two doubles, two triples, and a home run in its eight-run rout of the Bacharachs, leaving Hilldale atop the standings with a 14–5 record. The Bacharachs remained in third place at 11–8.[54]

On July 4, William E. Clark opined in the *Age* that the Eastern League would best be served if someone not affiliated with any particular team was placed in charge so as to avoid collapse. Clark's concern was over the refusal of players like John Harper, who flatly refused to play for Jim Keenan and his manager, Jude Gans. Clark noted that Gans had allegedly convinced Keenan early in the season to cut the pay of certain players and to let Gerald Williams and Bunny Wilson go because they asked for more money. Whether Gans had in fact done this or not, Keenan did cut ties to the players, and Clark believed that players around the league were now boycotting the Lincolns because of it. Something had to be done, Clark believed, because the fans were starting to "look upon the Eastern Colored League as a farce."[55]

This issue, along with the above noted lack of competition, may have been a reason why coverage of the Eastern League in the African-American press dropped precipitously in 1925. It got worse as several of the league clubs suffered financially through their worst seasons yet, so much so that the league's credibility was damaged. It was not just the smaller teams like Wilmington that were hurt, but the larger ones such as Brooklyn and New York. Fortunately for the Royals and Lincolns, their owners were thought to be able to take the hits without risk of failure. Wilmington could not. The *Age* reported that if league commissioners found it necessary to go back to a six-team circuit, then Wilmington and the Cuban Stars would most likely be dropped.[56]

It did not take long for the first shoe to drop. On July 25 the Wilmington Potomacs, established by Ben Taylor in Washington D.C. three years earlier before being sold to George Robinson, who moved the team to Wilmington, went "to the wall," folding up amidst its financial crisis. Robinson refused to absorb the financial strain that the losing club placed on him and opted to break up the club, with three of his players — Washington, Lindsey and Chambers — going to the Lincoln Giants, and pitcher Red Grier to the Bacharachs. League commissioners had met in Philadelphia to see if something could be done to salvage the club, but nothing definite was decided, so Robinson shut things down.[57]

A week later the *Age* reported that persistent rumors were making the rounds that another team would be dropped from the Eastern Colored League and that according to Oscar Charleston, manager at Harrisburg, it would be the Lincoln Giants. Jim Keenan, however, was "emphatic" in denying that his team would quit, stating that Charleston was not only mistaken but would be in for a shock when his club arrived for the pending series in New York. In fact, the Lincolns had been bolstered by the arrival of the new players obtained from Wilmington, as well as John Harper, obtained via trade. The fact that Keenan was the Secretary-Treasurer of the league, and that his team played in New York, the league's largest market, made Charleston's claims "ridiculous."[58]

As if to prove Keenan's point, a record crowd turned out that following week, "filling every available seat" to watch the Lincolns take on "Pop" Lloyd and the visiting Bacharachs. The Lincolns had things comfortably their way into the ninth inning before "Lloyd's sluggers" drove home four runs, taking all of the "want-to" from the Lincolns and winning 10–8. Lloyd led the way with three hits for the Bacharachs, including one in the ninth resulting in the go-ahead run. Game two proved the same with the Bacharachs clobbering the now listless Lincolns, 13–6. Keenan, incensed with his team's performance, promptly dropped both of his venerable, older pitchers, "String Bean" Williams and "Steel" Taylor. With the victories, the Bacharachs improved their overall record to 22–19, good enough for fourth place in the standings.[59]

In late August, Jude Gans, having seen enough of the Lincoln Giants, and having taken enough of the blame for its downfall, resigned, prompting Keenan to acknowledge the hard work Gans had put forth. Keenan also cut ties with George Scales, sending the team captain on his way over personal differences, and named Bill Lindsey, formerly of Wilmington, as captain. Gans' departure also sparked gossip that Lloyd would be leaving the Bacharachs to take over the helm of the Lincolns. According to William E. Clark, Lloyd had commented that his contract, which was set to expire at the end of the 1925 season, was likely not to be renewed. "The Lincolns now have a wealth of young material," Clark wrote, "who, under the guidance of an experienced leader and player such as Lloyd might develop into the championship combination New York fans have dreamed of.... Because of his record as a player and his known ability as manager and leader of men, the New York fans would be especially proud if he were called to develop a championship club in this city."[60]

It was an opportune moment for such a discussion as Lloyd and his crew were just then entering the city for a Sunday afternoon doubleheader with the Lincolns. They proved to be two of the best games played at the Oval that year. Orville Singer was the star for the home team in game one, banging a homer, triple and a single in five at-bats, just a double shy of the cycle. The Lincolns had jumped to a 2–1 lead, but in the eighth inning, Chaney White, Lloyd and Lundy got hits, pushing two runs across to go up, 3–2. It was not enough, for in the bottom of the ninth, with Rich Gee on first, Singer ended things with a two-run, walk-off homer, greatly exciting the large Sunday afternoon crowd.[61]

In the second game, Chambers faced off with Farrell in a tight matchup until the eighth inning when the Lincolns knotted things at 3–3. Farrell, not to be denied, won his own game in the ninth by driving in Lloyd with the go-ahead run and then shutting down the Lincolns for the final three outs. The 41-year-old Lloyd, batting sixth for the Bacharachs, had three hits on the day, including a double and a stolen base. With Lloyd, managing was not the only thing the New York fans could look forward to.[62]

The Bacharachs took three more games over the next two weeks, twice besting a club from Bay Ridge, 3–2 and 6–2, and splitting a double dip with the Bushwicks, 13–15, and 16–6. Lloyd continued to pound the ball, getting two hits in the first game at Bay Ridge, then seven more in Brooklyn, including a triple and double. The old man was killing the ball and there seemed no let-up in sight, even while contemporaries such as "Cannonball" Dick Redding were rumored to be calling it a day.[63]

With the season winding down and the Bacharachs settling into fourth place, Lloyd's contract was set to expire on October 15. For Lloyd, that was the end date with no question that he was still bound to Atlantic City, but certain league commissioners disagreed, arguing that when his contract had expired, he must be released by the Bacharachs and purchased by another team. Lloyd and other commissioners insisted that because his contract was not that of a player but rather a manager, he should not be considered the property of any team, the way that a player was. As the Bacharachs were unwilling to pay him the salary he demanded, he had the right to go and manage any club that he chose. Some believed that the Bacharachs' refusal to let Lloyd leave was inspired by other clubs not wanting to see Lloyd in New York.[64]

Lloyd ultimately proved to the contentious commissioners that his managerial contract with Atlantic City had been voided by the club, not him, and in view of this fact, he was released to sign with whichever team he chose. Lloyd chose the Lincoln Giants. Formal announcement of the agreement was made in late January, 1926, following months of negotiations between Lloyd and Jim Keenan. The *Age* reported that the agreement reached between the two men gave Lloyd complete control of the team for at least two years. It would be up to Lloyd to build the kind of team he had put together at Hilldale, and ten years earlier in New York. With his immediate future ironed out and bat in hand, Lloyd headed south again to play winter ball in Cuba.[65]

EIGHT

You'd Think He Was Still a Young Man

Lloyd's time in Cuba during the 1925-26 winter season was cut short after San Jose, the league's third team, folded on December 22 because of money issues and bad weather. Some of the rain had come from the *Florida Hurricane*, forming in late November, nearly a month after the official end of the hurricane season. This was only the third hurricane to have developed after November 1 in the North Atlantic Ocean since 1886. While cyclone-force winds and sporadic rain were reported on the island, much of its impact was felt in Florida, where damages were estimated in the millions along with four fatalities near Tampa. Lloyd, keeping his powder dry, batted .387 in 163 at-bats, good enough for third in the league.[1]

That spring Lloyd took over as player-manager of the New York Lincoln Giants, batting .342 in 40 games. At third base for the Lincolns that season was George Scales, back from a brief sojourn with the Homestead Grays and Newark Stars, and having patched up his differences with team owner Jim Keenan; he remained one of the most consistent right-handed hitters in the league. Scales "feasted on curveballs." He was also a versatile fielder who could play anywhere. Scales was a bit on the "portly side and lacking speed," but "compensated by studying the hitters, positioning himself accordingly, and throwing runners out with his rifle arm." Scales had a great amount of respect for Lloyd's abilities. Years later, Scales recalled, "When I first met Lloyd, he was an old man. He was a line drive hitter, a big 'ol batter who just laid on the ball. The older he got, the better he knew how to play. You'd think he was still a young man."[2]

In late March and with the coming Eastern League season still in limbo, team owners turned out "en masse" for another meeting at the Christian Street Y.M.C.A. in Philadelphia to map things out. While it was thought that Hill-dale would once again have the best chance at a pennant, it was noted that the Lincoln Giants, with the "venerable" Lloyd at the helm, might put up some resistance.[3]

In April, Lloyd opted to play some preseason games to test his squad. Doing so, the Lincolns got off to a "false start" when they dropped a Sunday afternoon affair at the Oval, 6–5, to the Bronx Giants. Under frigid skies, and with a thin crowd of 1,500 in the stands, the two clubs were knotted into the ninth inning before the Bronx Giants pushed two runs across, then held on to win it. The freezing weather did not help, as most of the players had recently returned from Florida and Cuba. Lloyd, Lindsay, and Ramirez all had hits for the Lincolns, while Roberts, on for Simmons, allowed just three hits in five and a third innings. With a couple more practice series on tap, Lloyd promised that his new club, featuring Ramiro Ramírez, "the noted Cuban centerfielder," Joe Lewis and George Johnson, would "surprise the fans" with its play.[4]

Two weeks later, "playing a much improved brand of ball, but still getting the worst of the breaks," the Lincolns came from behind to tie the Bloomfield Elks, 4–4, before dropping another round to the Bronx Giants, 6–4. After two more difficult sets, another with Bloomfield and one with Tuckahoe, it was becoming clear that regardless of what the pundits were projecting, Lloyd's work was cut out for him in 1926.[5]

With the official season opener upon them, the Lincolns were trumpeted in the *Amsterdam News* as "Jim Keenan's New Diamond Stars, a team whom the eyes of the people of greater New York are centered and who carry their hopes for victory this season." Those hopeful eyes were promptly reddened, however, as the Lincolns were "outclassed" in both halves of the lid-lifting doubleheader with Hilldale, 14–8 and 17–1. Under ideal conditions, and in front of 6,000 fans, Lloyd chose to go with the young arms of Rube Chambers and Howard, both of whom struggled. Meanwhile, Clint Thomas, Hilldale's centerfielder, banged out two homers and a double in four at-bats in the second game to pace the Daisies. The Lincolns weakness, pitching, or a lack of experienced pitchers, hurt them all season long.[6]

If Lloyd's team was to put up wins, it would have to rely on its offense, and that is what happened the following week in a home doubleheader against the Bacharach Giants. After Red Grier held them to two runs in the first game, the Lincolns opened up in game two, winning 11–7. Nine of the Lincolns' 11 runs came in the sixth inning, when the Bacharachs were forced to use "the whole pitching staff" to retire the side. "Speed" Gilmore, one of Lloyd's "busher pitchers," making his first appearance in the Eastern League, "made good," holding the Bacharachs in check, especially with runners on base. "The visitors did their best to get Gilmore rattled, but he was cool under fire."[7]

The Lincolns continued to hit as they "made Hilldale look foolish," winning 13–6, before taking both ends of a weekend doubleheader from New Brunswick, 18–9, and a team from Pottstown, Pennsylvania, 12–4. Orville Singer feasted on Pottstown pitching, belting a homer, two doubles and a single in five at-bats, with Lloyd going yard as well. With the season slipping into June, the Lincolns were just two steps out of the cellar, at 3–4 in league games.[8]

By late June, however, injuries were taking a toll on the Lincolns, forcing Lloyd deep into the bush, bringing up Charlie Lewis, a 19-year-old shortstop to replace the retiring Bill Lindsey. Although making his first attempt in professional baseball, Lewis had impressed Lloyd as being an exceptional ballplayer. He was thought to be good on grounders, while at the plate he reminded Lloyd of Gerard Williams. Lloyd also brought in another young pitcher, Charlie Craig, a 21-year-old hurler, who in his first game beat Hilldale, 3–1. It was Craig's only win of the year, and he spent most of his career with lesser ball clubs.[9]

On June 27, the youngsters were on display at the Catholic Protectory Oval against Oscar Charleston and his first-place Harrisburg Giants. In the first game, Lewis played shortstop, alongside Lloyd at second, going 1-for-5 at the plate as the Lincolns routed Harrisburg, 14–7. Craig, with the win against Hilldale in his pocket, pitched game two but was shelled, losing 17–5. In baseball, you are only as good as your last game, and Lloyd, recognizing this, shuffled his lineup constantly, reaching and doing whatever it took to field a competitive team. But with youth comes inconsistency, and that is what Lloyd got, an inconsistent bunch that battled throughout the campaign but failed to overtake the more talented, experienced Bacharachs and Hilldale on anything resembling a regular basis.[10]

They did have their moments, however, such as a Fourth of July holiday doubleheader when they delivered a "double drubbing" to the "crack" Camden, New Jersey, club. In the first game the lefty Rube Chambers scattered three hits, fanning eight batters in the 9–1 victory. The Lincolns gathered 13 hits in the win, Berdell Young leading the way with two doubles and a single. The Lincolns had the game sewn up by the third inning when Young, leading off, doubled and scored on Willie Gisentaner's single. Lloyd's "two ply smash" and Bob Hudspeth's walk filled the bases, before Tom Finlay singled, scoring Gisentaner and Lloyd, Hudspeth going to third. Hudspeth scored on Rich Gee's sacrifice fly. The Lincolns posted three more runs in the sixth on two doubles, a single and a sacrifice fly. Camden cried uncle in the seventh, the remainder of the game called off by agreement.[11]

The second game, "a slugging match," was even better for the Lincolns as they won it in the ninth inning, 12–11. Going into the sixth inning the Lincolns were five runs down, but with the sacks full and two outs, "Pop" Lloyd drove a "mighty wallop" over the right field fence, clearing the bases with a grand slam. "Highpockets" Hudspeth then doubled and scored on George Johnson's single. Tom Finlay walked and Rich Gee singled, scoring Johnson with the tying run, bringing the score to 10–10. Camden scored in the top of the seventh to go ahead, but the Lincolns tied things in the eighth. With the game tied 11–11 in the ninth, Finlay walked and Rich Gee bunted safely before Tom Gee advanced both runners with a sacrifice. After Joe Lewis fanned with two runners in scoring position, Young, a part-time outfielder, singled to center, scoring Finlay with the game-winning run.[12]

In early August the Bacharach Giants, having won 15 of their previous 16 games and sprinting to the top of the league standings, came into the Catholic Protectory Oval for a double-header with the Lincolns. Lloyd's young squad surprised them, however, taking both ends, 4–0, and 7–5.[13]

Both games were pitching duels, with "Rats" Henderson and Rube Chambers battling in the first affair, and Red Grier facing Willie Gisentaner in the second. The Bacharachs' veteran hurlers had a slight advantage in the number of hits allowed, but the Lincolns gave their guys better support, bunching needed hits when it mattered most. Henderson allowed the Lincolns a scant four hits across eight innings in the lid-lifter, two of which went to Bill Mason, the Lincolns' newly acquired left fielder, the first a run-scoring single, followed by a triple. Red Grier had the Lincolns at his mercy into the sixth inning before losing command and allowing two men aboard. Tom Finlay then banged a three-run homer to tie things at 5–5 before the Lincolns pushed two more runs across in the eighth to seal the victory.[14]

The latter contest was marred somewhat when Oliver Marcelle was thrown out of the game by the umpire for arguing a call. When Marcelle refused to leave the field promptly, the umpire ended things, forfeiting the game to the Lincolns. Jim Keenan, however, a league commissioner as well as club owner, upon meeting with Lloyd and Dick Lundy, overruled this "too technical decision" and ordered the game completed, which it was.[15]

The doubleheader with the Bacharachs was the last good pitching Lloyd would see from his squad for a least a month. They returned to form, however, on Sunday, August 29, taking another doubleheader from Camden, 4–3 and 8–7. The Lincolns' Arthur "Rube" Chambers got the better of Camden's John "Rube" Chambers in the first contest, pitching his best ball of the summer and holding Camden to seven hits. He was supported on offense by Mason and Lloyd, both of whom hit home runs. Lloyd added two more hits in the second game, keeping his own marvelous season alive.[16]

Later that same week, the Lincolns, despite inclement weather, were able to take one game of a scheduled double dip from the Bronx Giants at the Oval, 9–1. With Rube Chambers, again in excellent form, and the entire Lincolns squad hitting better than usual, the Lincolns jumped out to an early lead. A wild pitch by Chambers in the ninth inning allowed the Giants' lone tally. Lloyd, playing second base, led the way on offense with three hits, while "Big Bill" Mason hit what many at the ball park that day believed was the longest home run ever hit there, a bomb that cleared the top of the trees in right center.[17]

In the middle of September it was announced that the Eastern League had extended its season to the end of the month, thereby allowing for the makeup of a last few games. In doing so, the Lincolns split a doubleheader with Hilldale, losing 8–1 before coming back strong, winning 11–1. They followed that up by splitting another deuce, this time with the Cubans, losing 13–7 and winning 5–4. Balls were flying out of the Oval that day as Martín Dihigo belted two homers in game one and George Scales hit three in the second. Two more splits came against Harrisburg, the Lincolns winning 14–1 and losing 10–8, and Hilldale, the Lincolns winning 5–3 before falling, 13–6. These final series brought the regular season to an end, the Lincolns finishing a distant fifth place in the east, with Lloyd's former club, the Bacharachs, winning it all.[18]

In New York, the big news was the anticipated city baseball championship between the Lincolns and the Bronx Giants. The Bronx Giants, a white team, looked to have Lou Gehrig, the New York Yankees' powerful first baseman in the lineup, while the Lincolns countered with Lloyd and "Cannonball" Dick Redding. It was even speculated that the mighty "Sultan of Swat," Babe Ruth himself, would appear for the Giants. The matchup was eagerly trumpeted in the papers, but the weather turned ugly, and by the time the scheduled doubleheader was actually played, in early November, Gehrig opted only to umpire the bases, and Ruth did not show. On the field the two teams split, Lloyd's club dropping the first, 4–2, but winning the second, 4–2. While another doubleheader between the two clubs was scheduled for the following week, it never took place, the weather continuing its late fall stumble.[19]

*　*　*

In January, 1927, the *Courier* announced that Oscar Charleston, the great outfielder and manager of Eastern Colored League rival Harrisburg Giants, was moving on, opting to play for Cum Posey and the Homestead Grays. Charleston had notified the *Courier* in a personal letter sent from *Egrido* 18, Havana, Cuba, where he was playing baseball that winter. On the subject of

Cuban baseball, Charleston noted that the season was not going well, "rather dull," he said. "The two factions working in opposition make it impossible for either to do much. There are about eight American players here and all are playing good ball," but the league itself was a mess.[20] Within two months Charleston's plans had changed and he was back with Harrisburg, demonstrating yet again the fragile nature of the Negro Leagues baseball contract, proposed or otherwise.[21]

Lloyd was in Cuba that winter as well, playing for Havana. Again he was a force at the plate, batting .353, good enough for third in the league, following only Jud Wilson at .424 and Martín Dihigo at .415. Dihigo, exhibiting his amazing versatility, also won four games as a pitcher, finishing 4–2.[22]

By January Lloyd and Lizzie, his wife, had returned to their home on Michigan Avenue in Atlantic City. From there, on March 17, he wrote the *Amsterdam News* that he was in great shape and ready to report for the season in a matter of days. "I feel as if I have been at a training camp all winter instead of the seashore. I feel like playing a game today." In the letter, Lloyd also noted that his club would be stronger in the coming season with the addition of Julio Rojo, the great Cuban catcher, coming over from Baltimore in exchange for Lindsey, who was thought to have retired, and Singer, as well as the continued development of the team's young pitching, including Chambers, Craig and Gilmore.[23]

Lloyd and Keenan continued to upgrade their club by trading the veteran "Highpockets" Hudspeth to the Royal Giants in exchange for Bob Douglas and Connie Rector. Douglas, the Royals' former manager, while viewed as a "crackerjack first baseman," had sat out the previous year after having suffered a nervous breakdown. The jury was still out on him. Connie Rector, on the other hand, was a pitcher of "established reputation" and was looked upon by Lloyd to strengthen an already sound pitching staff. It was also noted that Gerard Williams, who had "undergone the knife" for a second time, was rapidly recovering and was expected to join the Lincolns. With the Lincolns "recruited to its full strength," the club looked forward to the season opener.[24]

With Lloyd "whipping" his club into condition, the Lincolns bested a strong Camden team on April 17, 10–2. Despite an ominous threat of rain and chilly conditions, the Lincolns looked good, collecting 12 hits, including doubles by George Johnson and Bill Mason. Rector got the win for the Lincolns, striking out four while giving up eight hits in six innings.[25]

On the same day, the Bacharachs, led by Dick Lundy's two hits, proved again that they would be reckoned with in 1927, jolting Hilldale, 10–0. In spite of the Bacharachs showing, however, it was Alex Pompéz's Cuban Stars, led by the formidable young star Martín Dihigo, who were favored to win the Eastern League pennant that season. The Cubans, an itinerant band playing only road games for most of many seasons while based in Havana, found a home in 1927, playing their home games in Newark at David's Stadium. With Wilbur Crelin's Newark team "going on the rocks" the previous year, the new home had opened up for the Cubans.[26]

The season opened officially for the Lincolns with a May 1 doubleheader against Hilldale, one which found Lloyd's Giants hitting the ball to all parts of the park in sweeping both ends, 7–6 and 6–5. Three home runs were featured in the two games — Lloyd and Rojo in game one, followed by Mason's bomb to right in game two. The downside for the Lincolns was that both George Scales and Clint Thomas went out with injuries expected to sideline the players for a couple of weeks. Scales wrenched his knee rounding second on the way to third, while Thomas fractured a rib in a collision with George Dial at third. Connie Rector won the opener for the Lincolns, while Willie Gisentaner bested Phil Cockrell in game two. Lloyd, beginning what was heralded by the *Amsterdam News* as his 25th year in professional baseball, had two hits in each game.[27]

The Lincolns went on a "batting rampage" against the Cubans at Davids' Stadium in Newark, scoring 25 runs in winning both halves of a Sunday doubleheader, 13–6 and 12–7. The Lincolns were led by Esteban "Mayari" Montalvo, the big Cuban outfielder, who following a decision by league President Isaac Nutter denying a Western League protest and allowing him to play for the Lincolns, had five hits in six at-bats. Rojo, the other Cuban member of the Lincolns, also played well, blasting a triple. Nutter's reasoning in denying the protest was that the Negro National League had not listed him on its binding reserve list, showing no interest in Montalvo until after he had signed with the Lincolns. He further noted that Montalvo had been forced to stay in Cuba the year before when he could not come to an agreement with Alex Pompéz and the Cuban Stars, and that as no Western League team had attempted to sign him, he was free to play with the Lincolns. Pompéz felt that there were plenty of black players for the Eastern League to choose from and that he should have free reign over all the Cuban ones. Montalvo, however, did not see it that way, nor did Jim Keenan. Keenan, not seeking a baseball war with the west, briefly acquiesced a week later, dropping Montalvo from his roster in response to an order by Judge W. C. Hueston, president of the Negro National League, demanding that Montalvo be returned to the western league's Cuban Stars.[28]

That same week William Clark of the *Courier*, one of the most widely circulated of all black newspapers, predicted in his column that organized baseball would be desegregated "within the next ten or fifteen years." Clark's reasoning was that in places like the Bronx, the third largest borough in New York City, the Lincoln Giants were the neighborhood team, enjoying a 60–40 percent white-black ratio at its ballgames and within its fan base. Clark wrote that in the northern Bronx, white fans were just as attuned to the health of John Henry Lloyd as the most rabid Negro fan and worried more when Rube Chambers was in a pitching slump than his teammates did. "The race of their athletic idol," Clark surmised, "is lost sight of by the fans." It was a nice thought, but regardless of Clark's optimism and the fact that white managers such John McGraw and Connie Mack were on record as lusting for talented black players, it would be another 20 hardscrabble years before organized baseball allowed a black player — Jackie Robinson — to take the field in a major league contest.[29]

With Montalvo still in the lineup on May 15, not yet having been released, the Lincolns won their eighth and ninth consecutive home games, besting the Royal Giants, 7–2 and 6–2. It was Brooklyn's first appearance at the Protectory Oval in two years and a large crowd was on hand to witness it, despite inclement weather. In the first game, Connie Rector nearly shut out his former teammates before allowing two runs in the ninth inning. The Lincolns hit "Pud" Flournoy hard, winning the game with relative ease. Game two, however, was a different matter, a pitching duel between Bill Holland for Brooklyn and Lloyd's young ace, Charlie Craig. The Lincolns held a 2–1 lead into the ninth when Hudspeth slammed one over the right field wall, tying the score. The Lincolns, however, with their big hitters heading to the plate, broke the tie in short order. George Johnson, Bill Mason and Montalvo got on base with singles before George Scales ripped a walk-off grand slam over the right field fence to win it. It was Scales' seventh homer of the season. Lloyd got two hits in the first game before going hitless in the latter.[30]

Losing the hard-hitting Montalvo created a hole in the Lincolns lineup, spinning the club into a batting slump, evidenced by a doubleheader loss the following weekend against Harrisburg. With John Beckwith the new Harrisburg manager and Oscar Charleston leading the way at the plate, the Giants pummeled the Lincolns, 9–4 and 13–5. The Lincolns were then "humbled" by Hilldale, 9–2, before dropping a doubleheader to Atlantic City, 12–7 and 4–2. As the press continued to bemoan the Lincolns' loss of Montalvo, Lloyd was not outwardly discouraged, explaining that a reckoning was on the way and that his club should not be counted out.[31]

Lloyd's optimism notwithstanding, the Lincolns continued to struggle through May, dropping a pair to the Bacharachs on May 29 before the largest crowd of the season, despite the fact that the Yankees were playing at home in the South Bronx. With June, however, came the resurgence Lloyd hoped for as they walloped Hilldale, 7–4. By Independence Day — with Montalvo happily back in right field — the Lincolns put together a five-game holiday run, besting East Orange, Santop's Broncos, the Philadelphia Professionals, and White Plains. While the team's revival may have had more to do with its playing down in competition, Montalvo's return certainly provided a boost. But then the worm turned. Jim Keenan, tiring of the flack being dished his way in the dispute over Montalvo, "suddenly withdrew" from the league, piecing together an independent schedule for the remainder of the campaign. At the heart of this new schedule was Cum Posey's vaunted Homestead Grays, the best team in the west. Keenan signed them up for a home and home series to be waged over the next month.[32]

Rollo Wilson, in the *Courier*, was ecstatic over the east versus west match-up, as it was only the second time in the history of Pittsburgh black baseball that any of the big eastern teams had appeared there. He happily wrote that "at last the seaboard citizens are going to have an opportunity to see just how good the Grays are." While condescending to New York players such as Montalvo and "Jelly Bean" Gardner, calling them as good as any in the east, Wilson delivered a backhand gesture of sorts to Lloyd, asserting that while Lloyd, at his advanced age, ran the risk of getting his feet tangled up in his beard, he still managed to come up with the ball.[33]

Cum Posey, for his part, was more than confident, telling Wilson that "[w]e'll beat those birds." "Connie Rector can't stop my hitters," he said. "Spearman and Joe Williams know all about that bunch. And they will never hit Oscar Owens or Lefty Williams. Washington and Gray and Graham are better hitters than Beck or Charleston. Mason will be lucky if he gets a foul tip in the series. The boys may throw a 'cripple' to Lloyd now and then to give the old fellow a chance, but otherwise he will be helpless."[34]

The "helpless" Lloyd, every bit as confident of the outcome as Posey, led his team into Forbes Field the second week in August, but Posey's remarks proved prescient as the Grays simply "snowed under" the Lincolns, taking four of the five contests, the first three in Pittsburgh and the last two in New York.[35]

The three games at Forbes Field produced a "galaxy of thrills" for the home crowd. "Smokey Joe" Williams, the veteran hurler every bit Lloyd's contemporary, bested Connie Rector in a twilight affair, 4–2. Williams helped himself at the plate with a "ringing triple" which eluded Gardner in center field and put the winning run in scoring position. Williams also pitched masterfully, hitting his stride and getting better as the game went on. For the Lincolns, both Lloyd and Scales played well, soundly fielding their positions and hitting the ball hard. Scales had two hits while Lloyd had one. The game was marred somewhat when "Home Run" Mason, vehemently objecting to a called third strike with two outs and two on in the ninth, had to be restrained by a police officer who intervened to maintain order.[36]

The next day, in front of a crowd "nearer to 6,000 than 5,000," the Grays swept both ends of the doubleheader, winning an 11-inning nail-biter, 4–3, before taking the second game, 4–3. The Grays scored first in the opener, the result of a passed ball which rolled near the dugout and was ruled a two-base advance by the umpires. The Lincolns then scored a pair on three consecutive hits and a wild throw by Young. Lloyd's triple to left-center in that inning was the "hardest hit of the first game." The Lincolns scored again when Scales stole home on "Chippy" Britt's windup, taking a 3–2 lead. The Grays fought back, however, when with two down in the ninth inning and nobody on base, Bobby Williams sliced one into center field that skipped past Jelly Gardner, allowing Williams to come all the way around to tie things. The Grays won it in the 11th when Spearman, batting for Young, flied to deep right, bringing "Dolly" Gray home with the winning run.[37]

The Lincolns threatened again in the second game, Lloyd and Baynard combining to put across three runs, one of which was a result of Lloyd's "fine base-running." But again the Grays came back to tie things, before winning it in the tenth when Joe Williams belted a long sacrifice fly to score Red Ryan with the bases loaded and none out. Lloyd, relentless as August, put his glove on display in the second game, turning in several great plays, one a back-handed catch of a sizzling hopper near first base with a "daisy" throw to retire the runner by a step. Rollo Wilson, having jabbed Lloyd about his age earlier in the week, wrote in the *Courier* that "Lloyd is still one of the greatest — and a GENTLEMAN to boot."[38]

On Sunday the Grays topped the Lincolns, 8–6, in a game played before a smaller crowd than those witnessing the contests in Pittsburgh, largely because of threatening weather. The Bronx faithful, however, gave a rousing welcome to "Smokey Joe" Williams when he sauntered onto the field. Williams, a broad smile on his face as he waved to the crowd, clearly enjoyed the moment.[39]

It was the hitting and pitching of Bobby Williams and Lefty Williams, respectively, that won it for the Grays on Sunday. Bobby Williams got it going in the second inning when he singled to center and was driven home on "Chippy" Britt's "wicked double" to left. Britt came home on Montalvo's "costly" error at first. Lloyd doubled and scored for the Lincolns in the second, but the Grays came back in the third on a Vic Harris single, Riggins' double, and Gray's two-run single. Bobby Williams then lined to Scales at shortstop, but Montalvo dropped the toss that would have doubled up Gray. Britt popped out to Lloyd ending the inning.[40]

In the fifth inning Gray doubled and scored from second on Bobby Williams' grounder back to the mound, beating the throw in from first. After Britt grounded out to Lloyd, Lefty Williams hit one to Montalvo but Gisentaner, the pitcher, failed to cover first, putting men on first and third. Bobby Williams next scored on a double steal, with Lefty Williams advancing to third where he stood when the inning ended.[41]

In the bottom of the sixth, with no outs, Jelly Gardner nubbed an infield single, sliding safely head-first into the bag. Garcia doubled and Mason walked. With the bases loaded, Montalvo "enacting the hero role," bounced a double off the left field wall, scoring Gardner and Garcia while advancing Mason to third. Scales walked, and with the bases loaded, Lloyd grounded into a run-scoring double play. Both sides went out in order in the seventh, and both scored a run in the eighth to the set the table for a New York comeback in the ninth, but it fell short when with two men on, Rector, batting for Moe Harris, popped out to second and Gardner popped out to third.[42]

While in Pittsburgh, Lloyd, as manager of one of the league's keystone franchises and as a great baseball veteran, was interviewed by the *Courier* on the relative health of the Eastern League. Pulling no punches, Lloyd opined that "the league is hooked up all wrong, has no laws which are respected, and try to make a major issue out of the questions of players' salaries." A new league, he argued, properly supervised and controlled, with a high commissioner not directly interested in any club, would be the proper move for the following year. The *Courier* added that the league as presently constructed was a joke, in that there was no real league schedule and no one to oversee the dealings of the owners or to enforce a mandatory World Series between east and west. The arrangement left the players, who already felt underpaid, dissatisfied, believing that management did not respect the rules of the organization and was in no position to demand or command respect. Lloyd's statements served as a prophecy of sorts in that the Eastern Colored League stumbled badly throughout 1927 and folded in mid-season the following year.[43]

At the same time, word began filtering out of Georgia that a rash of marriages between whites and blacks had prompted passage of an anti-miscegenation law requiring registration of the ancestry of every person in the state, so as to "prevent the marriage of persons of Negro and white antecedents." Enforcement of the law was to rest with the State Department of Health, which would prepare forms on which every citizen of the state must give available information as to the race of his/her ancestors and any mixture which may have occurred. Marriage licenses could be refused if such proof of the "racial purity" of the applicants was not on file. This "savage law" came as a surprise to many in that most Americans labored under the impression that white people in Georgia were opposed to marrying blacks. "We had no idea," the Baltimore Sun commented, "that savage laws are required to prevent them from doing so."[44]

The Lincolns, at Glendale the final week of August playing against a Brooklyn team called the Farmers, staged a "swatfest," banging out four home runs, each with a man on base, winning it, 8–1. Mayari Montalvo started the ball rolling with a two-run shot in the first, followed by Mason's "Ruthian drive." In the fourth inning, with Berdell Young on base, Julio Rojo homered, and was followed an inning later by George Scales, who yanked the final two-run bomb of the day. For his part, Gisentaner allowed the Farmers 11 hits, but they could not capitalize, leaving 15 men on base.[45]

Over the next month, the Lincolns played a series of games against various local clubs including the Doherty Silk Sox, Philadelphia Hebrews, Bronx Giants, Chester, PA, and the Philadelphia Professionals. Many of the exhibitions were wild affairs, the Lincolns scoring 15 runs against the Hebrews, 11 against the Professionals, and ten against Chester, all victories. The games, resplendent in their gaudiness, yet necessary in that the Lincolns were now independent, gave fans in the north Bronx more to cheer about than would have been offered had the Lincolns stayed in the Eastern Colored League, which by late September was near collapse.[46]

On September 28 the *Amsterdam News* reported that Ed Bolden, secretary-treasurer of the league and manager of the Hilldale club, had suffered a nervous breakdown, forcing him to give up all work for an extended period of time. The breakdown was later diagnosed as a stroke. As the league's original promoter, Bolden had suffered a great deal of stress regarding the league's miserable state of affairs, and it was speculated that this had possibly led to his condition. Bolden's representatives, however, responded that his ill health was simply a matter of overwork and did not reflect the league's condition or that of the Hilldale club. With Bolden on hiatus, it was surmised that Nat Strong, "the big mogul of the organization," would move to kill off the league. "He has done nothing to strengthen the position of his club, the Royal Giants, during the past season, nor would he aid the other clubs financially." The *Amsterdam News* opined that it was very likely that the league would either be reorganized or disbanded.[47]

Amid rumors of the Eastern League's imminent demise came word that Cum Posey's Homestead Grays would again be traveling east to play the Lincolns Giants, this time in three games over the October 1–2 weekend. The first game would be played at the Elks Grounds, 48th and Spruce Street, in Philadelphia, giving fans in that city an opportunity to see the fabulous Grays, with their equally remarkable 116–26 record. Games two and three would be played in the Bronx at the Catholic Protectory Oval. Posey also let it be known that he would be bolstering his lineup with Biz Mackey, Hilldale's hard-hitting catcher, and Martín Dihigo, who some were already considering the best all-around baseball player on the planet. Lloyd, no slouch when it came to recruiting help, promised to add to his roster too, as well as welcome back Berdell Young, who had been out sick. "We'll be ready," Lloyd remarked.[48]

In game one, Jap Washington's first-inning error proved costly for the Grays, paving the way for a 7–3 rout by the Lincolns. With two out in the first, hard-hitting Jud Wilson, on loan from Baltimore, was safe when Washington dropped a perfect throw from Riggins at first. Scales walked, setting the stage for Lloyd, who doubled down the right field line, scoring both Wilson and Scales. In the second, Rojo singled, was sacrificed over by Burnett, Chambers walked and Jelly Gardner singled to score the Cuban. Chambers came home on Mason's sacrifice fly, Wilson walked, and Scales doubled, scoring Wilson. With the sacks juiced in the seventh, "Chippy" Britt walked Scales, forcing in the Lincolns' seventh run of the ballgame. Posey's bunch was held without a run until late in the day when Dihigo, playing second base for the Grays, "lofted one into Spruce Street." The homer capped Dihigo's day, one in which he batted for the cycle, belting a single, double, triple and homer.[49]

Smarting from the defeat, the Grays "unleashed the hounds of war" the next day, taking both ends of the doubleheader from the Lincolns, 16–5 and 7–5. So relentless was the attack against the Lincolns starter, Phil Cockrell — on loan from Hilldale, by way of Augusta, Georgia — in the first game that a technical knockout was called in the fifth inning. By the time Cockrell exited, 15 runs, 17 hits and eight bases on balls had been posted. The game had been salted away by the third when Biz Mackey, up for the second time that inning, belted a grand slam. The second game, a more closely fought affair, went eight innings before darkness halted it. Connie Rector and Lefty Williams faced off, but Rector was not up to it, allowing seven runs on 14 hits. Mason hit a bomb for the Lincolns in the eighth, but it was too little, too late for the home team.[50]

Martín Dihigo, a multifaceted player nicknamed "El Inmortál," has been called the "most versatile man ever to play the game of baseball."

As talk of another year-end series with the Grays washed out, the Lincolns season came to an end. Dick Lundy's Bacharachs, who again had the best record in the east, traveled west to play the Chicago American Giants in the World Series, but fell short, with five losses and a tie in nine games. Also of note came an edict, ultimately "unheeded," handed down by Kenesaw Mountain Landis, Commissioner of organized baseball, that white minor leagues would no longer be allowed to participate in Winter League baseball on the West Coast, under penalty of expulsion. White minor leaguers had long sought off-season income by playing in the league, but Landis was now determined to prevent it. The reason for his decision was that African-American ballplayers routinely played in the league as well. Landis was no longer willing to permit players under contract to his league to participate. The decision, heeded or not, was another blow to those hoping that organized baseball may have been on the cusp of allowing black participation in the white leagues.[51]

The Lincolns, with an abbreviated sub–.500 record of 21–22 in the Eastern League, still managed to finish the season ahead of Hilldale and Brooklyn. In a year of historic baseball feats — see Babe Ruth and the 1927 New York Yankees Murderers Row — Lloyd, at 43 years old, posted a .350 batting average and fielded his position like an all-star. In fact, had the Lincolns remained in the league, Lloyd may have earned a spot on the east all-star team which instead went to the emerging star, Martín Dihigo. With another season in the can, Lloyd was showing few signs of slowing down, especially at the plate. The old man could still rake, and he clearly loved playing baseball! The following season proved to be even better as Lloyd enjoyed one of the finest seasons of his remarkable career.[52]

*   *   *

The early word out of the Eastern Colored League offices in early 1928 was that it was disbanding. At a meeting in the Philadelphia offices of Alex Pompéz of the Cuban Stars, owners Jim Keenan, George Rossiter of the Baltimore Black Sox, and G. A. Washington of the Bacharachs agreed that it would be in their own best interest to play the season as independents rather than in mutual association. Nat Strong of the Brooklyn Royal Giants was not on hand, nor were representatives of the Harrisburg Giants, which had quit the league several months earlier, or Hilldale, which had withdrawn over the winter.[53]

Ed Bolden, still recovering from his stroke, was reported as favoring a league, just not one constructed in the present format. "I am always in favor of a league," Bolden said. "I sponsored it and still believe it is the right idea.

When one man quits this week and then comes back a few weeks later ... then it is time for a halt. Hilldale made plenty of money in the days of independent baseball and that is the reason we have gone back to our old methods, for last year the club dropped $18,000. I still am ready to join a real league, which I hope will be in existence some day."[54]

That day, at least to a majority of its members, came a week later, when the Eastern League "magnates" announced that they had reconsidered their earlier action and would resume play. They also decided that member clubs would be permitted to schedule games with Hilldale and Brooklyn, if they desired to do so. On another note, Alex Pompéz announced that Martín Dihigo had signed with Cum Posey and Homestead for "the largest salary ever paid a Negro ball hawk."[55]

With the league in play, Pompéz brought his Cuban Stars into the Catholic Protectory Oval for a doubleheader with the Lincolns, winning both, 13–8 and 9–4. Sporting a lineup which included Alejandro Oms, Báro and Herrera, it was believed to be the best team of Cuban Stars that Pompéz had yet presented. Yet it was Angel Alfonso, "the diminutive shortstop," who was the star in both games, going 4-for-4 with a homer and double in game one, and saving the second game with a "bare-handed" stop of a George Scales liner in the eighth. Nip Winters led the way on offense for the Lincolns in the first game with two hits, but was hit hard on the mound, allowing the Cubans 16 hits. Lloyd, after going hitless in the opener, had two hits in the second game.[56]

Hilldale came to the Bronx the following week for a two-game set, and it was the play of George Carr and Nip Winters, former members of the Hilldale team, that enabled the Lincolns to win the first one, 7–0. Both Carr and Winters hit Phil Cockrell like they owned him, Carr with a home run in the first inning and Winters with one in the third. Hilldale came back in the second game, however, winning 12–4. The Lincolns' Connie Rector and Gisentaner were both hit hard, with Clint Thomas picking up four hits for the Daisies. Lloyd led the Lincolns on offense with a home run, a single and a stolen base in four trips to the plate.[57]

The Bacharach Giants came to town on May 20, with Dick Lundy again at shortstop and Chaney White in centerfield. The Lincolns jumped to an early lead, scoring nine runs in the first two innings. They were led by Scales and Rojo, who each had three hits on the day, and Rector, who belted a homer. Meanwhile, White made things interesting, blasting two homers for the Bacharachs, but it was not enough, the Lincolns coasting to a 14–7 victory. The day's second game was called off due to threatening weather. The following day the Lincolns beat the Philadelphia Elks, 4–3 in 11 innings. Lloyd had four hits, including a triple and double, while Gisentaner kept the Elks at bay, allowing just three runs and driving in the winning run.[58]

Lloyd's performance against the Elks was just a warmup. The following week, before a big crowd at the Oval, he led the Lincolns in a doubleheader sweep of Pompéz's vaunted Cubans, 6–3 and 12–6. In the first game, Lloyd brought in three runs with a single and double, before homering twice in game two. His team was playing well. It was perhaps for this reason, with the Homestead Grays coming to town, that Lloyd uncharacteristically chose to go public with his pronouncement that the Lincolns were ready for them. Speaking to the *Amsterdam News*, Lloyd was quoted as saying that his team was prepared and that they would "give 'Cum' Posey something to think about on winter nights when the old stovepipes meet on Wylie Avenue."[59]

After besting two lesser opponents — the Farmers and Harrowgate — Lloyd and his team readied for Homestead, on the docket for a scheduled four games, two to be played in Pittsburgh and two in the Bronx, culminating with a Sunday doubleheader at the Oval on July 1. Getting the games in proved to be no easy task as "wild confusion," leading to a forfeit, ultimately gave the Lincolns a 3–1 victory in the set.[60]

The Lincolns defeated the Grays in the first game of the Saturday doubleheader played at Forbes Field in Pittsburgh, 4–3 before losing the second game. They beat them again the next day, 7–1, with Nip Winters allowing just six hits in going the distance. It was the second game on Sunday, however, where the fun was had. The game began as a free-hitting affair, with "Smokey Joe" Williams on the mound for the Grays, opposed by "Speed" Gilmore for the Lincolns. Gilmore was knocked out of the box in the sixth inning and Williams in the seventh, forcing Lloyd and Posey to the bullpen. The Grays were up, 11–8, coming into the last half of the ninth inning. Scales led off with a double, and Mason followed with a double of his own, scoring Scales. Joe Lewis then singled, and Rojo hit a hot one to Lefty Williams, on for Joe Williams. He threw to second in an attempt to get Lewis, but the throw was high, forcing Beckwith to almost jump to catch it. The umpire, a man named Seixas, ruled that Lewis was safe because Beckwith had his foot off the bag.[61]

Earlier in the game the Grays had been upset with some of the calls made by Seixas, to the point that Lloyd and Scales had to physically prevent Beckwith and Jap Washington from assaulting the umpire. When Seixas made the questionable call in the ninth, mayhem broke out, as Posey, getting no relief in arguing his point, led his team off the field to the loud boos and heckling of the Bronx fans, many of whom were irate over having bet the Grays to win and did not want to lose their money through a forfeit. Posey's actions, resulting in a forfeit, also led to all future bookings of the Grays at the Catholic Protectory Oval being cancelled.[62]

Over the next month the Lincolns rallied to beat the St. Louis Giants, 6–5, and Philadelphia's Kensington club, 6–4 and 5–1. During this period, Romeo Dougherty of the *Amsterdam News*, writing on behalf of the Eastern Sport Writers Association, spoke of the obvious need for a strong baseball league in the east. "Baseball in the east cannot prosper under present conditions," he wrote. "The need of a league is apparent. The public will never again patronize independent baseball as it did in the days before it knew the association brand of the game. Owners are losing money, players are recalcitrant, fans are dissatisfied. The game ... needs a strong, well-balanced circuit which will protect all of those involved." The time to start for next season, Dougherty said, "is now." And the man Dougherty proposed to lead the new league was Ed Bolden, "the biggest figure in our season board game." While Bolden would attempt to fashion the remnants of the east into a solid league, his efforts did not take and his dreams of a stronger Eastern League continued to fade.[63]

Hitting the ball to all parts of the diamond, the Lincolns won both ends of an August 19 doubleheader at the Protectory Oval against the Cuban Stars, 8–6 and 9–4. One of the largest crowds of the season came out to witness the contests. The Cubans fell behind in the opening game when San gave up six runs in the first inning. Pompéz brought in Oscar Levis, who held the Lincolns except for single runs in the sixth and seventh. Scales and Rojo had two hits each for the Lincolns, including a double by Rojo. San started again for the Cubans in the second game and lasted five innings before the Lincolns posted five runs to chase him. Mason hit a homer in game two, while Lloyd had two hits.[64]

With Lloyd guiding the tracks, the Lincolns continued to roll, winning their 17th double-header of the season, besting the Garfield team, 8–0, and Kensington, 16–6. Rojo belted a grand slam in the latter contest. At the same time, however, Jim Keenan was being called out by Syd Pollack, the booking manager for a Cuban team known as the Havana Red Sox. In an open letter published in the *Amsterdam News*, Pollack expressed his bewilderment over the fact that the Red Sox had been continually "disregarded" after his having personally communicated with Keenan on "twelve different occasions or more." Pollack argued that it was a match being demanded by the fans. Two weeks later Pollack wrote another open letter, this time alleging that Keenan had "failed the fans" for not booking the Red Sox. For his part, Keenan wanted none of it and worked closely with Alex Pompéz to keep the Red Sox out of New York, forcing them to take games in New Jersey against teams like Trenton and Coatesville. It is clear that Keenan, and Pompéz for similar reasons, desired to keep Manhattan and the receipts it produced for himself, finding no room on the island for a new erstwhile competitor.[65]

In early September, with 85,000 fans watching the New York Yankees tussle with the Philadelphia Athletics at Yankee Stadium, a large crowd of 5,000 turned out to watch the Lincolns take on the Philadelphia Professionals. The first game featured plenty of offense, the Lincolns winning, 17–10, while the second was a pitching duel, also going to the Lincolns, this time 4–0. The following weekend the Cubans turned it around when visiting the Oval for the final time of the season, winning the first game, 5–4, in 11 innings, before tying one, 7–7, in a game called on account of darkness. Lloyd, playing first base due to the departure of Scales, Bill Riggins, Rojo and Bejerano the prior Tuesday for Cuba, picked up a single in each game.[66]

The Lincolns played out the remaining two weeks of their schedule with replacements "Highpocket" Hudspeth, Cason and Jess Hubbard, all over from the Royals, as the 1928 black baseball season in New York gradually came to an end. Almost immediately talk arose of a potentially stronger Eastern League being forged the following year. "If Keenan and Strong should decide to bury the hatchet, possibly an Eastern league of baseball would become a possibility." It did not happen, and with Strong having already laid plans for his Hilldale squad in 1929, the Lincolns played on as an independent until ultimately falling victim to the Great Depression in 1931.[67]

The 1928 season had been a remarkable one for Lloyd, who at age 44 enjoyed one of the finest seasons at bat ever recorded, hitting a Negro Leagues record .528 and winning the batting title over Dick Lundy by a remarkable 116 points. Lloyd also led the remnants of the Eastern Colored League, which had disbanded at mid-season, in stolen bases, and was second in home runs, hitting 11 in 37 league games, equal to nearly 50 over a 162-game schedule. While his batting eye remained sharp and his batting averages proved it, his physical skills gradually waned over the coming three years; yet he still had games to win and pitchers to hit. For Lloyd it was all about showing up, making the day count, and with the 1929 season approaching, his 23rd in professional baseball, he planned to do just that.[68]

NINE

The Big House

In the winter of 1928-29 much of the United States was plagued by an aggressive strain of influenza, one that in the seven weeks ending January 5, 1929, killed 26,000 people. It was the most important of the six such epidemics since 1920 and roughly half as lethal as the Great Influenza Epidemic of 1918-19. At the main unit of Bellevue Hospital in New York City, which was then regarded as an indicator of the public's general health, influenza-related deaths were being reported at the highest level since 1918. Nearly 50,000 influenza-related deaths occurred in the United States during the epidemic of 1928-29, well in excess of the normal expected number from those causes. In Washington, D.C., a two-day Influenza Conference took place at which the U.S. Public Health Service pledged itself to enlist national support in securing increased appropriations from Congress for health defense.[1]

The Eastern Colored League, suffering with its own form of economic grip, collapsed in the spring of 1928 only to reemerge the following year as the American League of Negro Baseball Clubs. The ALNBC, formed in Philadelphia on January 15, 1929, was comprised of the Hilldale Daisies, Baltimore Black Sox, Bacharach Giants, Cuban Stars, Homestead Grays and Lincoln Giants. No less an authority than Negro baseball pioneer Sol White commented on the "favorable impression" offered and its chances for survival by remarking that "all the owners of the teams associated in the new league have been through the sharp periods and dull periods of the business, and by this time should have come very near knowing their options."[2]

Two months later, with the season on the cusp, the ALNBC announced that Homestead had shipped Martín Dihigo and George "Chippy" Britt, two of the league's finest players, to Hilldale for Rev Cannady and Jake Stephens. Stephens was generally considered to be the best young shortstop in the game, having the previous season "outshone Dick Lundy." Sol White, commenting in the *Amsterdam News* on the trade, remarked that "owners and players are satisfied with the deal, nothing having been heard to the contrary, and so far everything is lovely and the goose hangs high. What the season's play will show in these exchanges remains to be seen."[3]

In looking forward to the campaign, Lloyd, who hoped to spend more time managing than playing, announced the he was ready for "a bigger and better season this year," promising to lead his club and go on the diamond if "necessity so dictates." Lloyd then spoke highly of Bill Yancey, a young shortstop formerly with Danny McClellan's Philadelphia Giants and "one of the best basketball players of recent days," who Lloyd openly hoped would be good enough to keep him on the bench. The rest of Lloyd's veteran lineup included George Scales, Chino Smith, Bill Mason, Julio Rojo, Rich Gee, "Highpockets" Hudspeth, Bill Riggins, Bob Douglas, Charles Spearman, "Dolly" Gray, and Namon Washington. "Broadway" Connie Rector, Nip Winters, Bill Holland, Herb "Boy" Thomas, Zip Campbell, and Neck Stanley, the spitballer, would be on the mound.[4]

The largest opening crowd ever to grace the Catholic Protectory Oval turned out on Sunday, March 30, to watch the Lincolns pound a highly thought-of local team known as the Carltons, 5–1. It was also the first time in 20 years that Lloyd did not take the field with his team on opening day. With Yancey at shortstop, Scales at second and Hudspeth at first, Lloyd managed from the bench, where as noted he hoped to spend a majority of his time that season. The Lincolns cashed four of their runs in the third, while a combination of Nip Winters, Connie Rector, Thomas and Bill Holland held the Carltons in check. The game was not all mundane, as the Carltons threatened in their half of the final frame before "Dolly" Gray made a sensational catch in center field preventing two runs. Sol White commented that "Honus" Lloyd, along with Jim Keenan, "had not been idle during the winter months," doing a remarkable job of getting the Lincolns ready for the opener.[5]

Danny McClellan's All Stars made their first appearance at the Oval on Sunday, April 7, coming away badly beaten, the Lincolns winning, 11–10 and 11–1. "Highpockets" Hudspeth enjoyed a great day at the plate, belting a single and double in each of the affairs. Lloyd also got off the bench for the first time, replacing Hudspeth at first base late in the second game. The Lincolns faced the Carltons again the following weekend, losing 4–3 under chilly, cloudy conditions. Yancey continued to impress with two hits in the game, while Lloyd, choosing to conserve his pitching staff, used Thomas, Rector and Holland for three innings each. With the official opener of the American League of Negro Baseball Clubs just two weeks away, a home doubleheader against the Bacharachs, and more interest being shown in the Lincolns that at any time during the past few years," Lloyd, "the grand old man of Negro baseball," was exuding confidence that his club would be up to the campaign.[6]

Despite cloudy skies, the Lincolns and Bacharachs opened the season on April 27, before being washed out in the eighth inning of the first game of a scheduled doubleheader tied at 8. Before the game, Dr. John F. Condon, public school principle, veteran ballplayer and Lincoln Giants fan, threw out the first pitch, while the 369th Infantry Band, led by its conductor, Lieutenant Jacob Porter, furnished the music. The season's first run came in the bottom of the first inning when Dolly Gray turned a walk and three stolen bases into a score. The game also featured three home runs, one by Chino Smith and two from the visiting Mack Eggleston and Ben Taylor, the Bacharachs' veteran manager. While the Lincolns "played brilliantly at times," they made five errors, clearly something that irritated Lloyd, who was managing from the bench.[7]

The Lincolns absorbed their first loss of the season the next week, dropping a soggy, rain-shortened affair to the Cubans, 8–6. Nip Winters, hurling for the Lincolns, was "nipped" for 12 hits. Meanwhile the Lincolns, who trailed the Cubans throughout, doggedly persisted. A base on balls to Scales, singles by Rojo and Yancey, a double by Gray, Scales' theft of third base, and Yancey's steal of second gave the Lincolns three runs to tie things in the second. They scored runs in the fourth, sixth and seventh innings, but fell behind for the final time when the Cubans pushed two across in the bottom of the eighth. Regardless of his club having shown "a commendable spirit of aggressiveness," team owner Jim Keenan was "sorely disappointed," especially in light of the fact that Hilldale, stacked with Oscar Charleston, Biz Mackey, Judy Johnson and Martín Dihigo, was coming to town the next week. He should not have been concerned, as the Lincolns swept both games of the double dip that marked the return of Lloyd to the lineup following Hudspeth's leaving for Hilldale.[8]

The fact that Hilldale had four future Hall of Fame baseball players on its roster was, to an extent, indicative of the level of play in the Negro Leagues during the late 1920s. While even the Negro press, when comparing black ball to the organized game, relegated it to AA status, there were clearly teams that could have played with anyone. The Lincolns, for instance, often beat the Bushwicks, a barnstorming team of white major leaguers sometimes consisting of Lou Gehrig, Jimmie Foxx and others. Later players such as Dizzy Dean and Bob Feller would attest to the quality of black ballplayers, especially when competing against Satchel Paige or Josh Gibson. Nevertheless, while many of the black clubs did have a few players who were major league ready, the lineups top to bottom generally did not compare favorably with major league counterparts. That was clearly the view of Al Lopez, who having played against Negro leaguers in Cuba, and later managing some of the first black ballplayers in the major leagues, including Larry Doby, Minnie Minoso, Hank Simpson, Al Smith and Luke Easter, believed that there were individual big leaguers in the Negro leagues, "no question about it," but, on average, most of the teams were of AA caliber. One can imagine what Lloyd would have given for an opportunity to prove Lopez or anyone else feeling this way wrong.[9]

Lloyd's official debut actually took place the day before the Hilldale set, when the Lincolns traveled over to Bayonne, New Jersey, to play a team of local all-stars. While the game was called on account of darkness after the sixth inning, the Lincolns down 6–4 at the time, Lloyd had three of his team's five hits, including a home run and double.[10]

The Lincolns, with Lloyd once again ensconced in the infield, left town a week later on a two-week road trip taking them to Hilldale, Baltimore and Homestead. Many questioned whether or not Lloyd would remain in the lineup, but his strong defense, which steadied the infield resulting in fewer errors, became necessary. "Yes, Lloyd is going to play," proclaimed the *Amsterdam News*, and as usual he brought his bat with him. By the end of May, Lloyd's bunch found themselves in third place, close on the heels of Baltimore and Homestead. Meanwhile, Hilldale, stumbling out of the block, was near the bottom at four and eight.[11]

At the same time, Kid Chocolate, one of the great prize fighters of his era, demonstrated that he was the class of the bantamweights by punching his way to a decisive victory over Fidel La Barba, former king of the flyweights, before 18,000 rabid fans. With both fighters looking to send a message, the battling began at the bell, the fans being treated to ten fast, furious rounds. Kid Chocolate's longer reach, however, proved to be La Barba's undoing. Time and again La Barba barreled in, going to the body, only to be repelled by Chocolate's "brown fists." While La Barba was more aggressive, Kid Chocolate landed the more effective blows, earning the decision on a two to one vote.[12]

By mid-summer the Lincolns had punched their way into second place with a league record of 17–10, trailing only Baltimore at 21–10. On June 30, Hilldale traveled to New York to take on the Lincolns in a Sunday afternoon doubleheader at the Oval. With Lloyd cajoling his forces in his "high falsetto" voice, the Lincolns won game one, 9–6, before dropping the second, 10–7. It took three innings for the Lincolns to win the first game. Bill Yancey walked to lead off the third. After Neck Stanley fanned, Babe Melton walked, advancing Yancey to second. With two on, Washington hit one through the box for a single, filling the bases. Chino Smith followed with a grand slam over the right field wall, putting the Lincolns up, 4–3. The Lincolns scored two more runs in the seventh on Stanley's double, Namon Washington's walk and a double to right by Riggins. With the score tied 6–6 in the ninth, Melton walked, Washington bunted safely, Smith flied out to center, and Riggins hit a bomb over the right field fence to end it. Lloyd, having recently been out of the lineup with a "charley horse," was back in at first base, going 1-for-3, and according to Sol White, was hitting "in old-time form."[13]

Two weeks later the Lincolns swept a pair from the Bacharachs, 15–9 and 14–12, winning the second game late in prodigious fashion. In the bottom of the eighth, back-up catcher Charles Spearman went to the plate with two on and the Lincolns seven runs down. With Lloyd and Yancey on base pleading for him to do something, Spearman tapped the dirt from his spikes, looked out at the pitcher, "Rats" Henderson, dug in, lifted his bat and waited for the pitch. When it arrived, Spearman swung, sending it on a far, arching shot over the right field fence for a three-run homer, bringing the Lincolns to within four. With his teammates shouting encouragement, Dolly Gray stepped in to face Bob McClure, who was on for Henderson. Gray promptly lashed a single to center. With Washington up, McClure came inside looking to get him off the plate, but hit Washington instead, sending men to first and second. Chino Smith walked, loading the bases, bringing Bill Riggins up. With the crowd on its feet "Rig" did not disappoint, crushing one of McClure's "twisters" for a grand slam to tie things. Scales, who had started the inning with a double, came up for the second time and walked. He then stole second and scored the go-ahead run on Rojo's single to left. It was a hell of a comeback! Lloyd had four hits on the day, while playing first.[14]

By late August, coming off a split with Dick Lundy and the Baltimore Black Sox, 3–2 and 1–2, the Lincolns were in fourth place with an 11–12 league record.[15] On August 25, the Lincolns faced Homestead, which was in third place at 15–11, three games behind the front-running Hilldale. The Grays, who had won three straight games from the Lincolns the previous Thursday and Saturday, were looking to continue their winning ways. The Lincolns, however, rose up, besting the Grays 18–13 in a "weird game," before playing them to a five-all tie in game two.[16]

The Lincolns jumped on the Grays in the first affair, putting up ten runs in the first three frames off Streeter. In the fourth inning, Everett "blew up" allowing the Grays to post five runs. Stanley came on to pitch but failed to do any better, allowing the visitors to tie the score in the seventh. At this point Lloyd sent in his ace, Connie Rector, hoping to shut things down, which he did. Meanwhile, the Lincolns found their bats again. In the sixth Lloyd hit a home run, before coming back in the seventh with a run-scoring double. In the eighth, singles by Lloyd, Gray and Washington, and doubles by Riggins and Scales pushed four more runs across.[17]

It was the day's second game, however, which proved to be "one of the best seen at this park all season." Although both teams were exhausted from their overnight trip from Pittsburgh, they played all-out, giving the fans everything they could have asked for. Connie Rector again took the mound for the Lincolns, opposed by "Smokey Joe" Williams, who was quickly staked to a three-run lead on homers by Dennis Graham and Vic Harris and an RBI triple by Dennis Graham. The Lincolns cut the lead in the fourth when Scales got on with a fielder's choice and Rojo tripled, bringing Scales home. Rojo, savvy on the base paths, stole home for the team's second run. The Lincolns scored two more in the sixth, but the Grays scored again in the seventh, tying things at 4–4. "Broadway" Rector subsequently hit a homer to put the Lincolns up, 5–4, before the Grays battled back to tie the game again, Jackson getting on on an error and coming around on Buck Ewing and Jap Washington singles. With the score knotted, the game was called on account of darkness.[18]

While the Grays were in the East, Cum Posey and Jim Keenan agreed to a trade in which stalwart infielders George Scales and Johnny Beckwith were swapped for one another. Scales, batting .387, had been with the Lincolns for five seasons after coming to the Bronx from St. Louis in 1924, while Beckwith, a native of Chicago, had played for the American Giants, the Baltimore Black Sox and the Grays before being shipped to the Bronx. Of the two players, it was thought that Beckwith was the more versatile. He could play any position in the infield and was an excellent catcher. He also batted a robust .439 for the season. In his first plate appearance with the Lincolns, Beckwith signaled his arrival with a long home run, clearing the trees in center field.[19]

After taking one from the Farmers, 10–6, a game in which Lloyd went 3-for-5, the Lincolns welcomed Hilldale to town for a Sunday afternoon doubleheader. With Beckwith at third, the Lincolns swamped Hilldale by identical 11–3 scores in both games, the latter called in the seventh inning so that the "Darbyites" could catch a train. Chino Smith, the league's home run leader, paced the Lincolns with four homers spread over the two contests — three in the first, one in the second. Bill Riggins also homered twice, with Beckwith and Dihigo homering as well. In both games the Lincolns jumped to early five-run leads. It was the Lincolns pitching, however, especially in light of the Hall of Fame credentials of Hilldale's vaunted lineup, that turned things on this day. Bill Holland, on the mound for the Lincolns in game one, "let the visitors down" with six widely scattered bingles. Rector, the 20-game winner, was on in game two allowing the Daisies just seven hits. The same could not be said for the Hilldale staff. Wilbur Pritchett, responsible for the Lincolns' five-run onslaught to start game two, allowed a home run to Chino Smith and walked the next three batters before allowing a bases-clearing double to Rojo, who came around on Yancey's two-bagger.[20]

A week later the Lincolns swept two more, this time from the Bacharachs, 1–0 and 12–4. It was a ninth-inning triple by Rojo and a single by Rector that ended the first game, "one of the finest pitching duels" played at the Oval all season. Rector was opposed on the mound by "Rats" Henderson, who until the last inning held the Lincolns to six hits. Only once before the ninth did a Lincolns player reach third base. It was Henderson's only league loss of the season.[21] Yet as good as Henderson was, Rector was better, allowing six hits and driving in the winning run. The game was also one of the fastest played at the Oval that year, finishing in one hour and 40 minutes, difficult to imagine under today's norms. The fact that Lloyd and Ben Taylor, both playing first base, authored 15 and 12 putouts respectively indicates the number of grounders served up.[22]

While the first game had been "almost a perfect contest," the second, lasting just six innings, was marred by tired, shoddy defense on both sides. Bill Holland and his mixed bag of pitches, faced Ping Gardner, but both were hit hard, allowing a combined three homers, one by Lloyd, and eight doubles. Melton, Beckwith, Lloyd and Holland each had three hits for the Lincolns.[23]

The Lincoln Giants finished the season with a league best 38–18 record, a .679 winning percentage, just ahead of the Baltimore Black Sox, who while playing many more games posted at .646 winning percentage. Chino Smith led the league in batting at .464, homers with 23, and doubles with 27. Lloyd batted .362, remarkable in that he had not planned on playing any more than necessary when the season began. Along with teammates Johnny Beckwith, Connie Rector, George Scales, and Chino Smith, Lloyd was named by John Holway to the Eastern all-star team, another incredible feat for this 45-year-old man of steel. Yet it was the Lincolns and their progress that Lloyd took most pride in. He was always about his team and determined to drive this point home to his players, and if doing so meant providing an on-the-field example, he would continue to do that as well.[24]

*   *   *

The year 1930, overwhelmed by the onset of the Great Depression, represented a bellwether shift in the makeup of black baseball. Gone from the game were men such as Rube Foster, who died on December 9 of that year, José Méndez, who had died two years before, and C. I. Taylor, who passed in 1922 at the age of 47. Contemporaries such as Lloyd, Joe Williams, Oscar Charleston and Dick Lundy hung on, still pitching and swinging, but the finish line lay just ahead. By 1930 the baton was being passed to an even more

luminous lot, players such as Satchel Paige, Josh
Gibson, Martín Dihigo, Judy Johnson, Cool Papa
Bell, Turkey Stearnes, Willie Wells, Biz Mackey,
Ray Dandridge, and Leon Day.

It was this latter group, building on the backs
of men like Foster and Lloyd, who would set the
stage for "Baseball's Great Experiment," the desegregation of major league baseball with the Brooklyn Dodgers' 1945 signing of Jackie Robinson. The
"baton" is an apt symbol to describe this passage
in that all of these men were *Running for Freedom,*
as historian Stephen F. Lawson later described it,
running for equal rights and the ability to seek
and succeed at the highest possible level. Each
generation, greater perhaps than the one before,
worked toward this collective vision, ultimately
reaching the pinnacle of all they hoped to achieve
with the signing of Robinson and the landmark
awakening it afforded.[25]

Satchel Paige called Chino
Smith one of the two
greatest hitters in the
Negro leagues. In 1929, he
led the league in batting at
.464, homers with 23, and
doubles at 27. Tragically,
he died young.

Yet with the "Promised Land" in sight, the
nation's mores evolved only begrudgingly. Between
1889 and 1930, 3,724 people were lynched in the United States. On New
Year's Eve, 1928, another lynching brought Mississippi's record for the year
to four, nine nationally. Of the nine people lynched, five were taken from the
hands of officers outside of jails; one was taken from a jail. An NAACP report
on lynching acknowledged that the diminished numbers were correct, remarking that it was a positive reflection of the passage in Congress earlier in the
decade of the Dyer Anti-Lynching Bill. James Weldon Johnson, then executive
secretary of the NAACP, found encouragement in the fact that there had been
a steady decrease in lynchings, recalling that in 1889, the year in which the
NAACP began, and Lloyd was five years old, there were 175 lynchings. Like
Lloyd and A. Phillip Randolph, Johnson was raised in Jacksonville, Florida,
and spent his life helping others see beyond the narrow scope of institutional
racism. Achieving such progress, however, was a long haul, and certainly one
lynching was too many.[26]

In 1930, there was no organized league in the East as Hilldale sold its
grounds in Darby, Pennsylvania, with Ed Bolden choosing to opt out. The
Bacharach Giants were looking for new ownership, and Cum Posey had
decided to let the Grays go their own way, choosing to play an independent
schedule. That left only the Lincolns, the Cuban Stars and the Baltimore

Black Sox for the organization, which was not enough. As with the previous season, Lloyd hoped to give most of his time to managing in 1930, having recently acquired first baseman George Giles, formerly of the Kansas City Monarchs. Giles, once considered one of the finest first baseman in the West, had been a holdout in 1929.[27]

With Giles in the fold, the Lincolns boasted a "powerful lineup," one ready to take on all comers. On paper, their talent was alarming. Chino Smith, in right field, was considered by Satchel Paige to have been one of the two greatest hitters in the Negro leagues; the athletic Fats Jenkins, Yancey's future basketball teammate with the Harlem Rens, was in center; and Clint Thomas was in left. Larry Brown, who originally came to the Lincolns as a right-handed pitcher, and Julio Rojo were behind the plate, with Johnny Beckwith at third, Riggins at shortstop, Dick Seay or Rev Cannady at second, and Bill Holland, Connie Rector, Red Ryan and Nip Winters on the mound. Turkey Stearnes, the fast, hard-hitting outfielder over from the Detroit Stars, was with the team through June 16, before returning to the Motor City. And of course, Lloyd played when needed.[28]

Turkey Stearnes was a Hall of Fame home run hitter "with scorching speed." When he ran, he did so with long, "chopping" strides, his arms flapping wildly and his head bobbing like a hunted turkey. Considered one of the great all-around players in baseball history, Stearnes batted .400 three times and led the Negro leagues in homers seven times. He also won three batting titles, and against white major leaguers batted .313 with four homers in 14 games. Stearnes jumped to the Lincolns before the 1930 season began, leaving the Detroit Stars, where he had been since 1921, over a salary dispute. With the Lincolns he was batting .323 and leading the East in home runs when the Stars made him a strong offer to return to Detroit, which he did. The Stars had missed not only his bat but also his "leadership and ability to draw" a good crowd.[29]

Chino Smith acquired his

Turkey Stearnes, considered one of the greatest all-around players in baseball history, batted .400 three times, and led the Negro Leagues in homers seven times. He also won three batting titles, and against white major leaguers batted .313 with four homers in 14 games.

moniker because of the slant across his eyes, giving him an Asian appearance. Aside from being a terrific outfielder, the "dynamo" Smith was an incredible hitter, consistently draping "frozen ropes" all over the park. Arrogant at the plate and respectful of no pitcher, Smith "hit everything thrown to him." He would often feign boredom, spitting at an opposing pitcher's best stuff, waiting until there were two strikes before knocking the pitcher down with a liner up the middle. He was "as famous for his fists as for his bat." John Holway described an incident in Cuba where Smith walked up behind New York Yankees pitcher Johnny Allen, who had a temper as well, sneering "is that all you gonna throw? If that is all you gonna throw, I'm gonna murder you today." Allen had heard enough. When Smith came to the plate for the first time, Allen fired one right at his head. On the very next pitch, Smith lined a drive back at Allen, and soon "the two were pummeling each other on the ground." In a seven-year career cut short by his untimely death, Smith batted .423 in league play, enjoying similar gaudy numbers against major leaguers. He also hit .335 in Cuba, saying plenty about the competition faced on the island.[30]

Threatening weather on March 30 did not prevent a large number of Harlem and Bronx fans from turning out for the opening of the Lincolns' 1930 season at the Catholic Protectory Oval where they faced the Carltons, a regional white team. It was an exciting game, the Carltons pushing the Lincolns to the tenth inning before Lloyd's men wrapped it up, 9–8. Three homers accounted for six of the Lincolns runs, two by Johnny Beckwith, the other by Bill Yancey. The Carltons scored six of their runs in the fifth inning when Red Ryan tired, walking four and allowing the Carltons to bat around before Connie Rector came on to stop the bleeding.[31]

The Lincolns won again the following week, this time topping the Philadelphia Professionals, another white club, 3–2. Chino Smith's walk-off homer in the ninth inning, with Lloyd on first, capped things for the Lincolns. On display as well was the impressive arm of new catcher Larry Brown, who as noted above was brought in as a pitcher but was moved behind the plate by Lloyd. His powerful arm cut off several runners trying to steal second. Yancey, Brown, Turkey Stearnes and Smith all had hits for the Lincolns.[32]

The Lincolns won both games of their first doubleheader of the season, besting a team from Wilmington, Delaware, 14–1, and Danny McClellan's Quaker Giants, stacked with former Hilldale players, 7–1. Home runs by Stearnes, Cannady and Ryan paced the walkover in the first game. Against the Quakers, however, things were a bit more difficult. Bill Holland and the Quakers pitcher "Cannonball" Jackman, "a tall ... strong right-handed submariner with exceptional control," dueled through four innings, Jackman holding a slight advantage until two errors and four hits gave the Lincolns five runs in the bottom of the fourth. Two more runs came against the Quakers pitcher, Stanley, in the sixth, before darkness halted things in the seventh. Chino Smith led the way, going 3-for-4, while Brown added two hits, and Yancey, Stearnes, Cannady, Thomas and Lloyd one apiece.[33]

Over the next few weeks, the Lincolns stretched their season-long home winning streak to ten games, sweeping a club from Philadelphia aptly named the Phillies, 11–1 and 2–0, then beating the Philadelphia Professionals, 6–5, New Brunswick, 17–9, and the Brooklyn Royal Giants, 16–1 and 7–6. The latter contest with Brooklyn was a ten-inning affair ending with Rev Cannady stroking a game-winning in the tenth. With many of their season tune-ups out of the way, the Lincolns were now focused to begin play against teams more of their caliber, those formerly of the ALNBC and/or the ECL.[34]

The Lincolns pushed their home win streak to 12 games, topping Hilldale in both halves of a doubleheader, 14–3 and 22–13. It was Hilldale's first appearance in the Bronx that season, and a large crowd was on hand. In the first game, a walkover for the Lincolns, Cannady hit two home runs while Turkey Stearns added another. In the second game, a see-saw affair, the Daisies posted four runs in the seventh inning off Connie Rector, before the Lincolns bounced back in the eighth with 15 runs to salt things. In the frame, 19 Lincoln batters came to the plate, Clint Thomas belted a home run and single, Stearnes a triple and double, and Lloyd, Smith, Beckwith, Cannady and Rojo all hit doubles. Johnny Beckwith also belted a long home run earlier in the game.[35]

On the road during the next week, the Lincolns kept playing hard, winning four games in Philadelphia, besting Hilldale, 8–6, the Baltimore Black Sox, 11–4, the Cuban Stars, 11–8, and Hilldale again, 4–3. Back at home, however, they finally tripped up, losing one to the Cuban Stars, 11–6, after posting their 13th consecutive home win, 14–2, against the same team earlier that day. Lloyd, Yancey and Beckwith all homered in game one. In the second game, their bats were shut down, 13 proving a "jinx" as the Cubans played "ball like a different team." It was an 11-inning affair in which the veteran outfielder turned hurler, Alejandro Oms, whose side-armed delivery made the ball tough to pick out of the shadows, allowed the Lincolns eight scattered hits. Those hits seemed to be enough heading to the top of the ninth, as the Lincolns held a two-run lead. In that inning, however, Oms and Solis scored, knotting the game 6–6. In the 11th Oms, Solis and Dihigo made hits, which with an error by Yancey led to five runs, allowing them to hold on for the victory. Solis and Echegoyen had three hits each for the Cubans.[36]

After winning a doubleheader against the Brooklyn Royal Giants at Dexter Park, Brooklyn, on "Decoration Day," the Lincolns returned to the Oval, besting Hilldale in two one-sided affairs, 16–8 and 13–8. Johnny Beckwith and Chino Smith, the Lincolns' heavy artillery, blasted two home runs each in the first game, with Beckwith going a perfect 4-for-4 at the plate. Smith "was only able to get two hits out of three chances." In the second game, Turkey Stearnes led the way for the Lincolns with a homer, while Lloyd turned a nifty double play at second on a fly ball hit to Smith in center and relayed in before the runner, Lackey, could get back to the bag.[37]

On June 8, in a double dip against the Royals, John Beckwith hit his eighth home run in the previous five Sundays, leading the Lincolns to another sweep, this time 4–2 and 13–10. The Lincolns then went on the road, besting East Orange, 3–1, before heading back to the Oval where they took one game and tied another with the Baltimore Black Sox, 7–5 and 10–10. Lloyd, playing first base, got two hits.[38]

The Lincolns suffered a terrific blow in the Saturday affair at East Orange when Johnny Beckwith, the loop's leading home run hitter, broke his right leg while sliding into second base. Beckwith was subsequently taken to St. Vincent's Hospital in New York and the bone was set by the same physician who looked after the New York Yankees. His bat would be sorely missed by the Lincolns. (The resilient Beckwith was back with the Lincolns by August 17.)[39]

The biggest news of the day came with the incredible announcement that Colonel Jacob Ruppert, owner of the New York Yankees, had agreed to allow the use of the "gigantic" Yankee Stadium, "The House That Ruth Built," for a doubleheader between the Lincolns and the Baltimore Black Sox. The games, taking place on Saturday, July 5, were to benefit A. Philip Randolph's fledgling Brotherhood of Sleeping Car Porters (BSCP). "All Harlem is expected to turn out as it usually does when the popular Porters Union stages a benefit."[40]

The fact that this would be the first appearance of black professional ballplayers at Yankee Stadium was "significant in itself," but a benefit for the BSCP made the event "all the more noteworthy," according to historian Lawrence Hogan. The establishment of the BSCP, Hogan wrote, is one of the "epic stories in the annals of American labor and African American history." A. Philip Randolph, who like Lloyd and James Weldon Johnson was raised in Jacksonville, went on to become the first black vice president of the American Federation of Labor, and was the singular figure behind the threatened March on Washington in 1941 which prompted President Franklin D. Roosevelt to issue Executive Order 8802, eliminating segregation in defense factories. Randolph would also be the "inspiration" and a principal organizer for the March on Washington, 1963, continuing a push that culminated with the Civil Rights Act of 1964.[41]

With Beckwith out, the Lincolns added two more wins to "their imposing list of victories" by taking a doubleheader from the House of David, 11–
1 and 12–4. The House of David, a barnstorming team of religious zealots
from a commune in Benton Harbor, Michigan, fielded a competitive baseball
club that because of its peculiar grooming tendencies was popular, drawing
large crowds. While the need for a competitive lineup ultimately forced them
to sign men from outside of their community, these outsiders were asked to
comply with certain team rules such as growing long beards and hair.[42]

The *New York Age* announced that in preparation for the pending set at
Yankee Stadium, "Manager Lloyd" had moved "Fats" Jenkins, the star bas-
ketball player of the Harlem Rens and former outfielder of the Baltimore
Black Sox, into left field, while shifting Clint Thomas to center, replacing
Turkey Stearnes, who had rejoined the Detroit Stars (a tough break for the
Lincolns). With Beckwith out until August, the loss of Stearnes proved to be
the second difficult blow confronting Lloyd and his club over the past month.
It would be up to Chino Smith and Clint Thomas to jack up their power
numbers if the team was to continue on its present winning course.[43]

The day after Independence Day, July 5, dawned with the *Age* blanketing
headlines that no less than 35,000 fans were expected to see the four-game
set between the Lincolns and Black Sox, two of which would be played at
Yankee Stadium. Colonel Jacob Ruppert, owner of the New York Yankees,
announced his intention to be present at the games in the Bronx, as did many
city officials and notables of both races. The winner of the pending series was
to be presented with a silver loving cup, donated by the management of the
new Lincoln Swimming Pool.[44]

The Lincolns continued playing great ball during the series, reinforcing
their dominance in the East, winning five of the six games played over the
three days beginning July 4. On that day, the Lincolns swept the Black Sox
in a doubleheader before 10,000 fans at Dexter Park, 4–1 and 7–6. Red Ryan
let the Sox down with four hits in the first game, while "Fats" Jenkins was
"wonderful" in the field. The Lincolns bats arrived in game two with Chino
Smith getting a home run and Yancey a triple. With the score 7–3 in the
ninth, the Black Sox staged a rally bringing them to within a run of the lead,
before Farrell came in for Cox to close the door.[45]

In the benefit set at Yankee Stadium, "the colored players proved that
they could hit the ball just as hard as the big leaguers," the Lincolns winning
the first game, 13–4, and losing the second, 5–3. Dixon, Baltimore's big first
baseman, started the scoring in the first game, blasting a home run into the
right field bleachers. After the Black Sox scored a second run that inning, Bill
Holland settled in, allowing just five hits the rest of the way, winning 13–4.

In support, the Lincolns rapped 14 hits, including a pair of homers by Chino Smith, two of his three hits in the game. Lloyd and Riggins added three hits apiece. The second game, which went to Baltimore, was thrilling, as Lyman Yokely, who had been driven from the game by the Lincolns a day earlier, held the Giants in check, beating them, 5–3. Rapp Dixon carried the weight for Baltimore on offense, banging two long home runs and driving in four runs. In the ninth inning, Red Farrell, pinch-hitting for Connie Rector, drove a long hot liner destined for the right field bleachers, only to watch as Scrip Lee, known best as a side-winding pitcher, leapt into the air at just the right moment for the catch, robbing Farrell of a home run. [46]

In the two games at "the big house," Lloyd went 4-for-8, handled 24 putouts at first base, stole a base and was credited with a sacrifice. Not a bad day for an old man! In hindsight, his role in opening Yankee Stadium to black professional ballplayers has been given some attention, particularly at baseball's Hall of Fame, where one line of Lloyd's plaque reads "INSTRUMENTAL IN HELPING OPEN YANKEE STADIUM TO NEGRO BASEBALL IN 1930." The day must certainly have been a thrill for all of the players. Bill Yancey, at shortstop for the Lincolns, recalled being the first Negro player out on the field that day. "I suited up early, ran out to right field and stood where the Babe stood and pretended to catch fly balls like him. Then I took a bat and went to the plate and pretended I was hitting one into the right field seats like him. It was a bigger thrill than hitting my own first home run against the Paterson Silk Sox back in '24." It was a great day, with the benefit netting $3,500, after expenses, for the BSCP.[47]

The final games of the weekend came on Sunday, the Lincolns returning to the Oval and taking two easy victories from the Cuban Stars, 7–6 and 8–4. Martín Dihigo and Alejandro Oms had homers for the Cubans, with Red Farrell hitting one out for the Lincolns.[48] The Lincolns subsequently left town, traveling to Baltimore to play another set with the Black Sox, this time winning 5–2 and 2–0.[49]

The Lincoln Giants, "with the best team in their history," established a scoring record by plating 72 runs in four games played at the Oval on July 19 and 20. On Saturday the Lincolns tallied 47 runs against Hilldale and the St. Ann Club of Philadelphia, while on Sunday the Jersey City Red Sox were beaten, 17–5, and the Philadelphia Professionals, 8–5. Chino Smith was featured at the plate in the first game with Hilldale, going 5-for-5 with two home runs, a double and two singles, but twice missing on the cycle. In the second game "Fats" Jenkins led the Lincolns in batting with three hits. It was thought that the Black Sox, who were scheduled at the Oval for the following weekend, would have Satchel Paige in the lineup along with several other players over from the West. With Paige a no-show, however, the Lincolns and Black Sox split the deuce, 17–5 and 8–6.[50]

On Sunday, August 3, in a high-scoring semi-professional affair held in the Flushing, Queens section of New York, "a volley" of bricks and stones ended a game between the Flushing Orioles, a Negro team, and the Flushing Eagles, a squad of white players. With the Orioles coming to bat in the last half of the ninth, the Eagles up 21–7, a group of young men leapt from three automobiles on the sidelines and began throwing missiles at the Orioles players. "A Negro, who was standing at the plate, ducked a brick. A moment later a stone broke his arm. His teammates either ran or were beaten, the assailants escaping in the cars. The two injured men, Fred Ehel and Ernest Woods, were taken to Flushing Hospital for treatment."[51]

The same day, the Lincolns bested the Mayfair nine and the Legion nine of Frankfort, 7–1 and 14–2. Six home runs were featured on August 10 in a doubleheader against the Cuban Stars, the Lincolns winning both, 7–6 and 15–5. Four of the homers came in the first game, with Ramon Bragaña, Dihigo and Oms connecting off of Holland, and Chino Smith off Bragaña. Clint Thomas and Dihigo added two more in the second game. "Fats" Jenkins broke up the first game in the tenth when his single scored Yancey from first. The two wins pushed the Lincolns record to 79–10–1 for the season.[52]

Playing before another large crowd at the Oval, the Lincolns split yet another double-header with the Black Sox, this time losing the first, 16–8, while winning the second, 7–1. Red Ryan, who had earlier defeated the Black Sox both in Baltimore and in the Bronx, was "a bit" off form in the opener, being driven from the box after allowing ten hits to the visitors. Ryan's poor pitching was matched by Bill Yancey's shoddy fielding, the shortstop committing three of the Lincolns' four errors. Yancey, however, did hit his team's only homer. In the second game the Lincolns played stout defense behind Bill Holland's near shutout, Baltimore's lone run coming when catcher Larry Brown, attempting to pick Lundy off of third, struck Eggleston's bat, which caused him to throw wildly into left field. Bill Holland, the Lincolns ace in 1930, went 25–1 over 26 starts that season. Holland, who hailed from Indianapolis, originally came to the Lincolns six years earlier, after beginning his career with the Detroit Stars and a stint with the Chicago American Giants. The weekend also marked the return of Johnny Beckwith, who after having been out for two months with a broken leg entered the first game as a pinch-hitter.[53]

At the end of August it was announced that beginning on September 14, the Lincolns would use Yankee Stadium as their home grounds, playing games on Saturdays and Sundays for the remainder of September and the first two weeks in October. Jim Keenan completed the arrangements for the use of "the big house" with Ed Barrow, business manager for the New York Yankees. There was even some talk of a pending series pitting the Lincolns against the Yankees, with a naïve hope that Commissioner Kenesaw Mountain Landis would give his approval for a series of exhibition games following the big league season. The series did not happen, but the use of Yankee Stadium, for economic reasons involving the Great Depression, continued a trend in which major league owners, while refusing to desegregate their own enterprise, profited from the sporadic popularity of the Negro game, which was strongest in the Bronx with Lloyd and the Lincoln Giants.[54]

Playing between showers and on a wet field at the Oval, the Lincolns took another doubleheader from Hilldale, 10–9 and 7–6. Red Farrell not only bested Phil Cockrell in the opener, but also led the Lincolns in batting with a homer, triple and single in three trips. The second game featured strong outfield performances by Jenkins, Thomas and Smith, thrilling the crowd "by going back to the fence for one-handed catches." The Lincolns then went on the road, beating a team from Wilwood, New Jersey, 1–0, despite Wilwood's pitcher, Wimble, tossing a no-hitter at them, before returning home to split a doubleheader with the Philadelphia Professionals, 4–5 and 13–1.[55]

Since midsummer, Sol White had championed in the New York press a championship series to be played between the Lincolns and the Homestead Grays, the best teams in the East and West respectively. It would be "a moneymaker," White wrote, one that would generate a "powerful impetus toward a greater interest in the grand old game." The problem, however, was that Jim Keenan and Cum Posey could not seem to check their considerable egos long enough to organize the set. "Can't they still do some business?" White asked. The question was answered on September 13 when "[a]fter weeks of negotiations," a series of ten games between the two clubs was finalized. The series was to start in Pittsburgh on September 20 with a doubleheader at Forbes Field, home of the Pittsburgh Pirates. Immediately afterwards, the two teams would board Pullman cars for New York where a Sunday afternoon doubleheader would be played at Yankee Stadium. Thursday and Friday afternoons, September 25 and 26, single games were to be played in Philadelphia, the two teams returning to the Bronx for the final two-game sets scheduled for "the big house" on September 27 and 28. Jim Keenan also announced that "[a]ny colored soldier appearing at the Stadium in uniform will be admitted free." The series, to quote John Holway, would be "one of the most memorable of all time in either white or black ball."[56]

The *Courier's* Rollo Wilson, every bit as excited at Sol White regarding the match-up, wrote of the series that the thing he wanted most was for good "sportsmanship" from the ballplayers. "They are to participate in a baseball classic and I want them to be worthy representatives of their group during every minute of every game. If everyone plays fair the better team will win, the fans will be satisfied and there will be no nasty aftermath of criticism from the jackals who glory in dishing the dirt."[57]

The Lincolns came into the series boasting one of the most potent offenses of "any colored team in the country," with a team batting average over 48 home games of .350. Johnny Beckwith led the way at .546, followed by "Fats" Jenkins at .500, Chino Smith .488, Rev Cannady .370 and Lloyd .357. Even the pitchers hit, with Bill Holland batting .419 in 43 at-bats and Red Farrell .474 in 38.[58]

An axiom in baseball is that you play your best today, because there may not be a tomorrow. It is proven wisdom, borne out time and again. In Pittsburgh, however, to begin this important set, Lloyd ignored it, opting to bypass Bill Holland, Red Farrell, Red Ryan and Connie Rector to start Tom Hannibal, who had not won a big game all year, against Lefty Williams, who had not lost one. The decision was inexplicable, given that Lloyd had ridden his big four all season long, and now, in the biggest series of the year, he chose to go with the seldom used Hannibal.[59] The only thought here is that with a pending ten-game set, and having just come off a series with the Cuban Stars, Lloyd believed the rested Hannibal presented a better road option. In front of 3,000 fans at Forbes Field, the Grays proved him wrong, jumping on Hannibal with 14 hits, beating the Lincolns, 9–1. Oscar Charleston led with the way with a big fly for the Grays, while Vic Harris and George Scales gathered three hits each. The Grays followed up in game two, beating Connie Rector, who was on for Red Farrell, in a ten inning affair, 17–16. Josh Gibson, Homestead's 18-year-old catcher who was in for an injured Buck Ewing, blasted a home run and a triple, the bomb being the first ever hit over the 457-foot center field fence at Forbes Field.[60]

With the set in Pittsburgh complete, the two teams jumped Pullman cars back to the Bronx, where the third and fourth games were played. In front of 10,000 fans, which must have seemed sparse in the cavernous Yankee Stadium, the Lincolns and Grays split the doubleheader, 6–2 and 3–2. Both games were pitching duels. "Smokey Joe" Williams and Bill Holland went at it in game one, each allowing six hits, including a timely triple by Lloyd, and two singles and a home run by Rev Cannady. In the second game, Red Farrell and Chippy Britt went to the hill respectively for the two clubs, Britt baffling the Lincolns' heavy hitters, allowing five well scattered hits. With the Grays up by two runs in the eighth inning, the Lincolns tied things on singles by Lloyd and Brown, followed by an error by Jake Stephens at shortstop and a wild pitch by Britt. Stephens made up for his error in the tenth, however, when he walked, stole second and came home with the winning run on Red Farrell's second throwing error. Lloyd and Brown had two hits each for the Lincolns, down in the series, three games to one. When asked about his club's predicament, Lloyd confidently replied that his team would return to the Stadium the following Saturday with the series tied.[61]

Lloyd's confidence must have taken a hit in Philly as the Lincolns were blasted at Shibe Park in game five, 11–3, before rebounding on Red Ryan's arm in game six, winning 6–4. In game five, "Smokey Joe" Williams held the Lincolns to seven hits, while Bill Holland, perhaps feeling the stretch run, allowed 12 hits, including another homer to Josh Gibson. Following game six, the two teams headed back to the Bronx for their final weekend set at Yankee Stadium, the Grays up 4 games to 2.[62]

With the series on the line, the two teams again faced off in Yankee Stadium, the Lincolns taking game one, 9–8. With the Grays up 8–5 in

In 1930, Josh Gibson, an 18-year-old catcher with Homestead, blasted the first home run ever hit over the 457-foot center field fence at Forbes Field in Pittsburgh. He would become the greatest slugger in black baseball history (courtesy NoirTech Research, Inc.).

the ninth inning, Lefty Williams put two men on base with walks, before rolling a double play, forcing the Lincolns to their last out with a man on third. Williams walked two more to load the bases, with Julio Rojo, pinch-hitting for Yancey, stepping in. Cum Posey, having seen enough, went to the bullpen for "Smokey Joe" Williams. Rojo, the Cuban catcher, lashed Smokey Joe's first pitch into deep right field for a bases-clearing triple. Connie Rector singled, bringing Rojo in with the winning run.[63]

The Grays fought back in the second game, largely behind the offense of George Scales and the rookie, Josh Gibson, winning 7–3 and clinching at least a tie in the series. With Connie Rector on the hill for the Lincolns,

Gibson hit a home run that went on a line into the left field bullpen, between the grandstand and the bleachers, a distance of "460 feet." The *Age* reported it as "the longest home run that was hit at Yankee Stadium by any player, white or colored, all season."[64]

Larry Brown, the Lincolns catcher, later told historian John Holway that when Gibson came to bat, Brown had advised Rector not to give him anything inside. Rector was a "master slow ball pitcher" having one pitch that "walked" to the plate and another that "crawled." Rector's command was not as good as it should have been, because when he came in with the pitch Gibson was looking for, the catcher sent it to the farthest reaches of the Stadium. Hall of Famer Judy Johnson would later attest that the ball had actually cleared the roof, sailing out of Yankee Stadium, something no one had ever accomplished. Others, including Gibson, recalled that it banged its way into the bullpen, as reported in the *Age*. Regardless, it was a shot, one that is still reverently spoken of today.[65]

The next day showed what an "Iron Man" Lloyd had in his ace, Bill Holland. Pitching on two days' rest, Holland started both halves of the doubleheader, easily winning the first, 6–2, before dropping the second, 5–2. In game two, his fourth game in eight days, Holland held the Grays to one run before weakening in the eighth, allowing four runs on four hits. He blew up "like an umbrella," Clint Thomas later recalled.[66] Lloyd went down fighting as well, with many "old-timers" who had watched him play saying that they "never saw him play better than in this series." Lloyd went 3-for-3 in the first game on Sunday, bringing his average for the series to .375, while continuing to be a "tower of strength" on defense. Larry Brown batted .385, but the Lincolns' big guns, Chino Smith and Johnny Beckwith, were "shut down," batting .214 and .125 respectively.[67]

As "shadows gathered" over Yankee Stadium and the 1930 season on that Sunday evening, September 28, the Homestead Grays clinched their claim to the eastern championship, having taken six games to four. That night, these same Grays—the veterans Williams, Charleston, Johnson and Scales, the rookie Gibson—"piled into their bus" to go play their third game of the day, against the International League All-Stars, losing 8–2. It was a remarkable testament of how driven these men were—some near the ends of their careers—to make ends meet. If there was a baseball game to be played and a dollar to be earned, they played it. How many players or teams could do that today or would do it? During the Great Depression, "Smokey Joe" Williams, Oscar Charleston, and John Henry Lloyd, they played ball to eat.[68]

Within a week, Adolfo Luque, star Cuban "twirler" for the Brooklyn Robins, organized a team comprised of white and colored stars, traveling to

Havana to play in the Cuban winter league. Sailing just two days after completion of the series with Homestead, Lincolns players Clint Thomas, Larry Brown, Rev Cannady and Chino Smith traveled south to form a team with Martín Dihigo, Dick Lundy, Judy Johnson, Alejandro Oms, and Ramon Bragaña. They were joined by Luque's rookie battery mate at Brooklyn, Al Lopez, the Spanish-speaking catcher from the Ybor City section of Tampa, Florida. Julio Rojo, Connie Rector and Bill Holland were also expected to play in Cuba that winter, as was Lloyd, but business first.[69]

On November 15, it was announced that when the 1931 season rolled around, it would be Johnny Beckwith, the versatile, hard-hitting infielder, who would lead the team, rather than Lloyd. Just before leaving for Cuba to play winter ball, Lloyd announced that he had tendered his resignation. Differences between Lloyd and Keenan had come to a head during the final series with Homestead for the eastern championship. Keenan's apparent disappointment at losing the series was said to have been so intense that he showed a "sudden coolness" toward Lloyd and several of the players, remarking that Clint Thomas, Bill Holland and Larry Brown were the only players in the lineup doing their best. The insinuation was resented by the other players, resulting in Keenan and Rev Cannady almost coming to blows when Cannady called him a "poor sport."[70]

With players taking sides in the dispute, the internal conflict became so "rife" that a final doubleheader scheduled for October 18 was cancelled. The *Age* clearly took a stand, noting how sorely Lloyd would be missed, both as manager and as a player. "Not only has Lloyd given his best as a player, but he worked hard to develop the team from the low position in which he found it, to the present ranking as one of the best in the country." Lloyd brought Chino Smith to the Bronx, developing him into one of the greatest power hitters in black baseball. Lloyd was also responsible for the development of Bill Yancey, Larry Brown and several other younger players. Connie Rector and Bill Holland "enjoyed their best years of pitching under Lloyd's tutelage." Financially, the Lincolns were the most successful colored baseball team in the east in 1930, and many argued that it was ungrateful of Keenan to overlook this fact. Lloyd, having left for Cuba, was not around to comment any further on the matter.[71]

With Lloyd in Havana that December playing with Almendares, word came from Chicago of Rube Foster's death at age 52. Foster, "the mastermind of baseball, perhaps the most colorful figure the game has known, was called out by Umpire Father Time after a vain effort to regain his health." Foster, Lloyd's mentor and friend, had been at the state asylum in Kankakee, Illinois, for four years after suffering a nervous breakdown in 1926. Having taken a bath and retired for the evening, he was later found dead by the attending nurse. While some have written that Foster died "raving about winning one more pennant," it was not reported as the case. Foster was a presence, "the most famous black man in Chicago." Fans and admirers lined up for three days to view his casket at Washington's Undertaking Parlors, on the corner of Chicago's St. Lawrence Ave and 17th Street. His "mammoth funeral" at St. Marks M. E. Church, where he was a member, was attended by over 3,000 mourners, many of whom stood outside the church in the falling snow as Foster's casket was carried out to voices singing "Rock of Ages." His burial followed at Lincoln Cemetery. There could be perhaps no more fitting a symbol of the passing of the torch taking place in this seminal year for black baseball than Andrew "Rube" Foster's death.[72]

TEN

The Right Time

The following spring Jim Keenan, who for nearly two decades was "an outstanding figure in colored baseball," retired from the game. Citing a constant bout with rheumatism, Keenan turned over the reins of the club to Marty Forkins, an executive with the RKO theatrical circuit who for 25 years was the manager of Bill "Bojangles" Robinson, the tap dancer. Forkins also had the backing of Ed Barrow, business manager of the New York Yankees, who had arranged for Forkins' team to play games at both Yankee Stadium and the Polo Grounds, home of the New York Giants, when the major league clubs were out of town. Lloyd, back from Cuba and at that moment in the South "gathering material for his team," was, as expected, named manager of the new team.[1]

Regarding his roster, Lloyd announced in mid–April that he had signed "Fats" Jenkins, Chino Smith, Bill Holland, Red Ryan, and Connie Rector, all of whom had comprised the heart of the previous season's Lincoln Giants. Lloyd also brought in a young arm described as a "sensational youngster," Henry McHenry, who had pitched for the Kansas City Monarchs the previous season. The team was invited to train in Jacksonville, FL, and a number of other new players gathered in the South before the club returned north to open the regular season at Yankee Stadium on May 9. Lloyd suggested to Forkins that the team be named the New York All-Stars, and it would initially be called this in the press, but the team would ultimately be known as the Harlem Stars and, at times, the New York Black Yankees.[2]

Lloyd worked on getting the team ready, and by the second week of May arrangements were being made for the "gala" premier of the New York All-Stars at Yankee Stadium where they would face a team from Lancaster, PA, led by Howard Ehmke, a former pitcher with the Philadelphia Athletics. Hundreds of invitations were sent out, imploring fans of the old Lincoln Giants to turn out and cheer "the return of John Henry Lloyd," this at a time when many felt that he had left baseball for good. Having turned in his resignation at the end of the previous season, there had been concern that New Yorkers had seen the last of Lloyd, but with Keenan's retirement and Forkins' assumption of team control, Lloyd could not resist another go-around. Arrangements had also been made whereby "the leading Negro clubs of the country will be brought to the Stadium.... "Negro fans will for the first time ... be able to lend their support to a Negro team ... at Yankee Stadium."[3]

The baseball season finally began with a Sunday, May 10 doubleheader, the previous day's regularly scheduled opener being washed out. In attendance, among a sparse crowd of 3,000 fans, was Bill Robinson, having revealed himself as the principal club owner rather than Marty Forkins. "Bojangles" Robinson, possessing no small amount of confidence and incredibly fast feet, was ready to play, dressing for the game just in case Lloyd called him down from the crowd. On the day the All-Stars swept two white semi-professional teams, the Lancaster Nine and the Philadelphia Professionals, 17–0 and 8–6. With Howard Ehmke — the winning pitcher in game one of the 1929 World Series — on the mound for Lancaster, the All-Stars banged out 15 hits, including two by Lloyd, who managed two more hits in the second game. A week later, the All-Stars, playing in front of 15,000 fans at Dexter Park in Brooklyn, split a double dip with the Bushwicks, dropping a close one, 5–4, before winning the second, 9–6.[4]

The first reference in the *Age* to the new team being called the "Black Yanks" came on May 30, when it was announced that "Lloyd's new team" would be playing a "Decoration Day" doubleheader at Dexter Park against "Cannonball" Dick Redding and his Brooklyn Royal Giants. The second such reference came a week later, in reporting that the "Black Yankees" had dropped an 8–1 affair to Hilldale.[5]

With a rainy Sunday keeping many baseball fans indoors on June 7, a mere 1,500 fans in attendance at the Polo Grounds, the "Harlem Stars" swept both ends of an exciting double-header against the House of David, 4–3 and 5–3. As Jazz legend Cab Calloway entertained the fans between innings, Clint Thomas, playing second base for the Stars, blasted homers in each of the games, while Connie Rector and Bill Holland scattered eight hits each over the two contests. "Fats" Jenkins pitched in as well, getting five hits on the day, bunting safely three times in game two. Lloyd, playing first base, had two hits in the opener.[6]

Two weeks later the "Harlem Stars" went on the road where they were three-hit by Paul Carter, Hilldale's new pitcher, losing 4–1. Back at the Polo Grounds for the July 4 weekend, Lloyd's club split a benefit doubleheader with the House of David, 8–3 and 15–2, before splitting another twin bill, this time with the Cuban Stars, 10–5 and 6–3. They then swept a two-game set at Yankee Stadium from the Royals, 7–2 and 4–3. Dick Redding, the "once famous Cannonball," was knocked out of game one in the fourth inning having allowed seven hits, a walk and a hit batter. With the New York Giants playing a doubleheader at the Polo Grounds, attendance at Yankee Stadium was again disappointing, only about 1,500 fans turning out. Bill Robinson again called in favors to get Harlem entertainers "Buck and Bubbles, Putney Dandridge, and several other well-known colored dancers" to entertain the crowd between frames.[7]

With rumors circulating that Lloyd's team was on the rocks financially, it was reported that major league baseball would no longer allow Negro teams to play their games at major league parks. This was a devastating blow to those hoping that such games would increase the likelihood of black players crossing over into organized baseball. But to the powers that be in white baseball it was about money, nothing else. Ed Barrow and the other general managers determined that their cut of the gate was not up to their expectations given the low attendance being recorded in the east. One reason Lloyd's team had survived to this point in the season was that Bill Robinson had been passing the hat at games, the meager receipts being divided among the players. The Harlem Stars/Black Yankees had been a test pilot of sorts for major league baseball, and having proved unsuccessful in drawing decent crowds, the stadium owners found the venture no longer worth the effort.[8]

Why didn't the fans turn out? It was speculated that the one dollar price of admission was too steep, especially given the poor competition that was being brought in to face Lloyd and his bunch. Why would a baseball fan pay $1 to watch the "Black Yankees," one wag asked, when he could pay the same amount to watch the real ones? A more stinging indictment was directed toward Lloyd, who was criticized for building a "mediocre" squad — albeit on short notice — one that failed to attract fans or publicity. Add to this the collapsed economy, and a perfect storm had geared to insure that ballclub's failure.[9]

As the storm clouds swirled, it was reported that John Powers, one of the principal owners of the Harlem Stars, had announced that he was pulling the plug on the team, withdrawing financial support. Yet at the same time, Lloyd's crew kept swinging, taking two games against the Providence Colored Giants, 6–4 and 8–1. A reduction in the price of grand-stand admission to 50 cents for the game resulted in a much larger turnout at the Polo Grounds, bearing out the aforesaid concerns with ticket prices. With the Baltimore Black Sox and Hilldale Daisies scheduled for games in the near future, it was thought that "record crowds" might possibly start to turn out, but until it happened, no further games would be played at Yankee Stadium or the Polo Grounds.[10]

The storm ebbed somewhat the following week when Nat Strong, "well known booking agent and owner of the Bushwicks, Royal Giants, and other semi-pro baseball teams," stepped in to assist the financially strapped Harlem Stars. Strong announced that he would continue to promote the team for the remainder of the year as a traveling club, playing in Brooklyn and possibly touring out West. But remarkably, by the middle of the month, Strong had them back in Yankee Stadium, playing another benefit for the BSCP, this time against Hilldale.[11]

Thus, it was amid great anticipation that the bottom fell out. Where 15,000 fans had attended the 1930 benefit for the BSCP at Yankee Stadium, an announced 3,000 showed up for the August 16, 1931, affair, one in which the Harlem Stars, with Larry Brown behind the plate and Holland and Rector pitching, bested Hilldale, 3–1 and 11–3. The competition was there, the games were well played, but the fans were absent; rows of empty seats piled on one another in a cavernous arena. Rector and Carter opposed each other in the first game, "Broadway" Connie proving the better, allowing the Daisies five scattered hits. Hilldale's only score came in the third inning on a double by Eggie Dallard and a single by Rap Dixon.[12] Game two was a pitching duel between Holland and Oscar Levis until the sixth when Levis blew up, walking three men, hitting one, and allowing the Stars to push seven runs across. Mitchell was rushed to the mound in relief of Levis, but to no avail, as he became wild too, walking four batters, all of whom scored on hits by Livingston and Turner. The play of the game came early when former Lincolns infielder Rev Cannady made an incredible stop of Lloyd's hot liner up the middle in the first inning. Lloyd, playing first base, was 1-for-4 in the first game, going hitless in the second.[13]

Adding insult to injury, Lloyd and his players were not even paid. A. Philip Randolph, in a statement to William Clark of the *Age*, admitted that the team had not been paid inasmuch as it had signed a contract to split the proceeds, and since there had been a deficit, nothing was due them. Clark, stunned to learn this, wrote that "[i]n my ten years experience with baseball players and managers, this is the first contract I have ever heard of that did not give the teams playing the game — making the benefit possible — a minimum guarantee and a percentage on the net above a certain amount. If John Henry Lloyd signed such an agreement, he is a poorer business man that I had supposed."[14]

When questioned as to why the benefit had proved such a monetary failure, Randolph defended the benefits organizers, noting that the New York Giants and St. Louis Cardinals had been at the Polo Grounds and a big Elks parade had taken place at the same time, thereby negating attendance. "Thus, it was nobody's fault," Randolph offered. Clark, not buying it, argued that the organizers had dropped the ball, doing very little to ensure that the local press was involved in advertising the series, and citing sources close to the benefit as saying that the *Amsterdam News* had threatened to withdraw all support if the *Age* was allowed to run a single advertisement regarding the benefit. It was certainly no way to promote a benefit. That said, and newspaper wars aside, a lack of attendance —1,877 paid rather than the announced 3,000—bespoke the many issues the club dealt with that season.[15]

Up against it, his team on the ropes, Lloyd led the Harlem Stars into his old stomping grounds, the Catholic Protectory Oval, for a doubleheader sweep of the Carltons. The wins were emblematic of the team's hard play, something that Lloyd demanded of his ball club regardless of its financial standing. Lloyd and his players held together, and in fact were playing good baseball when word came from Atlantic City that Lizzie Lloyd, Pop's devoted wife, had died suddenly on September 15 from an attack of acute indigestion. Lizzie had apparently been in good health all summer, and her death came as a shock to a host of friends. It must have devastated her husband. A native of Pittsburgh, Lizzie Lloyd had lived in Atlantic City since coming there with her husband when he had first played for the Bacharach Giants. Funeral services were held that Friday with internment in a cemetery located just outside Atlantic City, in Pleasantville, New Jersey.[16]

In the wake of his wife's death, Lloyd unpacked his suitcase, finally, choosing to stay near her grave that winter in Atlantic City. Not ready to leave the following spring either, he signed with the local Bacharach Giants.[17] The Bacharachs, struggling with the economy, played an abbreviated, independent schedule in 1932, after which John Henry Lloyd, one of the great figures in the history of the game, quietly retired from professional baseball. Whether because of his wife's death or perhaps road fatigue, Lloyd chose to accept a janitorial position with the Atlantic City Post Office, rather than take one of at least two managing jobs offered him for the following season. Nan Lloyd, Lloyd's third wife and widow, speaking with Robert Peterson in 1967, asserted that Lloyd ultimately stayed in Atlantic City on the advice of a minister, one who reminded him that he already had a job and a home. "I wouldn't take it," Nan recalled the minister saying about a particular offer to manage a team. And so he did not.[18]

Lloyd later moved to a janitorial job at the segregated Indiana Avenue School in the Atlantic City school district. "He wanted to be around kids," Nan Lloyd said. Lloyd did just that, becoming a hero to the local kids, and "a familiar figure along the Boardwalk." He did not, however, retire from baseball entirely, managing and playing first base for the semi-professional

Atlantic City Johnson Stars — later renamed the Farley Stars — until 1942, when he was 58 years old.[19]

After Lizzie's death, Lloyd briefly married again, this time to a woman named Dorothy, of whom very little is known. In 1942, at age 58 and registering for the draft, Lloyd listed "Dorothy Lloyd" of 128 N. New York Ave, Atlantic City, New Jersey, as the person who would always know his whereabouts. At the same time, however, his own address was listed as 1623 Arctic Avenue, Apartment C-2, Atlantic City, N.J., indicating a possible separation. As Lloyd had no children, or siblings living in Atlantic City, it can be surmised that Dorothy Lloyd was the ex-wife mentioned by Nan Lloyd in her 1967 conversation with Robert Peterson. According to Nan, the marriage ended in divorce, "then I got him."[20]

Nan had never heard of John Henry Lloyd when he was a player. Having spent many summers during her childhood away from the city, in Cape May, she seldom had an opportunity to go to a baseball game. But then, while attending a game with a friend in Philadelphia in 1942, she and Lloyd were introduced. Lloyd was working at the Atlantic City Post Office and managing the Johnson Stars at the time, and was in town to visit friends and enjoy a game. Meeting this older, clean, immaculate man — a happy man that everyone was always glad to see — did the trick for her, and the two were married a short time later.[21]

Atlantic City's north side, where Lloyd lived and worked, was a cultural Mecca for African Americans in the community at that time. There were 250 black-owned businesses — boarding houses, barbershops, bars, churches — in the area. African Americans living there enjoyed "an oasis of racial harmony" at a time when segregation, much of it via custom, was in force. "We had everything we needed on this side of Atlantic Avenue," Sidney Trusty, an Atlantic City native and historian, explained in 2004 to Chuck Darrow in the *Atlantic City Press*. The heart of Atlantic City's north side was Kentucky Avenue, where whites and blacks mingled in an area not unlike Harlem, one where vibrant sounds, colors and smells emerged from the district's entertainment venues. "When it came to Kentucky Avenue, it was an altogether different ballgame," Trusty said. "Color didn't matter. Everyone was here for the same thing: the entertainment." Nat "King" Cole, Lena Horne, Ray Charles, Pearl Bailey, Count Basie and tap dancing legend Peg Leg Bates were regulars at venues like Club Harlem, the Wonder Gardens, the Cliquot Club, and Weekes' Lounge and Tavern. According to Michael Everett in a 2001 interview with Marvin Beatty, "Sammy Davis, Jr.'s mother was a barmaid at Belmonts." Even out in the streets, the people traffic was incredible. "Kids would be on the roofs watching the action. People would listen through open windows.... Bands would step into the alleys during breaks and kids would listen in.... There were bars everywhere!" Atlantic City native Ted Dobson recalled, "There was nothing you needed to do on the south side of town, unless you worked in the hotels." While Lloyd may have enjoyed the vibrancy of the place, being an active member of the Asbury United Methodist Church on Arctic Avenue, he did so in moderation.[22]

During this period, Atlantic City operated on a seasonal schedule, with people coming to town for work during the summer and the place emptying out after Labor Day. "You could ride bikes for days, go on the boardwalk and no one bothered you," Mack Thompson, another Atlantic City native, remembered. "Old men with home-made push carts would go around collecting junk to sell for booze money.... We went to the dump, it was like the mall, lots of good stuff." There was also a Farmer's Market where at the end of the day the vendors would give kids the produce that they had not been able to sell. "We ate more watermelon!" said Thompson. "It was the same at the docks, where white folks would catch big fish, take pictures ... then us kids would take it home, put it on ice."[23]

The Johnson Stars were named for its principle benefactor, a former sheriff and local syndicate boss named Enoch "Nucky" Johnson. The son of former Atlantic City sheriff Smith Johnson, the younger Johnson heeded the wisdom of his father and that of well-known racketeer Louis Kuehnle, his father's friend and confidant, that politics came easier than tending a field. Nucky Johnson was elected Atlantic County Sheriff in 1914 and County Treasurer in 1924. In these roles Johnson facilitated a reputation as the kind of guy one went to when needing something, but for a price.[24] He was the proverbial guy that a guy knew. He also played a central role in local politics, one that might have paved the way for a former all-star ballplayer like Lloyd to get a job at the post office and later with the school district. After all, it would not have been the first time that ballplayers were brought into communities with promises of employment when the season was over. And if Johnson needed a veteran manager for his club, he would have looked long and far for one with Lloyd's credentials.[25]

The Johnson Stars played their games at Laurel Park, a venue where "old men would sit on tomato baskets, or knock holes in the wood fence" to watch the games. It was an "easy park to sneak into," Mack Thompson remembered. Games were also played at the New York Playground at New York and Adriatic Avenues. The games were played on Sunday, after church, and "all the colored folks" arrived "hurrying for their space, but only those who had been at church because if you did not go to church, you did not show your face at the games."[26]

The atmosphere at Laurel Park also featured local impresario "Big Boy" Jones, a celebrity of sorts, serving as host and announcer, using a "big horn like a cheerleader. "On these grounds today," Jones would announce, "playing first base, Harvey Moore." "The fans were great," Thompson recalled. "If you didn't have a nickname they would give you one." The games were played hard, "no relief pitching, designated hitters, helmets, chest protectors, nothing ... it cost too much." Fouls balls were brought back; batters used taped, nailed bats. Ted Dobson remembered that "if you didn't return the ball, left fielder Jesse Robinson would come out flying, chase you down to get the ball back."[27]

Max Manning, an outstanding pitcher with the Newark Eagles, once recalled how Lloyd taught him to pitch when they were together on the Johnson Stars. He "taught me how to pitch, how to stand on the rubber, all the little techniques." Manning also remembered how Lloyd, even in his fifties, could still hit. "He was playing first base, and he could still hit the ball. He used to have a rag he'd oil the bat with. In a close game he'd say, 'I guess I got to do something about this,' and he'd get a hit and win the ball game."[28]

Lloyd clearly left an impression on the youngsters living in Atlantic City,

Pop Lloyd with Anderson and Ward of the Farley Stars. The Stars played their games at Laurel Park, a venue where "old men would sit on tomato baskets, or knock holes in the wood fence" to watch the games (courtesy John Henry "Pop" Lloyd Committee).

through either his work at the school or in his role as Little League commissioner. "We all worshipped Pop," Ted Dobson remembered. "He had been in the big time." Lloyd was generous, not just with his time but with whatever else might be needed. Dobson recalled Lloyd giving a friend of his a baseball glove. "Pop took him down to the basement and gave him his glove." Lloyd was someone the kids looked up to. "He always carried himself with such dignity, such honor," said Marvin Beatty. When Lloyd was once asked why he had not yelled back at a guy in the stands who had been heckling him, he replied, "The Lord gave us all two ears and just one mouth. So I think he wanted us to listen more than we talked. So that's what I do."[29]

In an era of constant, unrelenting racism, depression and war, many of Atlantic City's children lacked the guidance necessary to avoid pitfalls that surely awaited them. "There weren't many role models in Atlantic City in those ... years of decline. The old hotels were fading ... eclipsed by newer, bigger, more distant resorts ... everything ... wearing out or becoming cheap and tawdry, the city turned into a two-bit souvenir." Lloyd happily stepped into this void, showing many of these kids the difference between right and wrong, teaching them the hard truth that no one owed them anything, and that it would be up to each one of them to make of their lives what they could, good or bad. He would not accept excuses; hard work and determination would take them where shortcuts and laziness could not. "Anyone who would come under his influence didn't go wrong," said Marvin Beatty. "Whatever he told you just stayed with you." Former Atlantic City Councilman Walter Collette, who first met Lloyd while a youngster in school, added that "he taught us to play baseball, not race ball." These lessons transcended the "ragged" ball fields where the children played. "He taught us to adjust, to adapt," Collette said. "He didn't dwell on the injustice of the fact that he wasn't allowed to play in the majors. He just didn't dwell on it, and he wouldn't allow us to let race stand in the way of our achievements."[30]

John Henry Lloyd in 1951, at 67 years old, in the uniform of the Farley Stars, Atlantic City, New Jersey (courtesy John Henry "Pop" Lloyd Committee).

Marvin Beatty described Lloyd as an ideal person, one who commanded respect yet always had time to talk with kids. "He was a quality man, a role model in every sense of the word.... Winning was important, but it was how you played the game, no cheating, be a good sport; that meant something to him — sportsmanship. Were you prepared properly or not? Or could you just not take it? Anybody who met him had to be influenced by him. It wasn't a

matter of money, but the amount of character that he had." Jim Usry, Atlantic City's first African American mayor, and who first met Lloyd while umpiring games for the Farley Stars, agreed. When Usry was the principal at the Indiana Avenue School, where Lloyd worked, he would on a regular basis during the summer change into his trunks and cut the grass for the elder Lloyd. "I did not think Pop, being the person he was, should do that kind of work.... If he was white he would have gotten a better job."[31]

It was this legacy and the man's kindness that led so many in the community to revere Lloyd. "In my estimation," said Max Manning, "Pop Lloyd was one of the finest human beings I ever met. He was such a gracious kind of fellow, humble, kind and gentle. It was always 'young fellow this' and 'young fellow that.' He didn't drink, didn't smoke, didn't curse; he was really a role model."[32] In 1986, when working on a documentary about the history of

Pop Lloyd in semi-retirement. He ultimately stayed in Atlantic City on the advice of a minister who reminded him that he already had a job and a home. "I wouldn't take it," his wife, Nan, recalled the minister saying about a particular offer to manage a team elsewhere (courtesy John Henry "Pop" Lloyd Committee).

black baseball, historian Lawrence Hogan got a look at the run-down condition of "Pop Lloyd Field," a ballpark which had been dedicated while Lloyd was still alive, in October, 1949, and that by 1986 was in complete disrepair. With the help of Max Manning, educator Michael Everett and many others, Hogan formed a committee to raise the $450,000 necessary to rehabilitate the stadium, which was reopened on Lloyd's birthday, April 29, 1995. "Pop Lloyd Stadium," on the corner of Indiana and Huron Avenues in Atlantic City, with its exceptionally short porch in right field — something Lloyd the player would have abused — remains a "visible manifestation of Pop's memory," something that until then had "got lost in the shuffle someplace.[33]

Going beyond the realm of nostalgia, others in New Jersey formed committees, seeing to it that Lloyd was elected to the New Jersey Sports Hall of Fame, the New Jersey Black Hall of Fame, and ultimately the National Baseball Hall of Fame. "Every year I've sent 12 packages of clippings, stories, pictures and statistics to the Negro Leagues Committee so they could look it over and vote on him," said Ed Nichterlein, Sports Editor with the *Atlantic City Press*. It finally paid off. Upon learning of Lloyd's selection to the Hall of Fame by the Negro Leagues Committee, Nichterlein became so excited that he cancelled a trip to Philadelphia so that he could let everyone know.[34]

Induction into the National Baseball Hall of Fame at Cooperstown, had been Lloyd's dream when still alive, and it was carried on by Nan, who died two years before his selection, and ironically on the eve of his being inducted into the New Jersey Black Hall of Fame in 1975. Lloyd joined Satchel Paige, Cool Papa Bell, Oscar Charleston, Josh Gibson, Judy Johnson, Buck Leonard, Monte Irvin and Martín Dihigo as the only players having played a majority of their careers in black baseball to have been inducted in Cooperstown at that time.[35]

The day of Lloyd's induction, August 8, 1977, was a "beautiful day for a ballgame," according to fellow inductee Ernie Banks. It was a day on which a clearly moved Jim Usry, accepting the honor on behalf of Lloyd, extolled that "He belongs up here with the best — because we think he is the best!" In sharing his memories of Lloyd with the thousands of baseball fans gathered at Cooperstown that day, Usry made it clear that "Pop was an exceptional player and great teacher, but, above all, he was a humanitarian. I accept this," Usry continued, "with mixed emotions.... I feel deep humility, mindful of the great baseball talent up here (on the stage), and reverence.... But I also feel profound sadness and regret that Pop and his wife, Nan, are not here to see his fondest dream come true. But I know he is looking down on us with his warm, wide smile." With Usry that afternoon for the ceremony was a small contingent of Atlantic City residents including Ed Nichterlein, James

"Mickey" McCullough, who along with Senator Hap Farley had served on the Lloyd induction-campaign committee, Arthur Ayo, a 75-year-old one-time teammate of Lloyd's, and Oliver Small, a 68-year-old former infielder to whom Lloyd once gave a tryout with the Lincoln Giants. Lloyd would have enjoyed himself.[36]

*   *   *

John Henry Lloyd never overtly permitted the fact that he was not allowed into major league baseball to get him down. He practiced what he preached. He was also openly happy, showing no frustration or bitterness, when Jackie Robinson crossed baseball's color barrier, signing in 1946. In fact, Lloyd and Nan once traveled to Philadelphia to see Robinson play. If it bothered him some to know that time had run out on his own career, he kept it to himself, proud in the role that he had played in leading the way for Robinson and others.[37]

When asked in 1949 at the dedication of "Pop Lloyd Stadium" if he thought that perhaps he had come along too soon, Lloyd replied, "I feel it was the right time. I had a chance to prove the ability of our race in this sport, and because many of us did our best for the game, we've given the Negro a greater opportunity now to be accepted into the major leagues with other Americans."[38] This final truth is unassailable. Had Lloyd and the others played the role of jilted suitors, becoming sullen and angry over the way in which they were treated, the opportunity that Robinson and those who followed him enjoyed would have been forestalled. An excuse to extend segregation was all that was necessary, and that of an angry black male presented the easiest sell of all. But when the excuses, lacking merit as they always had, were no longer good enough to justify the money being lost to big league owners because of the ban, the major leagues opened its doors to African Americans. And on that day, Lloyd smiled.

John Henry Lloyd died on March 19, 1964, following a two-year bout with arteriosclerosis, one month before his 80th birthday. "It's amazing he had a heart attack as slow as he moved," Nan Lloyd wryly recalled. At the time of his death he resided at 800 N. Illinois Avenue in Atlantic City, leaving to his wife a postal savings account worth $570 and an $850 Metropolitan Life Insurance policy.[39] During his illness Lloyd had kept busy helping at one of the local high schools, "handing out towels, nothing strenuous," but his level of alertness had waned, to the extent that he lost interest in baseball, something that had not occurred prior to that point. His funeral was a "big one" with plenty of dignitaries, as well as former players and teammates Bill Yancey, "Rats" Henderson, Judy Johnson and Chance Cummings in attendance. Cummings, who as a boy in Jacksonville had carried Lloyd's glove for him just to get into the ballpark, was the last to leave, tossing the "final handful of dirt onto the grave." Lloyd was buried next to his first wife Lizzie — a few feet away from where Nan was laid to rest 11 years later — in the small cemetery just north of Atlantic City, New Jersey, off the Black Horse Pike in Pleasantville. It is a long way from Palatka.[40]

A dapper Pop Lloyd in October, 1949, taking in the scenes at the opening of Atlantic City's Pop Lloyd Stadium (courtesy the John Henry "Pop" Lloyd Committee).

When asked to summarize Lloyd's legacy, Marvin Beatty responded, "Ethics, pride, do your best, be a good sport — win or lose — don't ask for a handout, give all you can give, keep on trying, hustle and work hard ... always be a gentleman." That was the essence of the man. Lloyd was a great baseball player and manager, but as Jim Usry said at Lloyd's Hall of Fame induction in 1977, it was the cut of the man that stood out. "Above all, he was a humanitarian," Usry said.[41] Lloyd was an exceptional husband, teacher and ballplayer, one who gave everything he had to making a difference. At Cooperstown and on ball yards, Lloyd is remembered for it.

Chapter Notes

Chapter One

1. Whitey Gruhler, "Lloyd, Colored School Janitor, Is Baseball's Greatest Player," *Atlantic City Press*, October 2, 1938.

2. Gruhler, "John Lloyd Best Candidate for Post as Eagles' Pilot," *Atlantic City Press*, 1948; Lawrence Hogan, "The Black Wagner: John Henry Lloyd," Unpublished manuscript provided by Hogan to the author.

3. Robert Peterson, *Only the Ball Was White* (New York: Oxford University Press, 1970), 75.

4. While *Bemba* can mean "fat lips" or "nigger lips," Cuban baseball historian Roberto Echevarria does not believe the Cubans applied it to Lloyd with hard connotations (Echevarria email to author, October 10, 2007); Lloyd was also known as Sam Lloyd in Cuba, short for the racist "Sambo." It is probable that Cuchara and Sam began as racial slurs, with the former later changed to a compliment about his fielding.

5. John B. Holway, *Jose and Satch: The Life and Times of Josh Gibson and Satchel Paige* (Westport, CT: Meckler, 1991), 28.

6. Interview: Al Lopez, with Wes Singletary, April 1996.

7. Peterson, *Only the Ball Was White*, p.75; Holway, *Josh and Satch*, 166 and 221; Morris Levitt and Dick Edwards, "John Henry 'Pop' Lloyd," *Black Sports*, April, 1973; Kevin Kerrane and Rod Beaton, "Judy Johnson: Reminiscences by the Great Baseball Player," *Delaware Today*, May, 1977; Hogan, 6.

8. Hogan, 2.

9. Peterson, *Only the Ball Was White*, 75.

10. Nan Lloyd, interview with Robert Peterson, September 20, 1967, Peterson Collection, National Baseball Hall of Fame Library & Archives, Cooperstown, NY.

11. Nan Lloyd, correspondence to Clifford Kachline, January, 1972; authors Alfred M. Martin and Alfred T. Martin, *The Negro Leagues in New Jersey* (Jefferson, NC: McFarland, 2008), 58, cite Nan Lloyd as their source for listing Gainesville as Lloyd's birth site, but cite Lloyd's birth date as April 18, 1884.

12. Florida Office of Vital Statistics, No Record Found statement, certified copy, April 21, 2006; the 1885 Federal Census for Florida reveals nothing, while the 1890 Federal Census was destroyed; Janice Mahaffey, Special Collections, Putnam County Library.

13. 1900 United States Federal Census, Duval County, Florida.

14. Application for Social Security Card Account Number, September 20, 1955; D.S.S. Form 1, Draft Registration Card, Serial Number 1051, 1942.

15. Gruhler, "Lloyd, Colored School Janitor, Is Baseball's Greatest Player"; Ed Nichterlein, memo to Clifford Kachline, National Baseball Hall of Fame, May 9, 1977, in support of Lloyd's consideration for entry into the HOF; Burtz Palatka Directory, 1912–13; de-Nazarie & Wells Palatka City Directory, 1915.

16. "Palatka: A Brief History," *Palatka Herald*, November 11, 1884.

17. Ibid.

18. 1850 United States Federal Census, Loudoun, Virginia; 1880 United States Federal Census, Precinct 6, Duval County, Florida.

19. 1900 United States Federal Census, Duval County, Florida, vol. 5, #70; Nan Lloyd, interview with Robert Peterson, September 20, 1967.

20. James B. Crooks, *Jacksonville after the Fire, 1901–1919: A New South City* (Jacksonville, FL: University of North Florida Press, 1991), 20–21.

21. 1900 United States Federal Census, Duval County, Florida; Hogan, 6; Interview: Napoleon "Chance" Cummings by John Holway, copy of manuscript provided to author by Lawrence Hogan.

22. Crooks, 17.

23. Crooks, 20–21, 27–28.

24. James B. Crooks, "The Changing Face of Jacksonville, Florida: 1900–1910," *Florida Historical Quarterly*, 62 (April 1984), 447.

25. The State Baseball Championship had been played in Tampa only a few years before, between the Tampa baseball nine, composed of Afro-Cuban cigar makers from Ybor City, and the Oak Hall club from Gainesville. Four hundred fans came by train from Gainesville to cheer their team. The Tampa "Colored Band" added to the festivities. The Tampa team won, 10–0. *Tampa Times*, May 16, 1894.

26. Peterson, 75; Hogan, 2; Interview: Napoleon "Chance" Cummings by John Holway.

27. Peterson, 76.

28. Stuart McIver, "Cooks to Catchers, Bellhops to Batters," *Fort Lauderdale Sun-Sentinel*, August 22, 1993.

29. Ibid.; William McNeil, *Black Baseball Out of Season: Pay for Play Outside of the Negro Leagues* (Jefferson, NC: McFarland, 2007), 6–9, 210.

30. Lloyd proved the only batter to maintain a career batting average exceeding .300 in the "Coconut League." McNeil, 17.

31. Nan Lloyd, interview with Robert Peterson, September 20, 1967.

32. The ascendancy of Lloyd made 1906 John Hill's last as a starter at shortstop. He finished his career the following season backing up Lloyd on the Philadelphia Giants, with Grant at second base.

33. John Holway, *The Complete Book of Baseball's Negro Leagues: The Other Half of Baseball History* (Fern Parks, FL: Hastings House Publishers, 2001), 52.

34. *New York Age*, August 16, 1906

35. *Age*, September 6, 1906.

36. Hogan, 7.

37. Holway, 55.

38. James Riley, *Biographical Encyclopedia of the Negro Baseball Leagues* (New York: Carroll & Graf, 1994), 203.

39. Hogan, 7.

40. Holway, 56; Johnson, who was the black game's premier shortstop prior to Lloyd's emergence, and who had once played along with Bud Fowler for a team comprised mostly of white players, the Findlay Sluggers,

would in 1911 move to second base in deference to Lloyd. John Henry Lloyd clippings file, National Baseball Hall of Fame Library & Archives, Cooperstown, NY.

41. Echevarria email to author, October 10, 2007.

42. Riley, 381–382.

43. Holway, 57.

44. Holway, 58.

45. Holway, 58; Hogan, 7. The "Rube Foster Award" was created by Holway for his *Complete Book*, in which he retroactively determined which players would have won the award if it had existed at the time.

46. Al Harvin, *Black Sports Magazine*, June 1973, John Henry Lloyd clippings file, National Baseball Hall of Fame Library & Archives.

47. Hogan, 8.

48. *Age*, May 27, 1909.

49. *Age*, June 10, 1909.

50. *Age*, June 10, 1909; July 1, 1909.

51. *Age*, July 8, 1909; Bill Bedford would be killed by lightning later that season when pitching a game against Atlantic City collegians. Holway, p. 63.

52. Earlier that season, Andy Coakley had been forced out of Chicago over his concerns regarding management not giving him a share of the previous year's post-season earnings. *Age*, July 22, 1909.

53. *Age*, July 22, 1909.

54. *Age*, July 29, 1909.

55. *Age*, August 5, 1909; As the Royal Giants had decisively bested the Philadelphia Giants in most head-to-head games that season, it is difficult to see how the affair would settle any championship; see, Philip J. Lowry, *Green Cathedrals: The Ultimate Celebration of Major and Negro League Ballparks* (New York: Walker & Company, 2006), 82.

56. Interview: Max Manning by Michael Everett, 1997; Interview: Marvin Beatty by Michael Everett, 2001. (Taped copies of interviews provided to author by Michael Everett, Atlantic City, NJ.)

57. *Age*, August 19, 1909.

58. Riley, 631–632.

59. *Age*, September 23, 30, 1909; Holway, 62.

60. Lloyd's previous trip in 1907 was to play a series, not to participate in the winter baseball season.

61. Interview: Nan Lloyd with Robert Peterson, September, 20, 1967.

62. Ibid.

63. Ibid.

64. Ibid.
65. Riley, 624.
66. Roberto González Echevarría, *The Pride of Havana: A History of Cuban Baseball* (New York: Oxford University Press, 1999), 135.
67. Hogan, 8.
68. Ibid.; Holway, 614; Echevarría, 136–137.
69. Both Mordecai Brown and Addie Joss would be inducted into the National Baseball Hall of Fame. Nap Rucker later became a scout for Brooklyn, signing in 1927 a young catcher from Tampa named Al Lopez. Sherry Magee was one of the top hitters of the Deadball Era, playing for the Phillies, Braves and Reds. He was also one of the few players who combined slugging and speed, finishing his career with a .427 slugging percentage and 441 stolen bases, including stealing home 23 times. During his career he posted 2,169 hits, a .291 batting average with 83 home runs and 1,176 RBI. He led the National League in RBI four times and in slugging percentage and total bases two times each.
70. Hogan, 9; Echevarría, 136.
71. Hogan, 20.

Chapter Two

1. See Philip Dray, *At the Hands of Persons Unknown: The Lynching of Black America* (New York: Random House, 2002); John "Pop" Lloyd, "Baseball's Greatest, Then and Now: Were the Old Timers Better Than Today's Stars?" *Our World*, July 1953, 2.
2. Lawrence Hogan, *The House That Ruth Built Is The House That Pop Opened!* 1998, 10.
3. See Lawrence Hogan, *Shades of Glory: The Negro Leagues and the Story of African-American Baseball* (New York: National Geographic, 2007).
4. Riley, pp. 363, 168; The confusion is especially true when attempting to research newspapers of the day, with their multiple references to Leland, irrespective of which team the paper may have in fact been covering.
5. *Chicago Defender*, January 1 and February 5, 1910.
6. Hogan, 10.
7. Riley, 434.
8. *Defender*, July 30, 1910.
9. *Defender*, August 12, 13, and 27, 1910.
10. *Defender*, September 3, 10, 1910.
11. *Defender*, September 10, 17, 1910; "Jap"

Payne is listed by Lloyd as one of the top three outfielders he ever played with. Lloyd, "Baseball's Greatest, Then and Now.
12. *Defender*, October 8, 1910.
13. Holway, 75.
14. Riley, 839.
15. Holway, 78–79; Charles C. Alexander, *Ty Cobb* (Oxford University Press, 1985), 98–99.
16. Holway, 79; Interview: Buck O'Neil, *Baseball: A Film By Ken Burns — Shadow Ball, Inning Five*, 1994.
17. Hogan, 10; Eddie Plank and Chief Bender are in the National Baseball Hall of Fame.
18. Hogan, 10; Jack Coombs won 31 games in 1910, plus three more in the World Series in six days.
19. Hogan, 11; *Age*, October 19, 1911.
20. Riley, 654.
21. *Age*, May 11, 1911.
22. Ibid.
23. *Age*, May 18, 25, 1911.
24. Riley, 545–546.
25. *Age*, June 1, 1911.
26. *Age*, June 8, 1911.
27. *Age*, June 15, 22, 1911; July 6, 13, 1911.
28. Age, July 13, 20, 1911; August 3, 1911.
29. Age, July 13, 20, 1911.
30. *Age*, August 3, 1911.
31. *Age*, July 13, 1911.
32. "Sunday baseball was illegal, so to see a game, fans had to buy a club membership ticket!" John "Pop" Lloyd, "Baseball's Greatest, Then and Now."
33. *Age*, August 10, 1911.
34. *Indianapolis Freeman*, February 20, 1915; Riley, 767–777.
35. *Age*, August 17, 1911.
36. *Age*, August 17, 1911; Philip J. Lowry, *Green Cathedrals*), 151–152.
37. *Age*, August 17, 24, 1911.
38. *Age*, August 31, 1911.
39. *Age*, August 31, 1911; September 7, 1911.
40. *Age*, September 21, 1911.
41. *Age*, September 21, 1911; Riley, p. 465; Kindle must have impressed the McMahons because by 1914 he was batting second in the Lincolns lineup between Poles and Lloyd.
42. *Age*, September 28, 1911.
43. Ibid.
44. Ibid.
45. *Age*, October 12, 1911.
46. Ibid.
47. Ibid.
48. Kerrane and Beaton, "Judy Johnson," *Delaware Today*, May, 1977; Wagner quoted

by sportswriter Hugh Fullerton, displayed at the National Baseball Hall of Fame.

49. Ibid.

50. *Age*, October 19, 1911; Hogan, 12.

51. *Age*, November 2, 1911.

52. Nan Lloyd, interview with Robert Peterson, September 20, 1967.

53. Burtz Palatka Directory, 1912–1913; *Age*, September 26, 1931; Lloyd is credited with bringing James "Lefty" Turner, a pitcher and native of Palatka, to Atlantic City to play for the Johnson All-Stars. www.nlbpa.com

54. Nan Lloyd, September 20, 1967.

55. *Age*, November 9, 1911.

56. *Age*, February 15, 1912.

57. Riley, 855–856.

58. *Age*, February 15, 1912.

59. *Age*, March 7, 1912.

60. *Age*, March 14, 21 and 28, 1912.

61. *Age*, April 11, 1912.

62. *Age*, May 2 and 23, 1912.

63. *Age*, May 30, 1912.

64. According to the account in the *Age* of May 23, 1912, the victim was a wheelchair-bound African American man from Georgia who had merely asked Cobb for an autograph.

65. *Age*, May 30, 1912; June 6, 1912.

66. *Age*, June 13, 1912.

67. Ibid.

68. Age, June 20, 1912; July 25, 1912.

69. *Age*, July 25, 1912; August 1, 1912; The irony involving Lloyd belting the homer off of Buckner is that James Riley credits Buckner as being with Rube Foster and Sol White in "discovering" Lloyd back in 1905. If so, he had an eye for talent. See, Riley, 131.

70. *Age*, August 8, 1912; Patricia O'Toole, *When Trumpets Call: Theodore Roosevelt after the White House* (New York: Simon & Schuster, 2005) 193–197.

71. *Age*, August 8, 15, 1912; Riley, 236.

72. *Age*, August 29, 1912.

73. *Age*, August 29, 1912; September 12, 1912.

74. Lawrence Ritter, *The Glory of Their Times: The Story of the Early Days of Baseball Told by the Men Who Played It* (New York: Macmillan, 1966), 154; *Age*, October 31, 1912.

75. *Age*, October 31, 1912; November 7, 1912.

76. *Age*, November 7, 1912.

Chapter Three

1. Lawrence D. Hogan, *The House That Ruth Built Is The House That Pop Opened!* 7.

2. *Age*, December 12, 1912; January 30, 1913; The first game of the hotel league that winter featured Wickware pitching the Breakers to a 4–3 win over Dizzy Dismukes and the Royal Poinciana team.

3. *Age*, February 13, 1912.

4. *Age*, March 27, 1913.

5. *Age*, January 16, 1913.

6. *Age*, June 12, 19, 1913.

7. *Age*, June 26, 1913; July 3, 10, and 17, 1913.

8. Holway, 94. In his *Complete History*, Holway retroactively chose "all-star" teams for each year in the east and west, though there were no official all-star teams or All-Star Games in black baseball until the 1930s. Holway also created a mythical "Fleet Walker Award" for this book, which he awarded retroactively to the player he regarded as the year's most valuable in black baseball. Lloyd was Holway's choice for 1913, the first of several such awards .

9. Buck O'Neil, *Baseball: A Film By Ken Burns—Shadow Ball, Inning Five*, 1994.

10. *Age*, July 17, 1913.

11. *Age*, July 17, 24, 1913.

12. Gonzalez-Echevarria, 144–146.

13. *Age*, July 17, 1913; Gonzalez-Echevarria, 144–146.

14. *Age*, August 7, 21, 1913.

15. Ibid.

16. *Age*, September 4, 11, and 18, 1913.

17. *Age*, October 2, 1913.

18. Ibid.

19. *Age*, October 2, 9, 1913; Hogan, 13; Holway, 95.

20. *Age*, October 16, 1913.

21. *Age*, October 23, 1913; November 6, 1913; Holway, 94.

22. Gonzalez-Echevarria, 148; Lloyd's World War I registration card had him registering for the draft in 1918, when he was 34 years old.

23. *Age*, April 9, 1914.

24. *Chicago Defender*, April 11, 1914.

25. *Defender*, April 11, 18, 1914.

26. *Defender*, April 25, 1914.

27. *Defender*, May 2, 1914.

28. Ibid.

29. *Defender*, May 8, 15, 1914.

30. *Defender*, May 30, 1914.

31. *Defender*, June 13, 20, 1914; July 4, 1914.

32. Riley, 228.

33. *Defender*, July 25, 1914.

34. Riley, 839.

35. *Defender*, August 15, 1914.

36. *Defender*, August 22, 1914.
37. *Defender*, September 5, 12, 1914; There was no mention of the cause of Bill Lindsay's death in either the *Defender* or the *Freeman*, however, John Holway cites the cause of death as tuberculosis in his *The Complete Book of Baseball's Negro Leagues*. See Holway, 101.
38. *Defender*, September 5, 12, 1914; Hogan, 13; *Indianapolis Freeman*, September 12, 1914; Having served as a pallbearer for Lindsay, Bill Monroe, the 38-year-old star second baseman for Chicago, died the following March while at his parents' home in Chattanooga, Tennessee. This was another significant loss for the Rube Foster's ball club. See *Defender*, March 20, 1915.
39. *Defender*, October 17, 1914; see Robert Peyton Wiggins, *The Federal League of Base Ball Clubs: The History of an Outlaw Major League, 1914–1915* (Jefferson, NC: McFarland, 2009).
40. Holway, 97.
41. *Age*, April 22, 1915.
42. *Age*, April 29, 1915; May 6, 1915; June 3, 1915.
43. *Age*, June 10, 17, 24, 1915.
44. *Age*, July 1, 1915.
45. *Age*, July 8, 1915.
46. Riley, 594–595.
47. *Age*, July 15, 1915.
48. *Age*, July 29, 1915; August 12, 1915; *Defender*, August 7, 14, 1915.
49. *Defender*, July 29, 1915.
50. *Defender*, July 31, 1915; Bowser was one of the Indianapolis club owners.
51. *Age*, August 26, 1915.
52. *Defender*, August 28, 1915; Holway, 106.
53. *Defender*, September 4, 11, 18, and 25, 1915; Riley, 837.
54. *Defender*, October 2, 1915; see Melvin Stokes, *D. W. Griffith's The Birth of a Nation: A History of "The Most Controversial Motion Picture of All Time,"* (New York: Oxford University Press, 2007).
55. *Defender*, October 16, 1915.
56. Ibid.
57. *Defender*, October 30, 1915; November 6, 13, 1915.
58. *Defender*, November 20, 27, 1915.
59. Ibid.
60. *Defender*, November 20, 1915.
61. *Defender*, November 27, 1915; December 4, 11, 1915.
62. *Defender*, January 8, 1916.
63. Holway, p. 109; Defender, February 12, 26, 1916.
64. *Defender*, March 11, 1916.
65. *Defender*, April 1, 1916.
66. Ibid.
67. Riley, 164–166.
68. Holway, p. 102–03; *Defender*, April 1, 1916.
69. Ibid.
70. *Defender*, April 8, 15, 1916.
71. *Defender*, April 15, 22, and 29, 1916.
72. *Defender*, April 29, 1916.

Chapter Four

1. William Martin, *Verdun 1916: They Shall Not Pass* (University Park, IL: Osprey Publishing, 2001), 7.
2. John Henry Lloyd (World War I) draft registration card, #31-9-167-C.
3. Wes Singletary, Interview with Art Hamilton and Harold "Buster" Hair, Jacksonville, FL, February 24, 2009. Hamilton and Hair played for the Indianapolis Clowns when Charleston was manager.
4. Mark Ribowsky, *A Complete History of the Negro Leagues, 1884 to 1955* (Bridgewater, NJ: Replica Books, 1995), 93; Riley, 242.
5. Ribowsky, 93.
6. Holway, 123.
7. *Defender*, September 23, 1916.
8. *Defender*, April 29, 1916.
9. *Defender*, May 13, 20, 1916; Johnson was known by his peers as "Schoolboy" for having attended Morris Brown College; *Indianapolis Freeman*, May 13, 1916.
10. *Defender*, May 20, 1916; *Freeman*, May 20, 1916; Robert Charles Cottrell, *The Best Pitcher in Baseball: The Life of Rube Foster, Negro League Giant* (New York: NYU Press, 2004), 102.
11. Defender, May 20, 1916; Riley, 837.
12. Riley, 787–788.
13. *Defender*, May 27, 1916; *Freeman*, May 27, 1916.
14. *Defender*, June 24, 1916; Lawrence Hogan, *Shades of Glory: The Negro Leagues and the Story of African-American Baseball* (Washington, D.C.: National Geographic, 2006), 132–133.
15. *Defender*, June 24, 1916; DeMoss soon was back with C. I. Taylor and his club.
16. *Defender*, July 1, 8, and 15, 1916.
17. *Defender*, July 15, 1916.
18. *Defender*, July 22, 1916.
19. *Defender*, July 29, 1916.
20. *Defender*, August 5, 1916; Hogan, *The Black Wagner*, 6.
21. *Defender*, August 12, 1916.

22. Ibid.
23. Ibid.
24. *Defender*, August 19, 1916.
25. Ibid.
26. Ibid.
27. Ibid.
28. *Defender*, August 26, 1916
29. Ibid.
30. Ibid.
31. Ribowsky, 91.
32. Ibid.
33. *Defender*, June 24, 1916; Ribowsky, 91.
34. *Defender*, September 2, 1916.
35. Ibid.
36. Ibid.
37. Ibid; *Freeman*, September 9, 1916.
38. Defender, September 9, 1916.
39. Ibid.
40. *Defender*, September 9, 16, 23, and 30, 1916; *Freeman*, September 30, 1916.
41. Riley, 242–243.
42. *Defender*, October 7, 1916.
43. Ibid; The Ananias Club was named for Ananias, who fell dead when he lied to the apostle Peter, and was an expression sometimes used by the press in place of liar.
44. *Defender*, October 7, 1916; *Freeman*, October 7, 1916.
45. Ibid.
46. Ibid.
47. Sam Crawford, in Lawrence Ritter's *The Glory of Their Times*, 56.
48. *Defender*, October 7, 1916; *Freeman*, October 7, 1916.
49. *Freeman*, October 14, 1916.
50. *Defender*, October 21, 1916.
51. Ibid.
52. Ribowsky, 92.
53. *Freeman*, October 21, 1916.
54. *Defender*, October 28, 1916.
55. Ibid.
56. On the same day as the actions in Jackson, Tennessee, the Ohio Supreme Court upheld Governor Frank Willis' decision to bar showings in that state of D. W. Griffith's "The Birth of a Nation."
57. *Defender*, October 28, 1916; *Freeman*, October 28, 1916.
58. Ibid.; Holway, 112; Jack Watts, filling in at catcher for the injured Russ Powell, nearly had the little finger on his right hand torn off by a Lloyd foul tip. It was feared that "he will never be able to use the hand again, as far as baseball is concerned."
59. Due to the forfeit, the official score was 9–0.
60. *Freeman*, October 28, 1916.

61. *Defender*, November 11, 1916.
62. *Freeman*, November 4, 1916.
63. *Defender*, November 4, 1916.
64. *Freeman*, November 4, 1916.
65. *Freeman*, November 4, 11, 1916 and December 2, 1916; *Defender*, November 11, 1916 and December 30, 1916.
66. Riley, 291.
67. *Freeman*, November 4, 1916.

Chapter Five

1. *Chicago Defender*, February 10, 1917.
2. La Lucha, January 3, 1917.
3. *Defender*, February 10, 1917.
4. Ibid.
5. Ibid.
6. *Defender*, February 17, 1917.
7. Ibid.; Holway, 117.
8. *Defender*, February 24, 1917.
9. Ibid.
10. *Defender*, March 3, 1917.
11. Ibid.; Riley, 796–97.
12. *Defender*, March 17, 1917.
13. Ribowsky, p. 92; *Defender*, March 17, 1917.
14. *Defender*, April 21, 1917.
15. Holway, 116; Hogan, 14.
16. *Defender*, April 21, 1917.
17. Ibid.
18. *Defender*, May 5, 1917.
19. *Defender*, May 26, 1917.
20. *Defender*, May 12, 19, 1917.
21. *Defender*, May 26, 1917.
22. Ibid.
23. Ibid.
24. *Defender*, June 2, 1917; Riley, 497.
25. *Defender*, May 30, 1917; June 2, 1917.
26. *Defender*, June 9, 1917.
27. *Defender*, June 16, 1917; June 23, 1917; June 30, 1917.
28. With a mortality rate of approximately 18 per 10,000 people, tuberculosis was a leading cause of death within the city of Chicago at the turn of the twentieth century. Chicagohistory.org.
29. *Defender*, July 7, 1917; Riley, 563–564.
30. *Defender*, July 7, 1917.
31. *Defender*, July 28, 1917; How have Dick Redding and Bingo DeMoss not been elected to baseball's Hall of Fame?
32. *Defender*, August 4, 1917.
33. *Defender*, August 11, 1917.
34. Ibid.
35. Ibid.
36. Ibid.
37. Riley, 862.

38. *Defender*, August 18, 1917.
39. Ibid.
40. Ibid; Redland Field was renamed Crosley Field by later Reds owner Powel Crosley and featured a warning slope just before the outfield wall, which reached 400 feet in center and right field. Lowry, Philip J. *Green Cathedrals: The Ultimate Celebration of Major League and Negro League Ballparks*. (New York: Walker & Company, 2006), 66.
41. *Defender*, August 25, 1917.
42. *Defender*, September 1, 1917.
43. Ibid.
44. Ibid.
45. Ibid.
46. *Defender*, September 8, 1917.
47. *Defender*, September 15, 22, 1917.
48. *Defender*, October 20, 27, 1917.
49. *Defender*, November 3, 1917; Morris Levitt and Dick Edwards, "Historically Speaking: John Henry "Pop" Lloyd," *Black Sports*, April 1973, 48; Peterson, *Only the Ball Was White*, p. 77; Hogan, *The Black Wagner*, 14.
50. Peterson, 77.

Chapter Six

1. Holway, 124–25.
2. Riley, 695–697
3. Ibid.
4. Riley, 749–750.
5. *New York Age*, May 25, 1918; Riley, 862–863.
6. John (Pop) Lloyd, "Baseball's Greatest, Then and Now: Were the Old Timers Better Than Today's stars?" John Henry Lloyd clippings file, National Baseball Hall of Fame Library and Archives.
7. *Age*, June 8, 1918.
8. *Age*, June 15, 1918; July 6, 1918.
9. Riley, 113.
10. *Age*, July 15, 20, and 27, 1918.
11. *Age*, August 17, 24, 1918; Riley, 282.
12. *Age*, September 21, 1918; Holway, 127; The ranks of black baseball had been thinned because of World War I. This fact, along with certain economic and political unrest in Cuba, led to no American blacks playing in Cuba that winter. See Echevarria, *The Pride of Havana*.
13. Lloyd, "Baseball's Greatest, Then and Now"; See, Timothy Gay, *Satch, Dizzy and Rapid Robert: The Wild Saga of Interracial Baseball Before Jackie Robinson* (New York: Simon & Schuster, 2010).
14. Brent Kelly, *Voices from the Negro Leagues: Conversations with 52 Baseball Standouts* (Jefferson, NC: McFarland, 1998) 19.
15. Lloyd, "Baseball's Greatest, Then and Now"; See Larry Tye, *Satchel: The Life and Times of an American Legend* (New York: Random House, 2009) and Timothy Gay, *Satch, Dizzy and Rapid Robert.*
16. The *New York Age* has Lloyd in the Royal Giants lineup on May 10, May 24 and June 7 and out of the lineup for the first time on June 14, 1919. He was out of the lineup again on June 21, before appearing with the Bacharachs by June 28. Redding appeared with the Bacharachs for the first time on August 8.
17. Holway, 130.
18. Interview: Napoleon "Chance" Cummings, by John Holway, copy of manuscript provided to author by Lawrence Hogan, 6. The team was named after Harry Bacharach, the colorful mayor of Atlantic City who was instrumental in bringing the team to the South Jersey Shore. Bacharach served as mayor for six months in 1912, and again from 1916–1920 and 1930–1935. In between his first and second terms in office, he served as City Parks Commissioner; during that time he was tried for election fraud dating to 1910. *New York Times*, January 26, 1914.
19. *Age*, August 2, 1919.
20. Ibid.
21. *Age*, August 9, 1919; R. J. Lesch, "Jeff Tesreau," The Baseball Biography Project, SABR. http://bioproj.sabr.org.
22. *Age*, August 16, 1919. Even though Wickware pitched most of the game reported in the *Age* on August 16, with Redding briefly in relief, the headline mistakenly read "Tesreau outpitches Dick Redding."
23. Holway, 132 and 139; Major league pitchers then utilizing the spitball were to be grandfathered in pursuant to the new rule; See Mike Sowell, *The Pitch that Killed: The Story of Carl Mays, Ray Chapman and the Pennant Race of 1920* (New York: Macmillan, 1989).
24. Interview: Napoleon "Chance" Cummings, by John Holway, copy of manuscript provided to author by Lawrence Hogan, 5; Holway, 131; many consider Willie Wells the best of all blackball shortstops.
25. *Age*, May 22, 1920.
26. Holway, 145; *Age*, April 20, 1920.
27. *Age*, August 7, 28, 1920, and November 6, 1920.
28. Holway, 147; with the Washington Senators training in Tampa, both Sam Rice

and Joe Judge would take time out of their schedules to work with the Sacred Heart High School baseball team, which was led by the Senators' teenaged batting practice catcher, Al Lopez.

29. *Age*, October 9, 1920.

30. Ibid.

31. *Columbus Dispatch*, April 14, 1921; Hogan, "The Black Wagner," 15; Nan Lloyd, interview with Robert Peterson, September 20, 1967; Dick Clark and John Holway, "Charleston No. 1 Star of 1921 Negro League," *The Baseball Research Journal*, Volume 14, SABR, 1985, 63.

32. *Columbus Dispatch*, May 24, 30, 1921 and June 1, 5, 1921.

33. Dick Clark and John B. Holway, "Charleston No. 1 Star of 1921 Negro League," *The Baseball Research Journal*, Vol. 14, SABR 1985, 65.

34. *Age*, February 18, 1922; June 24, 1922; Riley, 488.

35. *Age*, June 10, 17, 1922.

36. *Age*, June 17, 1922.

37. Ibid.

38. Wes Singletary, Interview with Bitsy Mott, July 30, 1994.

39. *Age*, June 24, 1922.

40. *Age*, July 8, 1922; Riley, 319.

41. *Chicago Defender*, August 12, 1922.

42. *Defender*, August 12, 1922; John Holway, in *The Complete Book of Baseball's Negro Leagues*, incorrectly gives the dates for the series as September 12–16, 1922. Holway, 170–171.

43. *Defender*, August 19, 1922; Holway, 170

44. *Defender*, August 19, 1922; Holway, 170; Riley, 789.

45. *Defender*, August 19, 1922; Holway, 170.

46. *Defender*, August 19, 1922; Holway, 170–71; Riley, 712.

47. *Defender*, August 26, 1922; Holway, 171.

48. Ibid.

49. *Defender*, August 26, 1922; Holway, 170; Riley, 665.

50. *Defender*, August 26, 1922; Holway, 171.

51. Ibid.

52. Ibid.

53. Ibid; Treadwell closed out his career pitching for the Chicago American Giants in 1928, a team managed by Dave Malarcher. See Riley, 789.

54. *New York Age*, August 5, 1922 and September 2, 16, 1922.

55. *Defender*, September 30, 1922 and October 21, 1922; *Age*, October 14, 1922.

56. *Age*, October 7, 1922

57. Riley, 233–235.

58. John Holway, *Black Diamonds: Life in the Negro Leagues from the Men Who Lived It* (New York: Stadium Books, 1991), 127.

59. Riley, 233–235; in 1977, Martín Dihigo was inducted into the National Baseball Hall of Fame, the same day as Lloyd; he had already been enshrined in the Cuban and Mexican Baseball Halls of Fame, the only player to have been so enshrined in all three halls.

60. *Age*, October 7, 1922.

Chapter Seven

1. The move proved to be short-lived as Lloyd, despite hitting .418 as player-manager and leading Hilldale to the pennant, fell from Bolden's "good graces" and left after the season, returning to the Bacharachs; Riley, 488.

2. Holway, 179.

3. Hogan, *The Black Wagner*, 15; Holway, 179.

4. Hogan, 16.

5. *Pittsburgh Courier*, April 7, 1923.

6. *Courier*, June 2, 1923.

7. *Courier*, June 9 and 16, 1923.

8. *Courier*, June 23, 1923.

9. *Courier*, June 30, 1923.

10. *Courier*, June 30, 1923; Juanelo Mirabal, after his playing days were over, became Alex Pompéz's right-hand man, moving into the front office and serving as president of both the eastern Cuban Stars and Pompéz's New York Cubans after they were organized. Mirabal, whose father had died when he was young, viewed Pompéz as both godfather and mentor. Riley, 556.

11. *Courier*, July 7, 1923.

12. *Courier*, July 14, 1923.

13. Ibid.

14. Ibid.

15. *Courier*, July 28, August 4 and 11, 1923.

16. *Courier*, August 25, 1923.

17. *Courier*, September 1, 1923.

18. *Courier*, September 8, 1923.

19. Ibid.

20. *Courier*, September 22 and October 6, 1923.

21. *Courier*, October 13, 1923.

22. *Courier*, September 29, 1923; *Philadelphia Tribune*, January 5, 1924.

23. Hogan, 16; Riley, 488; *Courier*, Sep-

tember 29, 1923; John Holway, *Black Dia-monds: Life in the Negro Leagues from the Men Who Lived It* (New York: Stadium Books, 1991), 9.

24. *Courier*, October 6, 1923.

25. Nip Winters actually played for Almendares that season.

26. *Courier*, October 20 and November 10, 1923.

27. *Philadelphia Tribune*, December 8, 1923.

28. *Tribune*, December 15, 1923.

29. *Tribune*, December 29, 1923; Riley, 568.

30. *Tribune*, January 12, 1924.

31. Holway, 184.

32. Hogan, 16; Riley, 488.

33. See Stetson Kennedy, *The Klan Unmasked* (Gainesville, FL: University Press of Florida, 1954).

34. See Alain Leroy Locke, ed., *The New Negro* (New York: Atheneum, 1968).

35. See Arnold Shaw, *The Jazz Age: Popular Music in the 1920s* (New York: Oxford University Press, 1987).

36. See Nathan Irvin Hudgins, *Harlem Renaissance* (New York: Oxford University Press, 1971).

37. Lawrence D. Hogan, *Shades of Glory: The Negro Leagues and the Story of African-American Baseball* (Washington D.C.: National Geographic, 2006), 214.

38. *New York Age*, May 24, 1924 and July 5, 1924

39. *Age*, July 5, 12 and August 30, 1924; Holway, 190.

40. *Age*, July 19, 1924; Holway, 189.

41. *Age*, July 26, August 9 and 23, 1924; Holway, 188 and 196.

42. Roberto Gonzalez Echevarria, *The Pride of Havana*, 182.

43. *Age*, January 31, 1925.

44. *Age*, February 14, 1925 and March 7, 1925.

45. See, E. David Cronon, *Black Moses: The Story of Marcus Garvey and the United Negro Improvement Association* (Madison, WI: University of Wisconsin Press, 1955, 1969).

46. *Age*, March 7,1925.

47. *Age*, March 7 and June 27, 1925; Holway, 203; Hogan, 17.

48. *Age*, April 4 and 18, 1925.

49. *Age*, May 2, 1925. This is the first time that I found Lloyd referred to as "Pop" in the press.

50. *Age*, May 9, 1925; Tom Fial, one of the league's few native New Yorkers, retired from

baseball two months later due to recurring trouble with a leg he had broken two years earlier.

51. *Age*, May 16, June 20, 27, and July 4, 1925.

52. *Age*, May 30, 1925.

53. *Age*, June 6, 1925.

54. *Age*, June 20, 1925.

55. *Age*, July 4, 1925.

56. *Age*, July 18, 1925.

57. *Age*, July 25, 1925; it was also noted that John Harper had reported to the Lincoln Giants.

58. *Age*, August 1, 1925.

59. *Age*, August 8, 15, 1925.

60. *Age*, August 12, 1925.

61. *Age*, September 12, 1925.

62. Ibid.

63. *Age*, September 19, 26, 1925.

64. *Age*, December 5, 1925.

65. *Age*, January 24, 1926.

Chapter Eight

1. Holway, 206; Gonzalez-Echevarria, *The Pride of Havana*, 182; *Monthly Weather Review*, "Storms and Weather Warnings," December, 1925, 540 (www.aoml.noaa.gov).

2. Hogan, 17; Riley, 699.

3. *New York Amsterdam News*, March 17, 1926.

4. *Amsterdam News*, March 31, 1926; Ramiro Ramirez is alternately noted as Ramero and Romerio by the *Amsterdam News* on this date, but the paper does correctly have him in center field. Ramirez never made it to opening day as this would be his only appearance that season for the Lincolns.

5. *Amsterdam News*, April 14, 21, 1926.

6. *Amsterdam News*, May 5, 1926.

7. *Amsterdam News*, May 12, 1926; the rookie Gilmore posted a 6–7 record in 1926. Holway, 214.

8. *Amsterdam News*, June 2, 1926.

9. *Amsterdam News*, June 30, 1926.

10. Ibid.

11. *Amsterdam News*, July 7, 1926.

12. Ibid.

13. *Amsterdam News*, August 4, 1926.

14. Ibid.

15. Ibid.

16. *Amsterdam News*, September 1, 1926.

17. *Amsterdam News*, September 8, 1926.

18. *Amsterdam News*, September 15, 22, and 29, 1926; October 6, 1926.

19. *Amsterdam News*, October 6 and November 10, 1926.

20. *Pittsburgh Courier*, January 1, 1927.
21. *Amsterdam News*, March 23, 1927.
22. Holway, 232.
23. Ibid.
24. *Amsterdam News*, March 30 and April 13, 1927.
25. *Amsterdam News*, April 20, 1927.
26. *Amsterdam News*, April 6, 1927; *Pittsburgh Courier*, April 30, 1927.
27. *Amsterdam News*, May 4, 1927 and April 27, 1927. The Amsterdam News erred in writing that Lloyd, like John McGraw, was entering his 25th year of professional baseball in 1927. Lloyd's professional career began with the Macon Acmes in 1905, prior to which he played semi-professionally with the Jacksonville Old Receivers. McGraw had been in professional baseball since 1890 as a player and manager.
28. *Amsterdam News*, May 11, 1927; *Pittsburgh Courier*, May 21, 28, 1927; Montalvo was back with the Lincolns by July 4, 1927, but his presence ultimately precipitated Jim Keenan's pulling the Lincolns out of the Eastern Colored League.
29. *Pittsburgh Courier*, May 12, 1927.
30. *Amsterdam News*, May 18, 1927; Martín Dihigo belted three home runs in one game for the Cubans against Hilldale that weekend.
31. *Amsterdam News*, May 25 and June 1, 1927; *Pittsburgh Courier*, May 28, 1927.
32. *Pittsburgh Courier*, June 4, 11, 1927; *Amsterdam News*, July 6, 1927; Hogan, "Shades of Glory," 202.
33. *Courier*, August 6, 13, 1927.
34. *Courier*, August 6, 1927.
35. *Amsterdam News*, August 17, 1927.
36. *Courier*, August 20, 1927.
37. Ibid.
38. Ibid.
39. Ibid.
40. Ibid.
41. Ibid.
42. Ibid.
43. "Lloyd Believes that New Eastern League Would Be A Success," *Pittsburgh Courier*, August 20, 1927; see Ray Anselmo, "The Black Wagner: John Henry Lloyd," *Shadow Ball: Negro Players in the Deadball Era, The Inside Game: The Official Newsletter of SABR's Deadball Era Committee* (Vol. 2, No. 2, November, 2001).
44. *Amsterdam News*, September 7, 1927.
45. *Amsterdam News*, August 24, 1927.
46. *Amsterdam News*, September 7, 14, 21, and 28, 1927.
47. *Amsterdam News*, September, 28, 1927.
48. *Amsterdam News*, September 14, 28, 1927; *Pittsburgh Courier*, October 1, 1927; Dihigo was ultimately elected to the baseball Halls of Fame in Cuba, Mexico and the United States.
49. *Pittsburgh Courier*, October 8, 1927.
50. *Courier*, October 8, 1927; *Amsterdam News*, October 5, 1927.
51. *Courier*, October 15, 22, 1927.
52. Holway, 226, 228.
53. *Amsterdam News*, April 25, 1928.
54. Ibid.
55. *Amsterdam News*, May 2, 1928.
56. *Amsterdam News*, May 9, 1928.
57. *Amsterdam News*, May 16, 1928.
58. *Amsterdam News*, May 23, 30, 1928.
59. *Amsterdam News*, June 6, 1928.
60. *Amsterdam News*, July 4, 1928.
61. Ibid.
62. Ibid.
63. *Amsterdam News*, July 18, August 15 and December 19, 1928.
64. *Amsterdam News*, August 22, 1928.
65. *Amsterdam News*, August 29, September 5 and 19, 1928.
66. *Amsterdam News*, September 12, 19, 1928.
67. *Amsterdam News*, October 10, 17, 1928; November 14, 1928; and December 19, 1928.
68. Ray Anselmo, "The Black Wagner: John Henry Lloyd," 7; Hogan, *The Black Wagner*, 17.

Chapter Nine

1. Selwyn D. Collins, Ph.D., "The Influenza Epidemic of 1928–1929 with Comparative Data for 1918–1919," *American Journal of Public Health and The Nation's Health*, vol. XII No. 2, February, 1930, 120; *Amsterdam News*, January 16, 1929; see John M. Barry, *The Great Influenza: The Story of the Deadliest Pandemic in History* (New York: Penguin Books, 2005).
2. *Amsterdam News*, January 23, 1929.
3. *Amsterdam News*, March 13, 20, 1929.
4. *Amsterdam News*, March 20, 27, 1929; in 1932 Bill Yancey became a guard with The Renaissance Five basketball team (a.k.a. The Rens), which was inducted as a unit into the National Basketball Hall of Fame in 1963. Yancey would later credit Lloyd with teaching him "position play," showing him "the right moves on the pivot and how to work cutoffs and relays." Charles Einstein, *The Third Fire-*

side Book of Baseball (Simon & Schuster, New York: NY, 1968), 395.

5. *Amsterdam News*, April 3, 1929; Sol White's reference to "Honus" Lloyd, referring to Lloyd's given moniker as the "Black Honus Wagner," is the first such reference in the black press that I have seen. Sportswriter Hugh Fullerton once called Wagner "the nearest approach to a baseball machine ever constructed." This would have been an apt description of Lloyd as well.

6. *Amsterdam News*, April 10, 17, and 24, 1929.

7. *Amsterdam News*, May 1, 1929.

8. *Amsterdam News*, May 8, 15, 1929.

9. *Amsterdam News*, March 20, 1928; Bill Yancey, in Einstein, *The Third Fireside Book of Baseball*; Interview: Al Lopez, with Wes Singletary, April 1996; see Larry Tye, *Satchel: The Life and Times of an American Legend*.

10. *Amsterdam News*, May 15, 1929.

11. *Amsterdam News*, May 15, 22, and 29, 1929.

12. *Amsterdam News*, May 29, 1929.

13. *Amsterdam News*, July 3, 1929.

14. *Amsterdam News*, July 17, 1929.

15. *Amsterdam News*, August 14, 1929.

16. *Amsterdam News*, August 28, 1929.

17. *Amsterdam News*, August 28, 1929; Holway, 248.

18. *Amsterdam News*, August 28, 1929.

19. *Amsterdam News*, September 4, 1929.

20. Ibid.

21. Certain statistical compilations have Henderson at 6–0 for 1929, but he lost this one.

22. *Amsterdam News*, September 14, 1929.

23. Ibid.

24. Holway, 247.

25. See Stephen Lawson, *Running for Freedom* (Columbus, OH: McGraw-Hill Publishers, Inc., 1990); Jules Tygiel, *Baseball's Great Experiment: Jackie Robinson and His Legacy* (New York, NY: Oxford University Press, 1983).

26. *New York Age*, January 5, 1928.

27. *New York Age*, February 8, 1930.

28. Hogan, *The Black Wagner*, 18; for the date on which Turkey Stearnes left the Lincolns, see *New York Age*, September 20, 1930; Larry Brown came to the Lincolns as a pitcher from Memphis. see *Age*, March 29, 1930.

29. detroitnews.com, February 8, 2008; Entertainment.howstuffworks.com/turkey-stearnes-hof.htm.

30. Holway, 264; Riley, 719, 720; Smith

died from an illness speculated to have been Yellow Fever.

31. *New York Age*, April 5, 1930.

32. *Age*, April 12, 1930.

33. *Age*, April 19, 1930; Riley, 411.

34. *Age*, April 26, May 3 and 10, 1930.

35. *Age*, May 17, 1930.

36. *Age*, May 24, 1930.

37. *Age*, June 7, 1930; Memorial Day was originally called Decoration Day, and is a day of remembrance for those who have died in the nation's service.

38. *Age*, June 14, 21, 1930.

39. *Age*, June 21, 1930.

40. Ibid.

41. Lawrence Hogan, "The House that Ruth Built is the House That Pop Opened," 1998, 3–4.

42. *Age*, June 28, 1930; see Joel Hawkins and Terry Bertolino, *The House of David Baseball Team* (Chicago, IL: Arcadia Publishing, 2000).

43. *Age*, June 28, 1930.

44. *Age*, July 5, 1930.

45. *Age*, July 12, 1930.

46. Ibid.

47. Einstein, *The Third Fireside Book of Baseball*, 395; Hogan, "The House That Ruth Built," 5; *Age*, July 12, 19, 1930.

48. *Age*, July 12, 1930.

49. *Age*, July 19, 1930.

50. *Age*, July 26, August 2, 1930; for more on Paige, see Larry Tye, *Satchel: The Life and Times of an American Legend*.

51. *Age*, August 16, 1930.

52. Ibid.

53. *Age*, August 23, 30, 1930; James Riley has Holland at 29–2 for 1930. Riley, 387.

54. *Age*, August 30, 1930.

55. *Age*, August 30 and September 6, 13, 1930.

56. *Age*, August 30 and September 13, 1930; Holway, 267.

57. *Pittsburgh Courier*, September 15, 1930.

58. *Age*, September 20, 1930.

59. Tom Hannibal is not listed in Riley's *Biographical Encyclopedia of the Negro Baseball Leagues*.

60. Holway, 267.

61. *Age*, September 27, 1930.

62. Holway, 268.

63. *Age*, October 4, 1930.

64. Ibid.

65. Holway, 268; *Age*, October 4, 1930.

66. Holway, 269.

67. Ibid.

68. *Age*, October 4, 1930; Holway, 269.

69. *Age*, October 11, 1930; Al Lopez entered the National Baseball Hall of Fame in 1977 along with Lloyd and Dihigo. Judy Johnson from this team had already been inducted in 1975, and were it not for his early death, Chino Smith might also have found his way to Cooperstown.

70. *Age*, November 15, 1930.

71. Ibid; Lloyd hit .236 for Almendares in Cuba that winter. In 13 seasons of winter ball in Cuba, Lloyd batted .329 over 1,327 at-bats. Ashland Collection, National Baseball Hall of Fame Library & Archive, Cooperstown, New York.

72. *Chicago Defender*, December 13, 1930; Holway, 271; Riley, 292.

Chapter Ten

1. *Age*, March 28 and April 11, 1931.
2. *Age*, April 18, 1931.
3. *Age*, May 9, 1931.
4. *Age*, May 16, 23, 1931.
5. *Age*, May 30 and June 6, 1931.
6. *Age*, June 13, 1931.
7. *Age*, June 27, July 4, 11, and 18, 1931.
8. Hogan, "The House That Ruth Built," 19.
9. *Age*, July 18, 1931.
10. *Age*, July 25, August 1, 1931.
11. *Age*, August 1, 1931.
12. *Age*, August 22, 1931.
13. Ibid.
14. *Age*, August 29, 1931; whether Lloyd signed the contract, or whether it was signed by Nat Strong cannot be determined from the available research.
15. *Age*, August 29, 1931.
16. *Age*, September 12, 26, 1931.
17. "No North American blacks played in Cuba that winter." Holway, 287.
18. Hogan, 19; Ray Anselmo, 7; Nan Lloyd, interview with Robert Peterson, September 20, 1967, Peterson Files, National Baseball Library and Archives. Lloyd had legitimate shots at managing the Newark Eagles and the Baltimore Elite Giants, but for varied reasons turned them down. See Whitey Gruhler, "John Lloyd Best Candidate for Post as Eagles Pilot," *Atlantic City Press*, 1948.
19. Ibid.
20. D.S.S. Form 1, John Henry Lloyd, Serial #1051, 1942.
21. Nan Lloyd, September 20, 1967.
22. Chuck Darrow, "Kentucky Ave. Was Mecca of Entertainment in A.C.," *Atlantic*

City Press, July 26, 2004; Mack Thompson, interview with Michael Everett, Atlantic City, NJ, 2002–2003; Ted Dobson, interview with Michael Everett, 2001; Marvin Beatty, interview with Michael Everett, 2001.

23. Mack Thompson, interview with Michael Everett.

24. Marvin Beatty, interview with Michael Everett.

25. See Grace Anselmo D'Amato, *Chance of a Lifetime: Nucky Johnson, Skinny D'Amato and How Atlantic City Became the Naughty Queen of Resorts* (Harvey Cedars, NJ: Down the Shore Publishing, NJ, 2001).

26. Mack Thompson interview.

27. Mack Thompson and Ted Dobson interviews; Max Manning gave the New York Avenue Playground site in *The Negro Leagues in New Jersey*, by Alfred M. Martin and Alfred T. Martin.

28. Holway, *Black Diamonds*, 120.

29. Ted Dobson interview; Jacqueline Urgo, *Philadelphia Inquirer*, August 19, 1999; "'Pop' Lloyd Enters Baseball Hall of Fame," *Atlantic City Press*, February 4, 1977.

30. Urgo, *Philadelphia Inquirer*, August 19, 1999.

31. Ted Dobson and Marvin Beatty interviews; *Atlantic City Press*, March 2, 1975 and October 1, 1994.

32. Holway, *Black Diamonds*, 120.

33. *New York Times*, April 26, 1992; *New Jersey Historical Commission Newsletter*, Volume 25, May, 1995.

34. *Atlantic City Press*, February 4, 1977.

35. Dihigo went into the Hall of Fame with Lloyd in 1977. Some Negro Leagues veterans such as Jackie Robinson and Roy Campanella who preceded Lloyd to Cooperstown had been elected following their major league careers.

36. *Atlantic City Press*, August 9, 1977.

37. Nan Lloyd, Interview with Robert Peterson, September 20, 1967.

38. Hogan, "The Black Wagner," 20.

39. Atlantic City Surrogate's Court Affidavit, Docket 39354, May 21, 1964; Lloyd's death date is often given as 1965, but this document and his headstone confirm that it was 1964.

40. Hogan, "The Black Wagner," 20; See Wes Singletary, "A Long Way From Palatka: The Early Career of John Henry Lloyd, *Black Ball: A Negro Leagues Journal*, Vol. 2, No. 1 (Spring 2009), 52.

41. *Atlantic City Press*, August 9, 1977.

Bibliography

Unpublished Sources

Ashland Collection, National Baseball Hall of Fame Library & Archives (NBL), Cooperstown, NY.

Atlantic City Surrogate's Court Affidavit, Docket 39354, May 21, 1964.

Beatty, Marvin. Interview by Michael Everett, Atlantic City, NJ, 2001. Video tape copy of interview provided by Everett to author.

Cummings, Napoleon "Chance." Interview by John Holway, copy of manuscript provided to author by Lawrence Hogan.

Dobson, Ted. Interview by Michael Everett, Atlantic City, NJ. Video tape copy of interview provided by Everett to author.

Florida Office of Vital Statistics, No Record Found Statement, Certified Copy, April 21, 2006.

Hair, Harold "Buster." Interview by the author, February 24, 2009.

Hamilton, Art. Interview by the author, February 24, 2009.

Hogan, Lawrence. "The Black Wagner: John Henry Lloyd," unpublished manuscript provided by Hogan to the author.

Hogan, Lawrence. "The House That Ruth Built Is The House That Pop Opened." 1998. Copy of manuscript provided by Hogan to author.

Lloyd, Nan. Interview by Robert Peterson, September 20, 1967, Peterson Collection, NBL, Cooperstown, NY.

_____. Correspondence to Clifford Kachline, January, 1972. John Henry Lloyd clippings file, NBL, Cooperstown, NY.

Lopez, Al. Interview with the author, April 1996.

Manning, Max. Interview by Michael Everett, Atlantic City, NJ, 1997. Video tape copy of interview provided by Everett to author.

Mott, "Bitsy." Interview with the author, July 30, 1994.

Nichterlein, Ed. Memo to Clifford Kachline, May 9, 1977. John Henry Lloyd clippings file, NBL, Cooperstown, NY.

Thompson, Mack. Interview by Michael Everett, Atlantic City, NJ, 2002–03. Video tape copy of interview provided by Everett to author.

Published Sources

Ancestry.com

1. John Henry Lloyd, Application for Social Security Card Account Number, September 20, 1955.

2. John Henry Lloyd, D.S.S. Form 1, Draft Registration Card, Serial Number 1051, 1942.

3. 1850 United States Federal Census, Loudoun, VA.

4. 1880 United States Federal Census, Precinct 6, Duval County, FL.

5. 1900 United States Federal Census, Duval County, FL, vol. 5, #70.

6. John Henry Lloyd (World War I) draft registration card, #31-9-167-C, January, 1918.

Anselmo, Ray. "The Black Wagner: John Henry Lloyd." *Shadow Ball: Negro Players in the Deadball Era*. The Inside Game:

The Official Newsletter of SABR's Dead-ball Era Committee 2, no. 2 (November, 2001).

Bak, Richard. *Turkey Stearnes and the Detroit Stars: The Negro Leagues in Detroit, 1919–1933.* Delight, AR: Gospel Light, 1995.

Barry, John M. *The Great Influenza: The Story of the Deadliest Pandemic in History.* New York: Penguin Books, 2005.

Burtz, Jesse E. *Palatka Directory, 1912–1913.*

Clark, Dick, and John B. Holway. "Charleston No. 1 Star of 1921 Negro League." *Baseball Research Journal,* Volume 14, SABR (1985): 63–70.

_____. "1930 Negro National League," *Baseball Research Journal* (1989): 81–86.

Coates, John M. "Smoky Joe Williams." *Baseball Research Journal* (1973): 54–55.

Collins, Selwyn D., Ph.D. "The Influenza Epidemic of 1928–1929 with Comparative Data for 1918–1919." *American Journal of Public Health and The Nation's Health,* Vol. XII, No. 2, February, 1930, 120.

Cottrell, Robert Charles. *The Best Pitcher in Baseball: The Life of Rube Foster, Negro League Giant.* New York: NYU Press, 2004.

Cronon, E. David. *Black Moses: The Story of Marcus Garvey and the United Negro Improvement Association.* Madison: University of Wisconsin Press, 1955, 1969.

Crooks, James B. "The Changing Face of Jacksonville, Florida: 1900–1910." *Florida Historical Quarterly* 62 (April 1984), 447.

_____. *Jacksonville after the Fire, 1901–1919: A New South City.* Jacksonville, FL: University of North Florida Press, 1991.

D'Amato, Grace Anselmo. *Chance of a Lifetime: Nucky Johnson, Skinny D'Amato and How Atlantic City became the Naughty Queen of Resorts.* Harvey Cedars, N.J.: Down the Shore, 2001.

Darrow, Chuck. "Kentucky Ave. Was Mecca of Entertainment in A.C." *Atlantic City Press,* July 26, 2004.

Debono, Paul. *The Chicago American Giants.* Jefferson, NC: McFarland, 2006.

_____. *The Indianapolis ABC's: History of a Premier Team in the Negro Leagues.* Jefferson, NC: McFarland, 2007.

Delaney, James. "The 1887 Binghamton Bingos." *Baseball Research Journal* (1982): 109–115

deNazarie and Wells, *Palatka Directory for the Year 1915.*

Dray, Philip. *At the Hands of Persons Unknown: The Lynching of Black America.* New York: Random House, 2002.

Echevarría, Roberto González. *The Pride of Havana: A History of Cuban Baseball.* New York: Oxford University Press, 1999.

Einstein, Charles. *The Third Fireside Book of Baseball.* New York: Simon & Schuster, 1968.

Figueredo, Jorge S. *Cuban Baseball: A Statistical History, 1878–1961.* Jefferson, NC: McFarland, 2003.

Fitzgerald, F. Scott. *The Great Gatsby.* New York: Charles Scribner's Sons, 1925.

Gay, Timothy. *Satch, Dizzy and Rapid Robert: The Wild Saga of Interracial Baseball before Jackie Robinson.* New York: Simon & Schuster, 2010.

Gruhler, Whitey. "John Lloyd Best Candidate for Post as Eagles' Pilot." *Atlantic City Press,* 1948. John Henry Lloyd clippings file, NBL.

_____ "Lloyd, Colored School Janitor, Is Baseball's Greatest Player." *Atlantic City Press,* October 2, 1938.

Harvin, Al. *Black Sports Magazine,* June, 1973. John Henry Lloyd clippings file, NBL.

Hawkins, Joel, and Bertolino, Terry. *The House of David Baseball Team.* Chicago: Arcadia, 2000.

Heaphy, Leslie. *Black Baseball and Chicago: Essays on the Players, Teams and Games of the Negro Leagues' Most Important City.* Jefferson, NC: McFarland, 2006.

_____. *The Negro Leagues, 1869–1960.* Jefferson, NC: McFarland, 2002.

Hogan, Lawrence. *Shades of Glory: The Negro Leagues and the Story of African-American Baseball.* New York: National Geographic, 2006.

Holway, John B. *Black Diamonds: Life in the Negro Leagues from the Men Who Lived It.* New York: Stadium, 1991.

_____. *Blackball Stars: Negro League Pioneers.* Westport, CT: Meckler, 1988.

_____. *The Complete Book of Baseball's Negro Leagues: The Other Half of Baseball History.* Fern Parks, FL: Hastings House, 2001.

_____. *Josh and Satch: The Life and Times of Josh Gibson and Satchel Paige,* Westport, CT: Meckler, 1991.

_____. "Judy Johnson a True Hot Corner Hotshot." *Baseball Research Journal* (1986): 62–64.

_____. "Louis Santop, The Big Bertha." *Baseball Research Journal* (1979): 93–97.

_____. *Smokey Joe and the Cannonball.* Washington, D.C., Capital Press, 1983.

Hudgins, Nathan Irvin. *Harlem Renaissance.* New York: Oxford University Press, 1971.

Kelley, Brent. *Voices from the Negro Leagues: Conversations with 52 Baseball Standouts.* Jefferson, NC: McFarland, 1998.

Kennedy, Stetson. *The Klan Unmasked.* Gainesville: University Press of Florida, 1954.

Kerrane, Kevin, and Rod Beaton. "Judy Johnson: Reminiscences by the Great Baseball Player." *Delaware Today,* May, 1977.

Kirwin, Bill, ed. *Out of the Shadows: African American Baseball from the Cuban Giants to Jackie Robinson.* Lincoln: University of Nebraska, 2005.

Kleinknecht, Merl F. "Blacks in 19th Century Organized Baseball." *Baseball Research Journal* (1977): 118–127.

_____. "East Meets West in Negro All-Star Game." *Baseball Research Journal* (1972): 78–79.

Lanctot, Neil. *Fair Dealing and Clean Playing: The Hilldale Club and the Development of Black Professional Baseball, 1910–1932.* Jefferson, NC: McFarland, 1994.

_____. *Negro League Baseball: The Rise and Ruin of a Black Institution.* Philadelphia: University of Pennsylvania, 2004.

Lawson, Stephen. *Running for Freedom.* Columbus, OH: McGraw-Hill, 1990.

Lesch, R. J. "Jeff Tesreau." *The Baseball Biography Project,* SABR. http://bioproj.sabr.org.

Lester, Larry, Sammy J. Miller, and Dick Clark. *Black Baseball in Chicago.* Chicago: Arcadia, 2000.

Levitt, Morris and Edwards, Dick. "John Henry 'Pop' Lloyd," *Black Sports,* April 1973, 48.

Locke, Alain Leroy, ed. *The New Negro.* New York: Atheneum, 1968.

Lowry, Philip J. *Green Cathedrals: The Ultimate Celebration of Major and Negro League Ballparks.* New York: Walker, 2006.

Luke, Bob. *Willie Wells: El Diablo of the Negro Leagues.* Austin: University of Texas, 2007.

Malloy, Jerry. "The Birth of the Cuban Giants: The Origin of Black Professional Baseball." *Nine* 2, no. 2 (Spring 1994): 233–247.

Martin, Alfred M., and Alfred T. Martin. *The Negro Leagues in New Jersey.* Jefferson, NC: McFarland, 2008.

Martin, William. *Verdun 1916: They Shall Not Pass.* University Park, IL: Osprey, 2001.

Mason, Herman "Skip," Jr. *African-American Life in Jacksonville.* Chicago: Arcadia, 1997.

McIver, Stuart. "Cooks to Catchers, Bellhops to Batters." *Fort Lauderdale Sun-Sentinel.* August 22, 1993.

McNeil, William. *Black Baseball Out of Season: Pay for Play Outside of the Negro Leagues.* Jefferson, NC: McFarland, 2007.

Michaels, Brian E. *The River Flows North: A History of Putnam County, Florida.* Dallas, TX: Taylor, 1986.

Moffi, Larry, and Kronstadt, Jonathan. *Crossing the Line: Black Major Leaguers 1947–1959.* Lincoln: University of Nebraska, 1994.

Nelson, Kadir. *We Are The Ship: The Story of Negro League Baseball.* New York: Jump at the Sun–Hyperion, 2008.

O'Neil, Buck. "Why Would You Feel Sorry For Me?" Interview in *Baseball: An Illustrated History,* edited by Geoffrey C. Ward and Ken Burns. New York: Alfred A. Knopf, 1994.

O'Toole, Patricia. *When Trumpets Call: Theodore Roosevelt after the White House.* New York: Simon & Schuster, 2005.

"Palatka: A Brief History." *Palatka Herald,* 11 Nov. 1884.

Peterson, Robert. *Only the Ball Was White: A History of Legendary Black Players and All-Black Professional Teams.* Englewood Cliffs, NJ: Prentice-Hall, 1970.

Rendle, Ellen. *Judy Johnson: Delaware's Invisible Hero.* Wilmington, DE: Cedar Tree, 1994.

Ribowsky, Mark. *A Complete History of the Negro Leagues, 1884 to 1955.* Bridgewater, NJ: Replica, 1995.

Riley, James. *Biographical Encyclopedia of the Negro Baseball Leagues.* New York: Carroll & Graf, 1994.

Ritter, Lawrence. *The Glory of Their Times: The Story of the Early Days of Baseball Told by the Men Who Played It.* New York: Macmillan, 1966.

Rivers, Larry Eugene. *Slavery in Florida: Territorial Days to Emancipation.* Gainesville: University Press of Florida, 2000.

Shaw, Arnold. *The Jazz Age: Popular Music in the 1920s.* New York: Oxford University Press, 1987.

Singletary, Wes. "A Long Way From Palatka: The Early Career of John Henry Lloyd," *Black Ball: A Negro Leagues Journal,* 2, no. 1 (Spring 2009), 52.

Sowell, Mike. *The Pitch that Killed: The Story of Carl Mays, Ray Chapman and the Pennant Race of 1920.* New York: Macmillan, 1989.

Stevenson, Brenda E. *Life in Black & White: Family and Community in the Slave South.* New York: Oxford University Press, 1996.

Stokes, Melvin. *D. W. Griffith's The Birth of a Nation: A History of "The Most Controversial Motion Picture of All Time."* New York: Oxford University Press, 2007.

"Storms and Weather Warnings," *Monthly Weather Review,* December 1925, 540. (www.aoml.noaa.gov.)

Tye, Larry. *Satchel: The Life and Times of an American Legend.* New York: Random House, 2009.

Tygiel, Jules. *Baseball's Great Experiment: Jackie Robinson and his Legacy.* New York: Oxford University Press, 1983.

Westcott, Rich. *Splendor on the Diamond: Interviews with 35 Stars of Baseball's Past.* Gainesville, FL: University Press of Florida. 2000.

White, Sol. *Sol White's History of Colored Baseball, With Other Documents on the Early Black Game, 1886–1936.* Compiled and introduced by Jerry Malloy. Lincoln, NE: University of Nebraska, 1995.

Wiggins, Robert Peyton. *The Federal League of Base Ball Clubs: The History of an Outlaw Major League, 1914–1915.* Jefferson, NC: McFarland, 2009.

Wright, Jerry Jaye. "From Giants to Monarchs: The 1890 Season of the Colored Monarchs of York, Pennsylvania." *Nine* 2, no. 2 (Spring 1994): 248–259.

Young, A.S. (Andrew Sturgeon). *Great Negro Baseball Stars, and How They Made the Major Leagues.* New York: A. S. Barnes, 1953.

Newspaper Citations

Atlantic City Press, **1938**: 2 Oct. **1975**: 2 Mar. **1977**: 4 Feb.; 9 Aug. **1994**: 1 Oct.

Chicago Defender, **1910**: 1, Jan.; 5 Feb.; 30 July; 12, 13, 27 Aug.; 3, 10, 17 Sept.; 8, 19 Oct. **1914**: 11, 18, 25 Apr.; 2, 8, 15, 30 May; 13, 20 June; 4, 25 July; 15, 22 Aug.; 5, 12 Sept.; 17 Oct. **1915**: 29, 31 July; 7, 14, 28 Aug.; 4, 11, 18, 25 Sept.; 2, 16, 30 Oct.; 6, 13, 20, 27 Nov.; 4, 11 Dec. **1916**: 8 Jan.; 12, 26 Feb.; 11 Mar.; 1, 8, 15, 22, 29 Apr.; 13, 20, 27 May; 24 June; 1, 8, 15, 22, 29 July; 5, 12, 19, 26 Aug.; 2, 9, 16, 23, 30 Sept.; 7, 21, 28 Oct.; 4, 11, Nov. **1917**: 10, 17, 24 Feb.; 3, 17 Mar.; 21 Apr.; 5, 12, 19, 26, 30 May; 2, 9, 16, 23, 30 June; 7, 28 July; 4, 11, 18, 25 Aug.; 1, 8, 15, 22 Sept.; 20, 27 Oct.; 3 Nov **1922**: 12, 19, 26 Aug.; 30 Sept.; 21 Oct. **1930**: 13 Dec.

Columbus Dispatch, **1921**: 14 Apr.; 24, 30 May; 1, 5 June.

Indianapolis Freeman, **1914**: 12 Sept. **1915**: 20 Feb. **1916**: 9, 30 Sept.; 7, 14, 21, 28 Oct.; 4, 11 Nov.; 2, 30 Dec.

New York Age, **1906:** 16 Aug.; 6 Sept. **1909:**
27 May; 10 June; 1, 8, 22, 29, July; 5, 19,
Aug.; 23, 30 Sept. **1911:** 11, 18, 25 May;
1, 8, 15, 22 June; 6, 13, 20 July; 3, 10, 17,
24, 31 Aug.; 7, 21, 28 Sept.; 12, 19 Oct.;
2, 9 Nov. **1912:** 15 Feb.; 7, 14, 21, 28 Mar.;
11 Apr.; 2, 23, 30 May; 6, 13, 20 June; 25
Jul.; 1, 8, 15, 29 Aug.; 12 Sept.; 31 Oct.;
7 Nov.; 12 Dec. **1913:** 16, 30 Jan.; 13 Feb.;
27 Mar.; 12, 19, 26 June; 3, 10, 17, 24 July;
7, 21 Aug.; 4, 11, 18 Sept.; 2, 9, 16, 23
Oct.; 6 Nov. **1914:** 9 Apr. **1915:** 22, 29
Apr.; 6 May; 3, 10, 17, 24 June; 1, 8, 15,
29 July; 12, 26 Aug. **1918:** 25 May; 8, 15
June; 6, 15, 20, 27 July; 17, 24 Aug.; 21
Sept. **1919:** 10, 24 May; 7, 14, 21, 28 June;
2, 9, 16 Aug. **1920:** 20 Apr.; 22 May; 2,
28 Aug.; 9 Oct.; 6 Nov. **1922:** 18 Feb.;
10, 17, 24 June; 8 July; 5 Aug.; 2, 16 Sept.;
7, 14 Oct. **1924:** 24 May; 5, 12, 19, 26
July; 9, 23, 30 Aug. **1925:** 31 Jan.; 14 Feb.;
7 Mar.; 4, 18 Apr.; 2, 9, 16, 30 May; 6,
20, 27, June; 4, 18, 25 July; 1, 8, 12, 15
Aug.; 12, 19, 26 Sept.; 5 Dec. **1926:** 24
Jan. **1928:** 5 Jan. **1930:** 8 Feb.; 29 Mar.;
5, 12, 19, 26 Apr.; 3, 10, 17, 24 May; 7,
14, 21, 28 June; 5, 12, 19, 26 July; 2, 16,
23, 30 Aug.; 6, 13, 20, 27 Sept.; 4, 11
Oct.; 15 Nov. **1931:** 28 Mar.; 11, 18 Apr.;
9, 16, 23, 30 May; 6, 13, 27 June; 4, 11,
18, 25 July; 1, 22, 29 Aug.; 12, 26 Sept.

New York Amsterdam News, **1926:** 17, 31
Mar.; 14, 21 Apr.; 5, 12 May; 2, 30 June;
7 July; 4 Aug.; 1, 8, 15, 22, 29 Sept.; 6
Oct.; 10 Nov. **1927:** 23, 30 Mar.; 6, 13,
20, 27 Apr.; 4, 11, 18, 25 May; 6 July; 17,
24 Aug.; 7, 14, 21, 28 Sept. **1928:** 25 Apr.;
2, 9, 16, 23, 30 May; 6 June; 4, 18 July;
15, 22, 29 Aug.; 5, 12, 19 Sept.; 10, 17
Oct.; 14 Nov.; 19 Dec. **1929:** 23 Jan.; 13,
20, 27 Mar.; 3, 10, 17, 24 Apr.; 1, 8, 15,
22, 29 May; 3, 17 July; 14, 28 Aug.; 4, 14
Sept.

New York Times, **1992:** 26 Apr.

Philadelphia Inquirer, **1999:** 19 Aug.

Philadelphia Tribune, **1923:** 8, 15, 29 Dec.;
1924: 5, 12 Jan.

Pittsburgh Courier, **1923:** 7 Apr.; 2, 9, 16,
23, 30 June; 7, 14, 28 July; 4, 11, 25 Aug.;
1, 8, 22, 29 Sept.; 6, 13, 20 Oct.; 10 Nov.;
15, 29 Dec. **1927:** 1 Jan.; 30 Apr.; 12, 21,
28 May; 4, 11 June; 6, 13, 20 Aug.; 1, 8,
15, 22 Oct.; **1930:** 15 Sept.

Tampa Times, **1894:** 16 May.

Index

Numbers in *bold* italics indicate pages with photographs.